Free Zone Scientology

Bloomsbury Advances in Religious Studies

Series Editors: Bettina E. Schmidt, Steven Sutcliffe and Will Sweetman

Founding Editors: James Cox and Peggy Morgan

Bloomsbury Advances in Religious Studies publishes cutting-edge research in the Study of Religion/s. The series draws on anthropological, ethnographical, historical, sociological and textual methods amongst others. Topics are diverse, but each publication integrates theoretical analysis with empirical data. The series aims to refresh the interdisciplinary agenda in new evidence-based studies of 'religion'.

Appropriation of Native American Spirituality, Suzanne Owen
Becoming Buddhist, Glenys Eddy
Community and Worldview among Paraiyars of South India, Anderson H. M. Jeremiah
Conceptions of the Afterlife in Early Civilizations, Gregory Shushan
Contemporary Western Ethnography and the Definition of Religion, Martin D. Stringer
Cultural Blending in Korean Death Rites, Chang- Won Park
Globalization of Hesychasm and the Jesus Prayer, Christopher D. L. Johnson
Innateness of Myth, Ritske Rensma
Levinas, Messianism and Parody, Terence Holden
New Paradigm of Spirituality and Religion, Mary Catherine Burgess
Orthodox Christianity, New Age Spirituality and Vernacular Religion, Eugenia Roussou
Post-Materialist Religion, Mika T. Lassander
Redefining Shamanisms, David Gordon Wilson
Reform, Identity and Narratives of Belonging, Arkotong Longkumer
Religion and the Discourse on Modernity, Paul-François Tremlett
Religion as a Conversation Starter, Ina Merdjanova and Patrice Brodeur
Religion, Material Culture and Archaeology, Julian Droogan
Secular Assemblages, Marek Sullivan
Spirits and Trance in Brazil, Bettina E. Schmidt
Spirit Possession and Trance, edited by Bettina E. Schmidt and Lucy Huskinson
Spiritual Tourism, Alex Norman
Theology and Religious Studies in Higher Education, edited by D. L. Bird and Simon G. Smith
The Critical Study of Non-Religion, Christopher R. Cotter
The Problem with Interreligious Dialogue, Muthuraj Swamy
Religion and the Inculturation of Human Rights in Ghana, Abamfo Ofori Atiemo
UFOs, Conspiracy Theories and the New Age, David G. Robertson

Free Zone Scientology

Contesting the Boundaries of a New Religion

Aled Thomas

BLOOMSBURY ACADEMIC
LONDON • NEW YORK • OXFORD • NEW DELHI • SYDNEY

BLOOMSBURY ACADEMIC
Bloomsbury Publishing Plc
50 Bedford Square, London, WC1B 3DP, UK
1385 Broadway, New York, NY 10018, USA
29 Earlsfort Terrace, Dublin 2, Ireland

BLOOMSBURY, BLOOMSBURY ACADEMIC and the Diana logo are trademarks of
Bloomsbury Publishing Plc

First published in Great Britain 2021
Paperback edition published 2022

Copyright © Aled Thomas, 2021

Aled Thomas has asserted his right under the Copyright, Designs and
Patents Act, 1988, to be identified as Author of this work.

For legal purposes the Acknowledgements on p. x constitute an extension
of this copyright page.

All rights reserved. No part of this publication may be reproduced or transmitted
in any form or by any means, electronic or mechanical, including photocopying,
recording, or any information storage or retrieval system, without prior
permission in writing from the publishers.

Bloomsbury Publishing Plc does not have any control over, or responsibility for, any
third-party websites referred to or in this book. All internet addresses given in this
book were correct at the time of going to press. The author and publisher regret any
inconvenience caused if addresses have changed or sites have ceased to exist,
but can accept no responsibility for any such changes.

A catalogue record for this book is available from the British Library.

Library of Congress Control Number: 2020950621

ISBN: HB: 978-1-3501-8254-7
PB: 978-1-3502-3299-0
ePDF: 978-1-3501-8255-4
eBook: 978-1-3501-8256-1

Series: Bloomsbury Advances in Religious Studies

Typeset by Deanta Global Publishing Services, Chennai, India

To find out more about our authors and books visit www.bloomsbury.com and
sign up for our newsletters

Contents

List of figures	vi
Preface	vii
Acknowledgements	x
1 Introduction: Researching 'Scientologies'	1

Part I From Scientology to Scientologies

2 The Church of Scientology and the 'Free Zone': A complex relationship	21
3 Auditing and the 'tech': The basics	40
4 'You are YOU *in* a body': Negotiating the self in Scientology	50

Part II Fluidity and boundaries

5 Authenticity and innovation: The 'true tech' and 'mistakes by Hubbard'	95
6 'Doing Scientology': E-Meters, objects and material culture	128
7 Moving forward: Reflections on Free Zone Scientology and the wider study of religions	152
8 Conclusion	160
Appendix A	169
Appendix B	171
Notes	173
References	176
Index	187

Figures

1.1	The Church of Scientology of London	9
4.1	The Purification Centre at the Church of Scientology of London	59
4.2	The treadmills at the Purification Centre in Saint Hill, East Grinstead	59
5.1	L. Ron Hubbard's Office at the Church of Scientology of London	100
6.1	The Mark Ultra VIII E-Meter at the Church of Scientology of London	131
6.2	The needle and display interface of the Mark Ultra VIII E-Meter at the Church of Scientology of London	136
6.3	The tone arm of the Mark Ultra VIII E-Meter at the Church of Scientology of London	137
6.4	The E-Meter canister of the Mark Ultra VIII E-Meter at the Church of Scientology of London	138
6.5	Inside the E-Meter canister of the Mark Ultra VIII E-Meter at the Church of Scientology of London	139
6.6	The Flag Building in Clearwater, Florida	143
6.7	The entrance to the Flag Building	144

Preface

In many ways, the origin of this book stems back to the spring of 2010. As an undergraduate student of Religious Studies, I visited the Church of Scientology of New York as part of a departmental field trip. Having recently become interested in the study of New Religious Movements (NRMs), it was an exciting opportunity to learn more about one of the most renowned NRMs that emerged in the twentieth century. We received a very warm welcome, which included a full tour of the Church, an opportunity to engage with the E-Meter through 'stress tests' and a lengthy question and answer session with Church of Scientology (CoS) staff members.

This welcoming CoS was a far cry from what some may expect. Like many others, my prior knowledge of Scientology came from the 'usual suspect' – the media. I had seen the leaked Tom Cruise CoS interview, *Trapped in the Closet* (the *South Park* episode lampooning Scientology and its beliefs), and the BBC's *Panorama* documentary (*Scientology and Me*) – featuring John Sweeney's infamous explosive outburst at CoS spokesperson, Tommy Davis. Hardly appropriate sources for developing a sound understanding of Scientology. Unfortunately, despite the best attempts of scholars, this simplistic view of Scientology continues to dominate public discourse surrounding the movement. Following our field trip, however, I was fascinated with the auditing process. More specifically, its use in Scientology as a combination of religious and secular-scientific elements. This practice is at the centre of contemporary Scientology, and is a focal point of this book.

It was during my masters studies that I became aware of the 'Free Zone', the umbrella category for the practice of Scientology outside and away from the CoS. An increasing number of former CoS members were beginning to use the internet to promote their view of Scientology as something that can exist outside the CoS and the Religious Technology Center. Marty Rathbun, the former Inspector General of the Religious Technology Center, was quickly becoming a popular online figure through his criticism of the CoS. What was perhaps more interesting, however, was his interpretation of Free Zone or 'independent' Scientology, where his disillusion with the CoS was based in institutional (not spiritual or philosophical) concerns. In a way Rathbun became the public face of the Free Zone. He was an independent auditor, practising Hubbard's work outside the institution Hubbard himself created. In Scientologist history, practising Scientology outside the CoS is, according to both the CoS and Hubbard's own policies, considered to be a controversial and heretical act known as 'squirrelling'. Footage of his interaction outside his home with the 'Squirrel Busters', a group of alleged CoS members wearing shirts emblazoned with squirrels featuring Rathbun's face, quickly went viral and gathered attention from the media.

I became intrigued – the notion of the Free Zone, and its turbulent relationship with the CoS, raised a number of questions:

What is 'Free Zone Scientology'?
How do Free Zone Scientologists operate and practise Scientology?
What is the cause of divisions between the CoS and the Free Zone?

During this period, I was writing a dissertation on media depictions of the auditing process, with the Free Zone quickly becoming a curiosity in the back of my mind. Meanwhile, the scholarly study of Scientology was experiencing a renaissance of sorts, with the publication of a relatively small number of edited volumes and monographs on the CoS during this period. This culminated in the 'Scientology in Scholarly Perspective' conference at the Faculty for the Comparative Studies of Religions and Humanism (Antwerp, Belgium) – the first academic conference purely dedicated to the study of Scientology. To this day it remains one of the best conferences I have attended, featuring papers from established senior NRM scholars and early career researchers, demonstrating that the study of Scientology was still alive and well. Following a number of interesting discussions over some excellent bolognese, I became certain that I wanted to conduct doctoral research on the topic of Free Zone Scientology, the results of which are contained in this book.

Throughout this book I use the auditing process as a case study to understand the complexities and nuances of contemporary Free Zone Scientology. This is a fitting approach; many of the 'Freezoners' interviewed throughout my research consider the auditing process and the notion of 'Scientology' to be interchangeable. To 'do' auditing is to 'do' Scientology. Accordingly, this emphasis on the core ritual of Scientology illuminates Free Zone practices and communities, allowing for a thorough study of the movement.

During the course of conducting this research, it is safe to say that I became captivated by the subject of Scientology, stretching as far as a visit to the CoS' Flag Headquarters in Clearwater during my honeymoon – a true testament to the patience and support of my wife. While spending a few hours speaking to a very helpful CoS staff member in the Flag Information Centre may not sound like the most romantic of honeymoon activities, it did emphasize the importance and usefulness of 'getting out there' and speaking to Scientologists. Indeed, this book has also enjoyed access to, and insights from, Scientologists across a range of what I call 'Scientologies' (different types of Scientology) – both within CoS and Free Zone spheres. Through field visits to the CoS of London and the Saint Hill Advanced Org (a significant location in Scientology history) and maintaining online communication with a range of Free Zone Scientologists (including independent auditors), the conclusions of this work are directly informed by the everyday practices and understanding of auditing.

By approaching this research through the method of lived religion, I frame auditing within the categories of the self, authenticity and materiality. Navigating through these aspects of contemporary Scientologies demonstrates that 'Free Zone Scientology' is an intricate category comprising of a large number of different interpretations and understandings of Scientology. Public discourse surrounding the Free Zone typically positions Freezoners as a singular entity of Scientologists directly opposing the institutional CoS (such as Marty Rathbun). However, through the journey of writing this book, I found the reality to be far more complex, with approaches to the auditing process directly impacting the production of boundaries and fluidity within different Scientologies, challenging approaches to the question of 'what is Scientology?'.

Ultimately, this book is about everyday Free Zone Scientologists, and comes back to my initial questions surrounding the Free Zone. It explores who Freezoners are, how they understand Scientology and what causes the boundaries between them and the CoS. This book is also part of a wider conversation. We are still enjoying the recent resurgence of academic interest in the topic of Scientology, with publications demonstrating the exciting directions in which the study can progress. The vast number of these publications, however, solely focuses on the institutional CoS, with very few scholars turning their attention towards the Free Zone. It is my hope that this book opens new questions and conversations surrounding contemporary Scientologies, while also offering valuable insights for the wider study of religions by providing a detailed case study of an NRM in transition and transformation in the twenty-first century.

Acknowledgements

There are many people without whom this book would not exist. My thanks goes to Marion Bowman and Paul-François Tremlett for all the wisdom, guidance and advice they provided throughout this research. My thanks also goes to Stephen Gregg, Suzanne Newcombe, Kim Knott, Greg Barker, George Chryssides, Donald Westbrook and the whole INFORM team for the conversations and insights which have enriched my study. I would also like to acknowledge all my fieldwork participants, both within the Church of Scientology and the Free Zone, for taking the time to share their invaluable stories and experiences.

I am deeply grateful to my parents, Rhys, grandparents and wider family for their support throughout this research. My thanks also goes to Gareth Cousins, Theo Wildcroft and Vivian Asimos for their conversations and comradery, in addition to my cats for their company while I wrote. Finally, I would like to give a special thanks to my wife, Victoria, who is my constant source of inspiration, love and encouragement. This book is dedicated to her.

1

Introduction
Researching 'Scientologies'

One evening in October 1983, a meeting was held at the Crown Hotel, a short distance from the Church of Scientology's British Headquarters in East Grinstead (UK). Captain Bill Robertson, a highly influential Scientologist and personal friend of Scientology's founder, L. Ron Hubbard, had gathered a group of Church of Scientology (CoS) practitioners. A gifted and charismatic speaker, Robertson passionately argued that the CoS had been infiltrated by government agents. Urging his fellow Scientologists to protect the work of Hubbard from corruption, he advocated the application of Scientology away from the institutional CoS. Insisting on what he viewed as 'authentic' Scientology according to Hubbard, Robertson claimed to offer no new approach to Scientologist praxis, simply an 'alternative way to be free' ([1983] 2012: online).

Fortunately for those interested in the subject of Scientology, much of Robertson's speech was captured on film and has been circulated online. The recording makes for compelling viewing, not least because it marks a significant moment in the history of Scientology. Independent groups using Scientologist practices had been emerging since the 1960s, yet Robertson's departure from the CoS marked the movement's first major schism, leading to what has now become known as the Free Zone. For Free Zone Scientologists (or 'Freezoners'), this is when 'Free Zone Scientology' truly began – with the idea that Scientology could be practised, understood and applied outside the institutional CoS. Robertson would go on to establish Ron's Org, which remains one of the largest and most successful Free Zone groups to this day, yet the category has become a broad umbrella term, usually encompassing all Scientologists operating outside the institutional CoS. Since Robertson's initial schism in the early 1980s, the Free Zone has become a significant aspect of contemporary Scientology, with a rising number of Scientologists practising in the Free Zone (Lewis 2016: 480). However, while the Free Zone is often perceived as a singular entity, united in opposition to the CoS, the reality paints a far more complex picture. One of the most defining features of the Free Zone landscape, as this book will demonstrate, is its largely unregulated and non-hierarchical environment, which has resulted in the emergence of a large variety of Scientologist groups, communities and independent practitioners.

To account for the diversity found within the Scientologist landscape, this book concerns the notion of 'Scientologies' – the existence of a several different types of Scientology. Understanding the dynamics of Scientologies is, as this book will lay out, best understood through the 'auditing' process. Auditing is a hybrid practice that combines psychology with religious and mystical notions of esoteric knowledge and experience, and it is a technique that enables Scientologists to make progress through pre-specified levels of achievement. The practice is positioned within Scientology (particularly the CoS) as an entirely scientific process, while simultaneously maintaining a religious status through its believed treatment of the spiritual self. Furthermore, its distinctive use of technology and its association with science fiction situates Scientology as a religion of an increasingly secular age. Accordingly, I approach Scientology in this work as a hybrid of religious and secular-scientific elements.

That auditing draws both from discourses of psychology and religious sources is a mark of contemporary Western cultures. Notionally impervious boundaries between religion and the secular-scientific have broken down, giving way to hybrid formations such as Scientology whose practices constitute negotiations of competing forces in Western societies. This book will therefore assist the scholarly understanding of Scientology as a varied belief system, featuring many Free Zone practitioners with different understandings of what it means to be a Scientologist, and how the auditing process is practised accordingly.

The bigger picture: The study of 'Scientologies'

The scholarly focus on the Church of Scientology

It would be remiss to ignore the fact that Scientology has been the subject of limited academic study throughout its history, with only a handful of monographs and edited volumes with which scholars can engage. The reasons for this are varied and closely tied with the methodological challenges facing scholars approaching Scientology as a research subject, as this chapter will go on to demonstrate. Recent years (from the late 2000s onwards) have seen a small pool of scholarship on the subject, with a number of doctoral students and scholars of New Religious Movements (NRMs) conducting more significant research on Scientology.

The first major publication on Scientology, however, was Roy Wallis's *The Road to Total Freedom* (1976). This work was an important milestone in the study of Scientology, outlining the 'cult phase' of Scientology (its Dianetics era), the theory behind its beliefs and its relations with society. However, it must be kept in mind that Wallis's work is surrounded by controversy. It is alleged that, while he pursued his research on Scientology, the CoS employed a representative to pose as a student at the University of Stirling, where Wallis was then employed, to gather information about him. Additionally, his colleagues and employers received letters (presumed to have been sent by the CoS) accusing him of a gay love affair and participation in a drug squad (Graham 2014; Lamont 1986: 87). Wallis acknowledges these difficulties in his work, stating that the CoS' vigorous attempts to countercriticism means that 'it seemed almost inevitable that [his] own final work would be the subject of lengthy and expensive litigation' (1976: vi). During a process of negotiation with the CoS, Wallis made a series of changes to his work, including amending that 'Hubbard was "obsessed" with communism, to read that he was "pre-occupied" by it' (1976: vi), and removing comparisons of the CoS with the Nazi Party which he deemed to be 'on reflection *unnecessarily* offensive to members of the Church of Scientology' (1976: vi, emphasis in original). Further to these amendments, *The Road to Total Freedom* contains, in an appendix, a commentary response written by a member of the CoS, Dr Jerry Simmons. It is therefore wise, despite the landmark nature of Wallis's monograph, to consider the limitations of *The Road to Total Freedom* in the context of a non-confessional and academic study of Scientology.

This controversy arguably contributed to the small amount of academic work on Scientology that emerged between Wallis's work and the recent resurgence of interest from the late 2000s onwards. However, there are now six prominent academic works on Scientology. These are Harriet Whitehead's *Renunciation and Reformulation: A Study of Conversion in an American Sect* (1987), J. Gordon Melton's *Studies in Contemporary Religion: The Church of Scientology* (2000), James R. Lewis's *Scientology* (2009b), Urban's *The Church of Scientology: A History of a New Religion* (2011), Lewis and Kjersti Hellesøy's *Handbook of Scientology* (2016b) and Donald Westbrook's *Among the Scientologists: History, Theology, and Praxis* (2019).

With the exception of Whitehead's work, which was written prior to (and published soon after) L. Ron Hubbard's death in 1986, the remaining five prominent works emerged during the past twenty years, marking a renewed interest in Scientology amongst the academic community. The three monographs by Urban, Melton and Westbrook could be categorized as general overviews of the CoS, its history and practices. For example, Urban's (2011) work provides a thorough history of Scientology, including details of auditing, the establishment of the CoS and the history of Scientology from the lifetime of Hubbard through to the current leader of the CoS, David Miscavige. Furthermore, Westbrook's (2019) work, directly informed by his ethnographic approach to the CoS, is significant in the number of interviews and level of access he was able to gain during his research.

The remaining two works are edited volumes. Lewis's (2009b) volume of essays, despite its broad range of topics, relates only to the subject of the CoS, and contains no significant research on Scientologies outside the institutional Church. This lack of scholarship on the Free Zone is addressed in Lewis's most recent edited work on Scientology with Hellesøy, the *Handbook of Scientology* (2016b). Noting that 'we are on the verge of experiencing a small tsunami of new scholarship on Scientology' (Lewis and Hellesøy 2016a: 2), their volume contains a plethora of chapters on Scientology that focus on the deeper aspects of Scientology beyond basic introductions, particularly aimed towards those with an already firm understanding of Scientology. Of particular note in this handbook are the chapters on Free Zone movements and schisms, notably Hellesøy's (2016) study of Ron's Org and the Dror Center, two prominent Free Zone organizations. These chapters remain a minority in the volume, however, with most contributions concentrating on the CoS.

The purpose of this book

While it is pleasing to see that academic work on Scientology is beginning to dig deeper than basic introductions to the movement, research on different Scientologies outside the CoS continues to be a minority pursuit. Indeed, the CoS presents itself as being synonymous with the category of 'Scientology', regarding the Free Zone and any other use of Hubbard's work outside its institution as a form of Scientological heresy. As I have previously argued (Gregg and Thomas 2019: 350), the scholarly community has, to a great extent, accepted the CoS' narrative of its position as the only 'official' form of Scientology, which in turn has resulted in many publications and monographs concerning only the institutionalized CoS.

This work is intended as a significant contribution to academic conversations surrounding Scientology, which has previously been dominated by CoS-centric understandings of 'what Scientology is'. In this book I argue that auditing lies at the core of contemporary Scientology, and that the ways in which different Scientologists understand, practise and engage with the process directly impacts the production of boundaries in Free Zone Scientologies. Although previous studies of Scientology exist, this study has benefitted from access to a range of auditing practitioners in types of Scientology beyond the CoS. I therefore provide an original account of auditing as it is practised in both the CoS and Free Zone spheres, examining the diverse nature of the auditing technique as a process that combines different series of procedures, material culture and both religious and secular elements pertinent to particular ideas about the mind, body and the self. A key distinction that emerges from this study is between the hierarchical, top-down and vertical authority-practice structure of the CoS, in contrast to the flatter, more horizontal forms of the Scientological authority-practice in the Free Zone.

During early stages of this research, it became clear that the notion of 'Free Zone Scientology' is far more complex than it may appear on the surface. While the Free Zone can be simply summarized as 'Scientology outside the CoS', the reality is a category comprising several understandings of Scientologist practices and belief. I argue that the category of 'Free Zone Scientology' is a fluid social environment, in which Scientologists unrestricted by administrative institutions use the opportunity to develop their own versions and applications of Hubbard's work. With this in mind, this book explores the topic of auditing in relation to notions of the self, issues of authenticity and innovation and use of material culture across Scientologies. This exploration demonstrates how key aspects and debates surrounding Scientologist practice not only play a part in boundary-making amongst Scientologists but can also lead to the emergence of new types of fluid and horizontal forms of Scientology.

This focus on more horizontal forms of Free Zone Scientology, in contrast to the institutional hierarchy of the CoS, raises further implications for the study of contemporary religion. Previous research on NRMs and Scientology in particular have tended to focus either on NRMs as indices of broad social processes such as secularization or globalization or (in earlier research) as exemplars of exotic processes such as charismatic authority and brainwashing. This book takes a completely different approach, using the auditing practice as a method of providing an in-depth case study of an NRM developing in the twenty-first century. Accordingly, this book aims to act as a framework for the study of similar movements formed in recent decades, allowing scholars of religion to contrast highly institutionalized and hierarchical environments of practice on the one hand (such as the CoS) with unregulated and fluid ones (such as the Free Zone) on the other.

Researching Scientologies: The methods

Beginning a study of Scientology

Approaching Scientology as a subject of study presents a series of distinctive challenges. First, scholars must familiarize themselves with 'the basics' of the movement. Despite its status as a new and emergent religion, Scientology has a rich and often controversial history, while also adopting a vast series of specialized practices and terminology collectively known as the 'tech' (which are explored in Chapters 2 and 3, respectively). Second, fully penetrating the topic of Scientology becomes difficult due to the existence of esoteric practices and information intended for practitioners only, in addition to the CoS' rigorous maintenance of its public image. Unsurprisingly, scholars can often feel discouraged from pursuing research on Scientology due to the 'methodological minefield' involved. I can attest, however, alongside other scholars who have recently adopted ethnographic approaches to the study of Scientology (Hellesøy 2016; Westbrook 2019), that these potential restrictions need not hinder one's studies, rather there are potential alternatives and approaches that can be adopted.

This book primarily draws from sociology and anthropology, combining qualitative aspects such as participant observation, interviews and engaging with material culture. I envisaged this research as an opportunity to understand the role and nature of auditing in a variety of Scientologies. Accordingly, data was gathered from discussions and interactions with a wide variety of participants who identify as Scientologists. This additionally includes participants who do not consider themselves Scientologists, yet still make use of the auditing process. Conducting this research involved the use of a number of well-known methods in the academic study of religions. While being aware of the sociological typologies associated with the study of new religions, data was gathered via methods including participant observation (at the CoS), and online interviews and email conversations (with Free Zone Scientologists). Additionally, this book involves analysis and interpretation of Free Zone web pages and Scientology documents, including Hubbard's vast writing on the auditing process. Indeed, as George Chryssides observes, 'according to [the Church of] Scientology sources, [Hubbard] wrote 40 million words on Dianetics and Scientology, [and] spoke 25 million words in 3000 lectures' (1999: 280). These texts and lectures are crucial to the study of Scientology – they lie at the core of Scientologist practices, and their interpretation illuminates how Scientologists 'do Scientology'. Altogether, this evidence base is analysed and interpreted through the method of 'lived religion' to fully engage with how the auditing process directly impacts the fluid nature of Free Zone Scientology.

Conducting fieldwork with the Church of Scientology

Roy Wallis's contested experience of working with the CoS during the 1970s might, on the surface, suggest that gaining access to conduct fieldwork at the CoS would be a demanding task for the scholar. The reality, however, is that there has been a notable shift in the relationship between the CoS and the academy in recent decades, with CoS members becoming increasingly welcoming of academics to tour their Orgs (Scientologist churches). Indeed, Westbrook (2019: 9) argues that Wallis's experiences with the CoS are unlikely to be repeated amongst contemporary academics. Noting the CoS' more relaxed attitudes towards scholars of religion conducting research within its facilities, Westbrook believes that scholars may feel more encouraged to study Scientology due to 'the church's apparent willingness to make itself and its members open to critical inquiry' (2019: 10). As he correctly observes (2019: 10), however, fieldwork with the CoS is still not an easy and simple affair. I thus approached my fieldwork aware of potential limitations due to the CoS' hesitation to work with outsiders (due to negative media coverage) and restrictions surrounding teachings and practices kept hidden from uninitiated members.

Throughout the course of this research, I conducted fieldwork at two CoS locations – the Church of Scientology of London, on Queen Victoria Street, and the Saint Hill Advanced Org at East Grinstead, UK. The Saint Hill Advanced Org (known simply as 'Saint Hill') acts as the CoS' British headquarters and includes the Saint Hill Manor, the former home of L. Ron Hubbard. In addition to being able to speak first-hand to CoS staff members who have undertaken auditing, visiting CoS Orgs gave me the opportunity for participant observation and direct contact with the material culture of Scientology, such as the E-Meter.

During the early stages of my research, I considered a potential visit to the CoS' Flag Land Base (often simply referred to as 'Flag'), the spiritual headquarters of the CoS at Clearwater, Florida, United States. Flag acts as the CoS' world headquarters. It comprises of several buildings across Clearwater that provide exclusive and advanced Scientology services. While this book predominantly concentrates on auditing in the Free Zone, it is important to examine the nature of auditing and its origin in the CoS, meaning that a field visit to Flag, particularly the Flag Building, would have been useful for this study. I had previously visited Flag in 2015 and spent a few hours speaking with a member of staff at the Information Centre. I was encouraged to arrange a formal visit during the fieldwork stage of my research and established contact via email with a Flag representative. After an initial conversation regarding my research, arrangements for a visit never reached fruition, with my emails unanswered.

While corresponding with the Flag representative, however, it was also recommended that I should visit Saint Hill due to its importance in the history of Scientology. Fortunately, an opportunity to do so arose in October 2016, at the INFORM (Information Network Focus on Religious Movements) Autumn Seminar, when I met a practising member of the CoS.[1] After an engaging conversation on my academic interest in Scientology, I was invited to visit Saint Hill and the CoS office in London.

Ahead of my first visit to the CoS of London, my initial participant requested to read an example of my previous work on Scientology. To establish a rapport with the CoS, I sent him a copy of my MA thesis, which focused on media accounts of Scientology. Upon my arrival at my first field visit to the CoS, I was greeted by my initial participant, in addition to two other high-ranking CoS staff members. I was surprised to learn that he had circulated my MA thesis amongst the two staff members. The staff were fairly critical of my work, insisting that media depictions of Scientology are always one-sided, and noted that there were some errors in my account of auditing practice and Scientologist belief, which they aimed to address during my research at the CoS. Nonetheless, by maintaining position as a balanced scholar and not as a journalist attempting to write an exposé, my participants invited me to take tours of the CoS of London and the Saint Hill Advanced Org.

It is in this regard that the CoS' reputation for rigorously attempting to control its public image was particularly noticeable in my fieldwork. My role as an outsider resulted in Donovan's (1999) understanding of the 'observer-effect', meaning that my presence directly influenced my participants' everyday behaviour and attempt to control the way I learnt about Scientology. My activities throughout all my field visits were constantly monitored and arranged by the

Figure 1.1 The Church of Scientology of London (photo by the author, 1 March 2017).

CoS, and I was always accompanied by at least one staff member throughout each visit, with little opportunity to interact with Scientologists not employed by the CoS. While some staff members encouraged me to take photographs, others did not allow photographs at certain times due to concerns regarding the photos being presented out of context. Further to the control of my visits and activities, conversations regarding solo auditing, a method of auditing conducted during the upper Operating Thetan (OT) levels, was restricted due to the confidential nature of what these levels entail. During my tour of Saint Hill, for example, I was shown the entrance to the Solo Technical Division, where OT levels I to III are managed but was unable to enter the rooms due to the confidential documents they were said to contain.

Despite certain limitations, I was able to adopt qualitative methods during my field visits to gain a rich understanding of auditing in contemporary CoS practices, particularly by engaging in participant observation, which allowed me to observe the CoS' 'activities and use of symbols in order to develop an understanding of its meaning and structures' (Knott 2005: 246). Throughout the course of four field visits, I was able to discuss auditing, Scientologist beliefs and other aspects of Scientology with my hosts, who were happy to answer my questions and engage in conversation. These discussions were also accompanied by videos, particularly in the CoS' Information Centre, a floor of the Church containing interactive video stands addressing different aspects of Scientology. I was also provided with several DVDs and literature, including interviews with Hubbard and overviews of various Scientologist practices, which prove to be an invaluable source of information concerning the tech and material culture of Scientology.

In addition to these conversations, I was given full tours of the CoS of London, the Saint Hill Advanced Org and Hubbard's Saint Hill Manor. During these tours, I was able to conduct participant observation of trainee auditors engaging with training exercises in the practical course room (using E-Meters) and theory course room (studying the theory of auditing and other Scientologist practices). This extended to non-staff members practising specialized repetitive routines in preparation for their auditing sessions. Of additional benefit to my research, I was able to witness Scientologists undergoing the Purification Rundown (which I will discuss in Chapter 4) while viewing videos in the Purification Centre and L. Ron Hubbard's former conservatory at Saint Hill.

Despite my role as an outsider limiting which aspects of the CoS my participants allowed me to view, they did allow me to access certain parts of the Saint Hill Manor that are not open to the public. As a researcher this was particularly welcome – Saint Hill holds a special place in Scientologist history not only because of its status as Hubbard's home during the 1960s but also due to the significant amount of CoS teachings and policies the founder developed during this period (Westbrook 2016b: 84–5). As a result, both the Saint Hill Advanced Org and Manor have become sites of pilgrimage for many Scientologists, giving them the opportunity to view Hubbard's personal home, possessions and working spaces. Perhaps the most notable aspect of my tour of the Manor was how it was extended to what my guide playfully described as the 'Scientologist tour' – referring to rooms that are not generally shown to non-Scientologists on public tours of the Manor. This included Hubbard's Research Room, in which he made some of the most notable breakthroughs in his research, including work on the state of Clear, OT I and OT II. I was surprised to be given the opportunity to view rooms, documents and personal possessions of Hubbard's that are usually only accessible to members of the CoS: it was a level of access I did not expect to receive. I was additionally offered the opportunity to take the CoS' Personality Test (the 'Oxford Capacity Analysis' test), which is offered to all newcomers to Scientology. Through these experiences I was given a valuable insight into a newcomer's experience of the CoS.

Online communication with Free Zone Scientologists

When approaching fieldwork with the Free Zone, there is very little previous scholarly data to draw inspiration from. Scholarly analyses of the Free Zone is a relatively new phenomenon, and apart from the example of Kjersti Hellesøy (2013, 2016), there are not many significant examples of scholars conducting fieldwork (nor attempting communication) with Free Zone groups. Hellesøy's work focused on two organized Free Zone groups Ron's Org and the Dror Center, and involved field visits to both groups in Switzerland and Israel, respectively. During these visits Hellesøy (2016) conducted interviews with staff members from both groups on their views on Independent Scientology, and subsequently maintained email correspondence with her participants.

Unlike Hellesøy, however, I intended to avoid focusing on specific Free Zone communities and instead directed my research towards the nuanced nature of the practice of auditing across a variety of Scientologies, including both established Free Zone groups and individual Free Zone Scientologists who practise independently. During one of my interviews, a Free Zone Scientologist claimed that many Freezoners avoid establishing public centres and communities for fear of legal retribution from the CoS, highlighting the need to position the Free Zone in my work as a fluid social environment, and not a series of hierarchical structures.

To achieve this, all my interviews and interactions with Freezoners were conducted via online methods, which I deemed to be particularly effective due to the scattering of Free Zone groups and individuals around the world. In an attempt to gather as wide a variety of Freezoners as possible, I was willing to interview anyone who identifies as a Scientologist outside the CoS, or makes use of the auditing process outside the CoS, regardless of whether they identify as Scientologists. The first challenge I encountered in my initial stages of fieldwork was how to identify, contact and establish communication and trust with Freezoners. The dispersed nature of individual Freezoners and Free Zone communities around the world makes it difficult to estimate the numbers of Scientologists practising Scientology outside the CoS. It is clear, however, that the established Free Zone groups (as opposed to Freezoners who operate independently) are significantly smaller in practitioner numbers than the CoS. For example, Hellesøy (2016: 454) reports that the Dror Center in Israel, one of the largest organized Free Zone groups, consists of eight full-time staff members and about fifty practitioners. Yet there is evidence to suggest that Free Zone groups are growing in popularity; Ron's Org centres can be found across Europe in countries including Denmark, Switzerland and Germany. Additionally, 'in Moscow alone, there are now seven Ron's Orgs' (2016: 452).

My concerns regarding successfully establishing connections with Free Zone Scientologists was short lived. Douglas Cowan notes that online fieldwork offers a 'considerably wider range of informants and a deeper pool of data than we might otherwise expect' (2011: 463), which is particularly applicable to the study of the Free Zone online. Most of my Free Zone participants use the internet to communicate with other Freezoners, to advertise their auditing services or to arrange auditing sessions with a professional auditor. Furthermore, some Freezoners use online methods to conduct their auditing sessions. These factors mean that the internet is more than simply a form of social media for many Freezoners, but is the medium through which their Scientologist practice is conducted. Shortly after contacting a community of Freezoners via the 'Independent Scientology' website (Iscientology.org), I began to accumulate a number of participants (spanning a range of Scientologies) via the snowballing method. Shortly thereafter I conducted a number of interviews via video calls (using programmes such as Skype, FaceTime and Zoom), written questionnaires and email conversations – depending on the availability or preference of the participant in question.

While there are limitations to digital fieldwork, most notably the lack of physical presence to conduct participant observation and engage with material culture, I believe that conducting fieldwork online presents a different set of rewards. On a basic level, digital ethnographic fieldwork is a more financially viable and time-saving method of research, while also reducing the environmental impact of travelling from country to country to speak to a number of fieldwork participants. In terms of the research itself, I was able to approach online interviews and conversations in the same way as I would approach formal face-to-face interviews. The most notable benefit, however, occurred in the weeks and months following the interviews through email contact with my participants. By maintaining email threads, I was able to seek clarification regarding certain terms that may have been used in our discussion and ask further questions that may have come to mind during my later analysis of the interviews. Additionally, since Hubbard's written texts are published by the CoS, and were originally written for application within the CoS, I was faced with the question of how these works are used by different Free Zone communities and individuals. This resulted in my conversations with participants on how these elements of Scientology are practised and interpreted in the Free Zone becoming an invaluable resource in understanding Free Zone Scientology.

Towards the end of my fieldwork, I had conducted online interviews with nine Freezoners across a range of different Scientologies. These included practitioners who identify as 'Free Zone Scientologists' and 'Independent Scientologists' who practise entirely independently, often as auditors, while other participants belonged to organized Free Zone groups or communities, such as Ron's Org. The varied nature of this sample makes for an insightful demonstration of the fluid and nuanced nature of contemporary Scientology, including different interpretations and methods of practising the auditing process, which this book will explore.

Hidden documents and practices

One of the most renowned challenges facing scholars wishing to study Scientology is the existence of leaked and confidential documents which have become a prominent aspect of public discourse surrounding the subject. Beyond engaging with Scientology in the field, the difficulty in approaching Scientology as a topic for research is amplified by the CoS' 'complex layers of secrecy' (Urban 2011: 2), concerning sacred texts and practices that they feel should be kept hidden from public view. When approaching his own study of Scientology, Hugh Urban argues that the secretive nature of the CoS raises an 'ethical and epistemological double-bind' (Urban 2011: 10), which he outlined in the following terms:

> This double-bind can be formulated as follows: first, how can one say anything meaningful about a group that is extremely private and regards portions of its teachings as off-limits to outsiders? Second, is it ethical to even attempt to penetrate the inner secrets of a religious community of which one is not a member – particularly one that sees itself as attacked and persecuted by media, government, and other critics? (Urban 2011: 11)

Urban's double-bind highlights the methodological challenges for both a basic approach to Scientology (understanding its practices and texts) and for attempting to engage with secretive groups more generally as part of a fieldwork project (including conducting interviews with highly critical former members). At its most basic, the study of Scientology's beliefs and practices can be challenging simply due to the fact that a significant portion of these are off-limits to not only outsiders but also Scientologists who have not sufficiently advanced along Hubbard's Bridge to Total Freedom. However, critically engaging with Scientology's beliefs and practices is arguably a minor problem compared to the overall challenge of conducting a thorough study of the movement, particularly due to the CoS' often hostile reaction towards the public disclosure of these beliefs and practices, and its attempt to control its public image. This is an issue that has continued to escalate for the CoS in the age of the internet and 'leaking' culture (the covert disclosure of confidential information in the public domain), which has led to former members leaking OT documents online for public scrutiny (Rothstein 2009: 368; Urban 2017: 19).

The Xenu documents, a space-operatic mythology which concerns the origin of human life on Earth, is arguably the most controversial leaked Scientologist document.[2] As the intention of the CoS is that the esoteric aspect of its faith, as specifically taught by Hubbard, should remain hidden from uninitiated members of the CoS who have not yet reached the required level on Hubbard's Bridge to Total Freedom (explored further in Chapter 4). It is here that the Xenu documents are allegedly made available to practising CoS members once they have reached the third level of Operating Thetan (OT III). The core of the mythology is a narrative which claims that Xenu, the head of the Galactic Federation, solved an overpopulation problem by sending thetans to Teegeeack (Earth), which has now resulted in the thetans being trapped in the material universe and constrained in physical bodies (Rothstein 2009: 373–4).

The examination of leaked and highly guarded Scientologist information, such as the Xenu documents, via the internet is not an entirely new concern for scholars, who are faced with a dilemma of whether to critically engage with these texts or not. The emergence and popularity of the internet has had a significant influence on this issue, not simply because of its increasing popularity and use in contemporary society, but also due to the potential of such documents to influence the wider public perception of Scientology. The information contained in leaked OT documents, specifically the Xenu narrative, is frequently featured in critiques and satirical lampoons of Scientology in an attempt to mock their beliefs. With this in mind, it becomes extremely difficult to ignore the presence of these documents, their influence on outsider perceptions of Scientology and the attempts of the CoS to remove them from public access. As Urban asks, 'should we frankly acknowledge that, in the internet age, little if anything can realistically remain "esoteric" for long and that Scientology's advanced tech should be analysed freely like any other publicly available religious material?' (2011: 13). This easily accessible nature of leaked data online creates an interesting boundary between outside scholars and CoS members. As practitioners are discouraged from reading or engaging with the documents until they have reached OT III, scholars (and outsiders more generally) have knowledge of Scientologist practices and texts that many on the inside do not (Gregg and Thomas 2019: 365).

In the first in-depth academic analysis of the Xenu mythology, Rothstein justifies the use of the leaked documents by arguing that 'pretending that the texts are *not* there is ridiculous, and acting as if anyone with potential interest in the subject is unaware of this material equally meaningless. The texts are there, almost waiting for scholarly inspection and analysis' (2009: 368, emphasis in original). In other words, scholars simply cannot turn their attention away from the Xenu documents based upon this request, particularly due to the widespread circulation of the writings online. Rothstein recognizes the potential hazards of the use of leaked online information, particularly concerning their true origin, and he argues that these concerns must be kept in mind when examining these documents, in addition to considering the accounts of former (often disillusioned) members of the CoS.

It is indeed possible that these documents could vary greatly from the genuine teachings of the CoS. The documents may have been edited to discredit and harm the movement, or even doctored by the CoS themselves to maintain the esoteric integrity of their texts (2009: 368). It is for this reason (and out of respect to members of the CoS) that I have chosen to not directly quote from any of the leaked OT III documents in this book. As Rothstein correctly observed, however, the existence of the documents cannot be ignored. Accordingly, this work's treatment of the documents will focus instead on their impact on contemporary Scientologist auditing, rather than on the complexities of the narrative itself (see Urban 2017: 15).[3] I will return to this issue in Chapter 4.

Chryssides (1999: 288) adds that the general response from members of the CoS is that leaked accounts of the OT III documents are merely distorted versions of accounts stolen from their British headquarters. They claim that these documents have been changed and quoted out of context in an attempt to discredit the CoS. Despite all the contested accounts of the Xenu mythology, however, it is known that Hubbard declared in 1967 that the root of human suffering can be found in an event that took place seventy-five million years ago, which had a lasting impact on the condition of the human spirit. The secrets and benefits of OT III are therefore aimed at undoing and preventing the effects of this event (1999: 288).

Through examining the experiences of other scholars that have studied Scientology, this chapter has already demonstrated the CoS' history of scepticism towards scholars taking an interest in Scientology. The secretive nature of the CoS, including practices and texts that are only revealed to insiders, places an immediate barrier between the CoS and scholars (Urban 2011: 11). Without becoming 'fully' immersed in the CoS by becoming a member, an outsider scholar will most often never receive the opportunity to witness secret practices and texts first-hand, making Kim Knott's (2005: 246) immersive category of 'observer-as-participant' (a scholar taking part in the activities they observe) impossible. This does not, however, compromise the value of the research of outsider scholars examining secretive organizations. For example, Lilith Mahmud (2013: 198), in her study of Italian Freemasonry, was initially encouraged by her participants to join a Masonic lodge to be able to view and take part in the esoteric ceremonies that would otherwise be inaccessible. Clarifying that her study considered Freemasonry as an organization, and was not concerned with its esoteric practices, Mahmud (2013: 199) was able to pursue a rich study of Italian Freemasonry through establishing a rapport with a variety of Freemasons across a number of different lodges, and without becoming a member. Similarly, by accepting that my participants at the CoS would never openly discuss the confidential details of the OT levels, I pursued conversations on the contemporary practice of auditing and the CoS' recent initiatives, such as the *Golden Age of Tech Phase II*, which they claim has made auditing a more efficient process.

I found that this refocusing of my fieldwork to not concern hidden practices did not limit my research. Much like Mahmud, who explains that 'tell-all books authored by disgruntled former Masons or profane spies' (2013: 198) shed light on esoteric Masonic practices, the confidential details of the CoS' OT levels 'have been made widely available by ex-Scientologists [who] seek to expose what they wish to present as "strange" beliefs' (Thomas 2017a: online). There is a potentially biased nature to these accounts, which poses a methodological challenge for scholars of religion, particularly when attempting a methodologically agnostic approach. Yet, as Chryssides (2017) explains, scholars of religion possess the skills to carefully evaluate and triangulate their sources, making these accounts invaluable in shedding light on aspects of new religions that would otherwise remain hidden.

Outline of chapters

Before commencing a study of Scientology, it is important to acknowledge the complexities of the subject matter. Chapter 2, 'The Church of Scientology and the "Free Zone": A Complex Relationship', is intended as an accessible summary of the key events and themes in the history of Scientology. Despite its status as a relatively 'new' religion, Scientology boasts an eventful and occasionally controversial history. This chapter begins with an account of establishment of the CoS and the influences of L. Ron Hubbard's early life, including his fascination with Freudian psychology and his near-death experience (documented in his *Excalibur* narrative), on his theories of Dianetics and Scientology. It moves on to consider the emergence of the Free Zone (under Captain Bill Robertson) during the early 1980s, including the CoS' opposition to Free Zone practice ('squirrelling') and its critics. The chapter concludes with an account of Scientology's turbulent relationship with the media, including its online critics (such as Anonymous), and wider popular culture – a vital part of understanding the contemporary Scientology in the twenty-first century.

As this book primarily concerns the auditing practice – more specifically its importance in contemporary Scientologies – Chapter 3 provides an introduction to the practice and Hubbard's Dianetic theory. Perhaps some of the most challenging aspects of conducting a scholarly examination of Scientology are the complexities of Hubbard's Scientological practices, collectively known as the 'tech', in addition to his use of Scientologist nomenclature (frequently referred to by Scientologists as 'Scientologese'). By examining Hubbard's theories behind the tech, and the basic purpose and application of auditing, this chapter acts as a foundation for the subsequent chapters in this book, which will consider the nuanced nature of auditing across Scientologies. Finally, the chapter will conclude by considering the hybrid nature of auditing as a combination of religious and secular-scientific elements – one of the process' most defining features.

With an appropriate explanation of auditing in place, Chapter 4 seeks to explore the Scientologist notion of the self. Since the primary purpose of auditing is self-development, this chapter involves a close engagement with Hubbard's theoretical work on the nature of the self, the belief in the spiritual thetan (the 'true' self in Scientology), and the goal of self-development in Scientology, that is, progression on Hubbard's Bridge to Total Freedom. Expanding on the importance of the self in auditing, this chapter also explores contemporary Scientologist practices related to the self, such as the Purification Rundown, a detoxification programme believed to prepare the body for effective auditing sessions.

Chapter 5, 'Authenticity and Innovation', builds upon the previous chapter by exploring the discourse of authenticity and innovation across contemporary Scientologies. This discourse concerns the notion of 'Standard Tech' and the application of auditing as it is perceived to have been intended by Hubbard. Drawing from my fieldwork with Free Zone Scientologists, I demonstrate the boundaries between Scientologists that emerge from different interpretations of Hubbard's writings and from different experiences of auditing.

In Chapter 6 of this book I examine the material culture of Scientology, particularly the objects pertaining to the auditing process. Amongst the material culture discussed in this chapter is the E-Meter, an electronic device used in auditing sessions. Used in both CoS and Free Zone spaces, the E-Meter is the most significant object in Scientology and is considered by many Scientologists to be essential to auditing. Building upon the previous chapter's discussion of authenticity and innovation, this chapter examines the use of the E-Meter in auditing sessions in contemporary Scientologies, including Free Zone approaches towards the device and customized E-Meter models that move away from Hubbard's original designs.

Following the analysis of contemporary auditing in the previous three chapters, particularly its influence on Free Zone spheres, Chapter 7 reflects on the implications of this research on the wider study of contemporary religions. It demonstrates that adopting a double-focus on the top-down hierarchy of the CoS and fluid-horizontal nature of the Free Zone opens new frameworks for the study of new religions. While former studies of NRMs have primarily focused on typologies, such as the brainwashing thesis and secularization, this work adopts the methods of 'lived religion' to consider the boundaries and fluidity of Free Zone Scientology outside institutional hierarchies. This chapter considers how the data gathered in this book demonstrates a breakdown in routinized charisma, and the ways in which lived religion allows scholars to view the emergence of schisms and emergence of new forms of contemporary religion through the innovative creativity of religious agents.

The final chapter draws together the data gathered and analysed in this book. Following this, I reflect on the contribution of this book to the sociology of NRMs and wider study of religions, and the potential directions for the future of the study of Scientology.

Part I

From Scientology to Scientologies

2

The Church of Scientology and the 'Free Zone'
A complex relationship

The early life of L. Ron Hubbard

It is not an understatement to say that Lafayette Ronald Hubbard, most commonly known as L. Ron Hubbard, had already lived an eventful life prior to his establishment of Scientology in the early 1950s. Indeed, the influences of his naval experiences, fascination with the human mind and work as a 'pulp fiction' author can be traced in Scientologist beliefs, practices and imagery. For the purposes of this study, I intend to provide a succinct summary of Hubbard's life prior to the publication of *Dianetics: The Modern Science of Mental Health* (*DMSMH*), outlining the key events which played a role in the development of Scientology.[1] Furthermore, a timeline outlining the order of L. Ron Hubbard's key publications and events related to the history of Scientology is also included in Appendix A.

Born in Tilden, Nebraska (United States) on 13 March 1911 to Methodist parents, Hubbard demonstrated signs of interest in non-Western spirituality and the psychology of the human mind at a particularly young age. At the age of six it is claimed that Hubbard befriended a Blackfoot shaman named 'Old Tom' (Westbrook 2019: 67), and that 'he became a blood brother of the Blackfeet, an honor [sic] bestowed on few white men' (The Church of Scientology International 1998: 28). Following his father's re-joining the US Navy 1917, his family eventually settled in Seattle, Washington. It was here that a twelve-year-old Hubbard became acquainted with Joseph 'Snake' Thompson, a US Navy commander and student of Sigmund Freud. Thompson is frequently credited with sparking Hubbard's interest in the human mind by introducing him to the psychology of the brain (Melton 2009: 18). While it is claimed by the Church of Scientology International that Thompson 'took it upon himself to pass on the essentials of Freudian theory' (1998: 29) to Hubbard, the extent of his teaching is unknown. However, Hubbard himself would remark in 1950 that Thompson 'had a tremendous influence upon [him]' (Hubbard, cited in Westbrook 2019: 67) and his interest in the treatment of the human mind.

Alongside his initial interest in the analysis of the mind, Hubbard became an active member of the Boy Scouts of America at the age of thirteen, and three years later began a series of expeditions in China, the West Indies and the Caribbean (Melton 2009: 18). Hubbard cited these journeys and the religious practices he witnessed as significant inspirations when developing his Dianetic theory (Urban 2011: 43), claiming that he had observed phenomena including 'a magician whose ancestors served in the court of Kublai Khan and a Hindu who could hypnotize cats' (Hubbard [1950] 2007a: 9). This period features heavily in Church of Scientology (CoS) biographies of Hubbard, which use Hubbard's encounters with various cultures and communities to not only position him as a person of exceptional character but also as events that inspired Hubbard to aid humanity through developing his science of the mind. The CoS' *'What Is Scientology?'* textbook outlines several anecdotes from his journeys, adding that 'for all the wonders of these lands and all his respect for those whom he encountered, he still saw much [human suffering] that concerned him' (The Church of Scientology International 1998: 34). Indeed, all aspects of CoS accounts of Hubbard's early life are presented as a trajectory towards the publication of *DMSMH*. In other words, Hubbard's encounters with Eastern religion/culture, fascination with psychological ideas and urge to improve the human condition all led him to conduct his Scientological work on the 'tech'.

Scientologist accounts of Hubbard's life, particularly from the CoS, are largely hagiographic in an attempt to legitimize Hubbard's work and authority (Christensen 2005: 243). To this end, the CoS has constructed a 'revisionist historical narrative' (Robertson 2016: 308), exemplified by evidence that Hubbard's 'war records [during the Second-World War] have been falsified to support his fraudulent claims to have been injured at duty and awarded medals of valour' (Robertson 2016: 308), while also omitting Hubbard's participation in occult work with Aleister Crowley in the 1940s (see also Urban 2012). These efforts to avoid mention of more controversial events in Hubbard's life create an image of Hubbard as a person of exceptional character, morals and intelligence. As Christensen, in her study of the *What Is Scientology?* hagiography, remarks, 'Hubbard is textualized and dehumanized in being considered an agent with special qualities and the only source of true salvation' (2005: 249). Accordingly, hagiographic accounts help establish Hubbard's authority and charismatic leadership in the CoS, and raises discourses surrounding authenticity across Scientologies (as I will discuss in Chapter 5).

Hagiographic concerns aside, it is known that Hubbard went on to pursue studies in molecular physics and civil engineering at George Washington University in 1930. This period is cited in the CoS hagiography as being the period which allowed Hubbard to utilize a 'scientific approach to solving the riddles of existence and man's spiritual potential' (The Church of Scientology International 1998: 35), prompting the double-axis between scientific method and Eastern spirituality which would become a defining characteristic of Scientologist techniques. However, Hubbard only pursued these studies for two years and later confessed to being a poor student (Urban 2011: 32; Westbrook 2019: 68). Soon thereafter Hubbard developed an association with *Astounding Science Fiction* magazine, through which he achieved significant success as a 'pulp fiction' author. Publishing at a significant rate, often through a nom de plume, Hubbard amassed hundreds of short stories and novels spanning genres including Westerns and supernatural fantasy, finding success with titles such as *Fear*, *Typewriter in the Sky* and *Final Blackout* (Westbrook 2019: 68). Despite this range in genres, Hubbard's work as an author of fiction is mostly closely associated with the genre of science fiction due to his success in *Astounding Science Fiction*, through which he published early work on Scientologist theory (Melton 2009: 21).

Further to the combined influences of his interests in Eastern spirituality, psychotherapeutic approaches to the mind and science fiction, Hubbard's Dianetic theories were also influenced by a spiritual experience. In 1938, while finding success as an author, Hubbard attested to a near-death experience while under the influence of anaesthetic during a dental operation. Described by the CoS as his 'entrance into the philosophic realm' (Bridge Publications 2012: 7), Hubbard is believed to have gained a hitherto unknown knowledge of the nature of humanity. In a manuscript titled *Excalibur*, Hubbard outlined the experience accordingly:

> It began with an operation. I took gas as an anesthetic [*sic*] and while under the influence of it my heart must have stopped beating, as in my terror I knew I was slipping through the Curtain [*sic*] and into the land of shades. . . . Though badly shaken I was quite rational when I was restored. The people around me looked frightened – more frightened than I. I was not thinking about what I had been through nearly so much as what I *knew*. I had not yet fully returned to life. I was still in contact with Something [*sic*]. And in that state I remained for some days, all the while puzzling over what I *knew*. It was clear that if I could but remember

> I would have the secret of life. This in itself was enough to drive one mad, so illusive [sic] was that just-beyond-reach information. And then one morning, just as I awoke, it came to me. (Hubbard, cited in Bridge Publications 2012: 11, emphasis in original)

The *Excalibur* narrative anticipates the religious inflection that Hubbard's science of the mind would take between the publication of *DMSMH* and establishment of the CoS. This is exemplified by notable themes such as the suggestion of a revelation of esoteric knowledge and exteriorization from the physical body, which are both central aspects of Scientologist belief and practice (Urban 2011: 38). Speculating further about the esoteric knowledge he believed to possess, Hubbard wrote:

> Suppose all the wisdom of the world were reduced to just one line; suppose that one line *were* to be written today and given to you. . . . There *is* one line, conjured up out of a morass of facts and made available as an integrated unit to explain such things. This line is the philosophy of philosophy, thereby carrying the entire subject back into the simple and humble truth. All life is directed by one command and one command only – SURVIVE! [sic]. (Hubbard, cited in Bridge Publications 2012: 13–14, emphasis in original)

Hubbard built upon this theory that all human action is directed by the pursuit of survival in *The Original Thesis*, which he circulated privately amongst friends and the science fiction community during 1948.[2] This helped him gain a small circle of supporters which led to his second publication on Dianetic theory, 'Terra Incognita: The Mind', published in *The Explorer's Club Journal* (Melton 2009: 21). Hubbard's ideas gained traction amongst the science fiction community, not least with John Campbell, Jr., the editor of *Astounding Science Fiction*. Campbell allowed Hubbard to publish his first article on Dianetics in the magazine under the title 'Dianetics: A New Science of the Mind', 'which was not presented as "astounding science fiction" but rather as a revolutionary new science of the human mind' (Urban 2011: 43). Campbell became an enthusiastic supporter of Dianetics and promoted the theory with *Astounding Science Fiction* readers, claiming that 'fifteen minutes of Dianetics can get more results than five years of psychoanalysis. . . . We've broken homosexuals, alcoholics, asthmatics, arthritics and nymphomaniacs' (Campbell, cited in Urban 2011: 45).[3] While Campbell was not entirely uncritical of Hubbard's work, allowing Hubbard to publish his Dianetic theory in his magazine became a significant factor to its success (Berger 1989: 125).

Hubbard's promotion of Dianetic practice in a science fiction magazine is highly significant to both the practice of Scientology and its perception amongst non-Scientologists. Dianetics was immediately successful within the science fiction community, to the extent that the auditing process was depicted in science fiction stories of the time, such as the way in which an auditing session was used to drive the narrative of Theodore Sturgeon's *Baby is Three* (Berger 1989: 139). Dianetics was not universally popular in the science fiction community, however, with some authors describing the practice as 'nonsensical' (Berger 1989: 124), and a potential detriment to the reputation *Astounding Science Fiction* had earned from its reporting on the development of atomic energy. This combined publicity was beneficial for Hubbard; in 1950 he was able to introduce the wider American public to his theories through the publication of *DMSMH*. The book was met with considerable commercial success, becoming an instant bestseller, prompting Hubbard to become a popular lecturer on Dianetics and the human mind with the general public (Bromley 2009: 87).

The establishment of the Church of Scientology

While *DMSMH* was finding popularity with an American market during the early 1950s, Hubbard continued his research on the human mind and self-development. Despite his previously critical stance on religiosity, Hubbard soon began to include religious elements in Dianetic theory.[4] This was due, in part, to a number of Preclears testifying to recollections of past life experiences during their auditing sessions. Exploring this issue further, Hubbard introduced the concept of theta beings (the spiritual and 'true' self in Scientology, also known as the thetan), stating that 'the theta being is the "I", it is WHO the preclear [*sic*] is' (Hubbard [1952] 2007c: 21, emphasis in original). Accordingly, the notion of Scientology was established, defined by Hubbard as 'the study and handling of the spirit in relationship to itself, universes and other life' ([1956] 2007: 5).[5] This marked the transition from Dianetic auditing and Scientology auditing, leading to an important distinction; 'Dianetic auditing treats the mind, while Scientology auditing treats the thetan in its spiritual development' (Gregg and Thomas 2019: 352) (this is explored further in Chapter 3). Indeed, Dianetic auditing was intended to be a purely psychological and psychotherapeutic endeavour, yet Hubbard considered Scientology to be an amalgamation of both his Dianetic theory of the mind and his research into the perceived spiritual nature of humanity. With this in mind, the concept of 'Scientology' is positioned as a series of techniques and methods which simultaneously lead to mental and spiritual fulfilment.

While preparing for the release of *DMSMH*, Hubbard established the Hubbard Dianetic Research Foundation to train auditors and coordinate Dianetic groups (Melton 2000: 9). He was correct in anticipating public appetite for his work; he soon amassed a following of supporters who enthusiastically attested to the benefits of auditing (Urban 2011: 52). Moreover, once Hubbard began the shift from the secular-scientific application of Dianetics to its use in Scientology, 'students of Dianetics and Scientology were already acknowledging that Scientology functioned for them as their religion' (Melton 2009: 23), providing the foundation for Hubbard to open the first CoS office in Los Angeles in 1954 (Lewis 2009a: 5). The transition from Dianetics to Scientology was not a universally popular decision amongst members of the Dianetic community, with some expressing concerns that the transition to religiosity would descend Dianetics 'into mystical mumbo jumbo' (Urban 2011: 11).

Nonetheless, Hubbard began to incorporate classically 'religious' elements to the structure of the CoS through the use of ecclesiastical terminology and ideas. For example, he ordained 'ministers' that were trained in the application of Scientology (Urban 2011: 66), and practising Scientologists are often referred to as Scientologist practitioners or parishioners (Westbrook 2016a: 30). Hubbard's decision to establish Scientology as a religion, and the apparent shift of auditing from its psychiatric and psychotherapeutic roots to its subsequent religious status, drew criticism from a number of sources outside the initial Dianetic movement. Some claimed that Hubbard's motivations were purely financial, with writers and acquaintances such as Lloyd Eschbach claiming to have witnessed Hubbard stating his wish to 'start a religion. That's where the money is!' (cited in Urban 2011: 58). Urban (2011) is keen to note, however, that it would be an error to categorize Hubbard's decision as being based on money-making or tax-evading schemes. Rather, he believes that the gradual shift Hubbard made towards religious or spiritual concerns was influenced by both internal and external tensions within the Dianetic movement.

Hubbard remained the leader of the CoS throughout his lifetime, during which he continued his research on the tech. Following a disengagement from public life in the early 1980s, Hubbard died of a stroke on 24 January 1986 at his ranch in Creston, California (Rigal-Cellard 2009: 326; Westbrook 2019: 168). The lack of details regarding the whereabouts of Hubbard in his final years, during which 'only a handful of Scientologists had even known where Hubbard was physically located' (Ruskell and Lewis 2016: 334), has resulted in much speculation regarding whether a coup of the CoS took place. This discourse surrounding Hubbard's passing, and criticism of CoS practices following his death, has remained a prominent issue across the spectrum of Free Zone Scientologies, as this book goes on to demonstrate.

Hubbard was succeeded by David Miscavige in 1987, a charismatic and ambitious young CoS staff member. Miscavige, who continues to lead the CoS to this day, holds the role of Chairman of the Board of the Religious Technology Center, an organization 'which owns all copyrights on the estate of L. Ron Hubbard' (Urban 2011: 131). Despite succeeding Hubbard in terms of leadership, Miscavige holds a significantly different position to the founder. Unlike Hubbard, he does not develop the tech, nor conduct Scientological research. Rather his position is characterized by two facets – legitimacy and legacy. As I will discuss further in Chapter 5, throughout the course of his leadership, Miscavige has run a series of projects and campaigns that have allowed the CoS to claim a position of legitimacy. On the one hand, this concerns religious legitimacy, with the ending of the so-called 'War' with the Internal Revenue Service in 1993 (thus securing tax exemption in the United States) (Westbrook 2019: 174), often viewed within the CoS as a milestone in securing public legitimacy as a 'real religion'. On the other, Miscavige's role concerns Scientological legitimacy and securing the CoS' status as the only acceptable form of Scientology. Through legacy projects such as the *Golden Age of Knowledge* and *Golden Age of Tech*, which aim to preserve the perceived 'true' application of Hubbard's work, further boundaries have been created between the CoS (presenting a legitimate form of Scientology) and the Free Zone (accused of Scientological heresy).

Captain Bill Robertson

The term 'Free Zone' is generally associated with Bill Robertson (often referred to as 'Captain Bill' or 'CBR'), an influential figure in the Scientology Sea Organization (Sea Org), the ecclesiastical order of advanced Scientologists. Established by Hubbard in 1967, the Sea Org is an organization of highly trained auditors delivering advanced Scientologist programmes to practitioners (Westbrook 2019: 140). The nature of the Sea Org stems from Hubbard's fascination with naval imagery and terminology, with the initial Sea Org members living aboard a fleet of ships, while making use of naval titles and uniforms (The Church of Scientology International 1998: 323).[6] Indeed, during his years in the Sea Org, Bill Robertson assumed the role of Captain of the Sea Org flagship, the *Apollo*. His promotion to the role of Captain was an award Hubbard only otherwise bestowed upon his wife, Mary Sue, suggesting a close bond between Robertson and Hubbard (Ron's Org Committee n.d.-a).

As previously discussed, Hubbard withdrew from public life in the early 1980s to focus on his Scientological research. In doing so, he established the Church of Scientology International in 1981, an organization that would manage the administrative duties of the CoS during his absence. Coinciding with this withdrawal, tensions began to rise within the CoS, resulting in much debate and disagreement over the character of the institutionalized nature of the CoS. This conflict caused a number of splits, with the various Scientologist communities that wished to be distanced from the CoS, while continuing to practise auditing and the teachings of Scientology, becoming collectively known as the Free Zone (Grossman 1995).

Differences in opinion in the CoS extend further than methods of auditing practice and Scientologist teaching, with the date of Hubbard's death being widely contested in the Free Zone. While there is no agreed date for Hubbard's disappearance amongst Free Zone groups, concerns have inevitably been raised regarding the validity of documents published under his name by the CoS, while Robertson subsequently claimed that he channelled further Scientologist teaching regarding higher OT levels from Hubbard after his death (Lewis 2013: 265).

Several online Free Zone sources suggest that Robertson was the recipient of extra-terrestrial knowledge in November 1982 through the form of an 'Official Decree' from the Galactic Grand Council. This decree declared that the planet Teegeeack (Earth), is a 'Free Zone' – free from any interference from any other part of the galaxy or economic interference from 'any non-planetary agency or power' (Galactic Patrol n.d.). Thus, the Free Zone movement had begun, distinct and in opposition to the CoS, yet still based on the teachings of L. Ron Hubbard.

Robertson's knowledge of and disenchantment with the CoS resulted in his establishment of Ron's Org in 1984, a form of Scientology that 'explicitly delimitates itself' from the CoS and other unofficial Scientology bodies (Ron's Org Bern n.d.: 3). Ron's Org aims to promote the core principles of Hubbard's technology and philosophy as a 'workable method to help the individual to form and improve the conditions of [their] life' (Ron's Org Bern n.d.: 3). Despite Robertson's coining of the term 'Free Zone', however, the Free Zone has evolved to become an umbrella term for all Scientologists who practise Scientology independently from the CoS (Ex-Scientology Kids n.d.), resulting in Ron's Org becoming just one part of the overall Free Zone movement.

The Free Zone, squirrelling and suppressive persons

Arguably the main principle of the Free Zone is that the practice of Scientology does not require a leader, nor a specific community or organization to which one must belong, as the primary focus of Scientology lies in the development of the individual practising it (Independent Scientology n.d.-b). A website that promotes 'Independent Scientology' argues that '"Scientology" does not equal "the Church of Scientology". . . . [And that] the problem with the CoS is their *actions* not their *beliefs*' (Independent Scientology n.d.-a, emphasis in original), wishing to draw a distance between the practice of Scientology and the institution of the CoS, and also directing attention towards its principle of providing auditing sessions at what it deems to be affordable prices. There are no strict guidelines or strong forms of community within the Free Zone, with many Freezoners choosing to practise Scientology independently. However, some groups of Scientologists have gathered to form their own strand of Scientologist practice, with Ron's Org being the most prominent example.

When responding to the criticisms of the Free Zone, the CoS accuses Free Zone Scientologists of 'performing the ultimate sin of *squirrelling* – practising the technology of Hubbard outside the sanctioned remit of the Religious Technology [Center]' (Gregg and Chryssides 2017: 26, emphasis in original), viewing any type of Scientology that exists outside the CoS to be illegitimate. In 1965 Hubbard issued a bulletin to CoS staff and members, titled *Keeping Scientology Working* (KSW), a ten-point policy which is not only significant for the management of the CoS but also allowed Hubbard to combat an increasing number of individuals adopting the tech outside the CoS (Schorey 2016: 341). Described by Westbrook as the 'crown jewel of Scientology's systematic theology' (2019: 124), KSW was Hubbard's endeavour to establish an orthodoxy within the CoS. It not only attempts to ensure a precise application of his vision of the tech throughout all CoS Orgs but also acts as a command which forbids the use of the tech outside the CoS.

As a result of KSW, members of the CoS frequently refer to Freezoners as 'squirrels', a derogatory term that originated from Hubbard (Cusack 2016: 485). In the bulletin Hubbard defined squirrelling as 'going off into weird practices or altering Scientology' (Hubbard 1965a: 6). This notion of changing or altering Scientology has been extended to the mere act of practising Scientology outside the CoS, making squirrelling 'an egregious crime against the Church, resulting in excommunication and shunning of members accused of perpetrating these activities' (Schorey 2016: 343). Hubbard expanded on KSW with another bulletin, titled *Safeguarding Technology* (1965b), in which he maintained that the tech is infallible, resulting in any changes to the tech being a detriment to the practice. Accordingly, Hubbard established that the act of squirrelling is potentially dangerous, describing it as 'destructive of a workable system' (1965b: online), while also deeming it entirely unnecessary due to his perception of the tech as a precise and workable method.

Despite this condemnation of squirrels in 1965, Cusack (2016: 503) argues that Hubbard could not possibly have predicted the age of the internet, in which his confidential materials would be freely available to Free Zone Scientologists, resulting in his squirrelling policy becoming a remnant of Scientologist history. With this in mind, Free Zone Scientologists often feel free to practise Scientology without fear of squirrelling, perceiving themselves as not being outside of Hubbard's core teaching. However, Hubbard's criticism of squirrels continues to result in an entire rejection of Free Zone Scientologies by the CoS. By attempting to respond to the criticism it faces from the Free Zone, in addition to its non-Scientologist critics, the CoS demonstrates 'patterns of organizational self-sabotage' (Lewis 2012: 140). Describing the CoS as 'its own worst enemy' (Lewis 2012: 140), Lewis highlights attempts by the CoS to silence or respond to their critics in ways that have resulted in further negative publicity for Scientology. These include the CoS' attempt to prevent the publication of critical books on Scientology (which only draw further attention to the publications), in addition to the extreme 'fair game' policy – the most notable CoS measure against its critics. The fair game policy has become notorious for its aggressive and heavy-handed nature, in which Hubbard outlined methods of silencing 'Suppressive Persons' (critics of Scientology, also known as SPs), stating that they are open to being 'tricked, sued or lied to or destroyed' (Hubbard, cited in Lewis 2012: 140). Hubbard defined an SP as an individual who 'will goof up or vilify any effort to help anybody and particularly knife with violence anything calculated to make human beings more powerful or more intelligent' and an 'Anti-Social Personality' [*sic*] (Hubbard [1968] 2007: 171).

It is the presence of SPs that has resulted in the Scientologist notion of 'disconnection' – 'a self-determined decision made by an individual that he is not going to be connected to another. . . . A severing of a communication line' (Hubbard [1968] 2007: 206). This has manifested itself in the CoS' disconnection policy, in which all SPs are to be cut off from all communication from their existing Scientologist family and friends (Lewis 2012: 140). Association with an SP can make a Scientologist a 'Potential Trouble Source' (PTS). In such a scenario the PTS is expected to attempt to resolve the situation. Should the PTS fail in doing this, and subsequently refuse to disconnect from the SP, they could also become SPs (Hubbard [1968] 2007: 206).

According to Lewis, the disconnection policy simply aggravates ex-Scientologists, thus resulting in 'many otherwise neutral to moderately critical ex-members [becoming] devoted enemies of the Church' (2012: 141). He also states that the combination of these controversies and hostility from the CoS have helped the Free Zone, with many Free Zone practitioners condemning the CoS' practices and policies, making it increasingly difficult for ex-members to re-join the CoS or engage with its practitioners once again. While Hubbard claimed to have abandoned this practice in the name of public relations, recent cases of harassment suggest that the policy is still active in the contemporary CoS (Gregg and Thomas 2019: 354). Perhaps the most notable example of the fair game policy being utilized is the highly publicized harassment of former CoS member Mark 'Marty' Rathbun, who during his time in the CoS held the prestigious and influential post of Inspector General of the Religious Technology Center. His encounter in 2011 with the 'Squirrel Busters', a group of Scientologists who accused him of squirrelling, resulted in significant media coverage of the footage of the incidents shared online by Rathbun (Gregg and Thomas 2019: 355).

Rathbun and his experiences of the Squirrel Busters and the fair game policy have more recently been a focal point of a major exposé documentary, *My Scientology Movie* (2015), by British filmmaker and journalist, Louis Theroux. The documentary features Rathbun providing first-hand experience of his time in the CoS, Scientologist practice, and makes accusations of misconduct towards the current leader of the CoS, David Miscavige. Throughout the course of the documentary, Theroux spends a prolonged period of time with Rathbun, discussing his experiences of Scientology and enlisting his assistance in re-enacting scenarios featuring Miscavige and alleged incidents of malpractice and abuse. Eventually the two are followed by camera crews maintaining a record of their activities for the purpose of an alleged response documentary produced by the CoS. The climax of the film involves a confrontation between Rathbun and a CoS member, who asks him intrusive questions about his personal life. Such hostile interactions between the CoS and former Scientologists suggest that the 'distancing from the fair game policy seems to be in name only' (Gregg and Thomas 2019: 354).

Central to Free Zone practice, as this book will demonstrate, is the use of the internet and the formation of online communities. Much Free Zone activity online is dedicated to levelling criticism towards the CoS, with many Freezoners viewing online activism as 'representing the total severance of their former loyalty to the church' (Schorey 2016: 351). However, a crucial aspect of the online presence of Free Zone Scientologists is expressing their belief in the validity of the philosophy of Hubbard, while additionally allowing these groups and individuals to promote their auditing services. There are online directories of Free Zone auditors and groups promoting their availability for auditing sessions, such as The Association of Professional Independent Scientologists (Freezone Auditors 2008; International Freezone Association Inc. n.d.). Lewis (2013: 265) notes that traffic between these Free Zone movements tends to be open, with unaffiliated Scientologists able to conduct sessions and train in multiple centres. This discourse between unaffiliated Scientologists is exemplified by the (now-discontinued) online magazine, *International Viewpoints*, a collection of articles written by Independent Scientologists. *International Viewpoints*, as Kyle D. Byron (2015: 129) explains, demonstrates the use of online communication by Free Zone Scientologists discussing various understandings of Scientologist practices. Indeed, the open nature of the Free Zone and its rise in popularity on the internet, particularly in relation to those who can advertise and offer their own auditing services to Free Zone Scientologists and others, marks an important step in the growth of the Free Zone community. Coupled with other independent Scientologist organizations that are categorized under the term 'Free Zone', such as Ron's Org, they appear as horizontal and improvised forms of Scientology practice in sharp distinction to the vertical-hierarchical relations favoured by the CoS.

Scientology and the media

When considering the history of Scientology, particularly the institutionalized CoS, it is important to understand the movement's controversial history in popular media, and its own use of the media in promoting Scientology. The CoS has often utilized various forms of media to promote its practices and to attract converts to Scientology. It is now possible to use the internet to take the CoS' personality test, formally known as the 'Oxford Capacity Analysis' test. Rigal-Cellard (2009: 330) compares the use of the personality test to attract new CoS members to the door-to-door evangelization of the Jehovah Witnesses and Mormon missionaries. The test is composed of 200 questions notionally used to understand the personality of the participant. Once the results have been analysed (usually instantly when done online), the response outlines the participant's shortcomings and the potential solutions offered by Scientology. The CoS has also invested time in creating advertisements for itself, such as the highly publicized Super Bowl television commercial aired in February 2020, encouraging viewers to 'rediscover the human soul' (Scientology 2020) through self-development.

Scientologist celebrities

In further promotional ventures, the CoS features a considerable number of celebrity adherents who not only act as role models for Scientologists but also a useful form of promotion for Scientology. This use of celebrity promotion dates back to Hubbard's 'Project Celebrity' in 1955, a campaign dedicated to attracting celebrities to Scientology. This subsequently led to the establishment of the first Scientology Celebrity Centre in 1969, which offered Scientology services exclusively to its high-profile members (Reitman 2011: 253; Urban 2011: 140). Celebrity Centres continued to grow throughout the 1970s and 1980s, with several celebrities eventually making considerable donations to the church in its attempt to 'de-abberrate Earth' in its 'Global Salvage' (a promotional project for the CoS) in 2007 (Urban 2011: 141). Placing an emphasis on nurturing talent has been a successful strategy for the CoS, with a number of high-profile celebrities (including John Travolta, Tom Cruise and Nancy Cartwright) being drawn to Scientology and crediting it with their success. For example, the *What Is Scientology?* handbook contains a number of quotations from celebrity practitioners, including John Travolta's statement that 'Scientology put [him] into the big time' (cited in The Church of Scientology International 1998: inside cover).

Carole Cusack (2009: 390–1) argues that the modern notion of 'celebrity' has taken on features and significance which are most commonly associated with religious figures. As a result, celebrities have become role models for many people in Western communities, who perceive their wealth and popularity as goals to be aimed towards through emulation. This raises the potential for individuals to engage with Scientology based on their admiration of the success of their favourite celebrities. Further to the appeal of Scientology based on celebrity endorsements, Cusack (2009: 405) argues that the presence of celebrity Scientologists has resulted in the normalization of Scientology, making Scientologist practice familiar and seemingly mainstream in the West. However, media coverage of celebrity Scientologists can be a double-edged sword for the CoS, particularly in terms of publicizing criticism of

Scientology from celebrity former members. For example, actor and former Scientologist Leah Remini stars in her own documentary series, *Leah Remini: Scientology and the Aftermath* (2016). *Scientology and the Aftermath* is notable in a number of ways; unlike documentaries such as *My Scientology Movie*, it is hosted by a former CoS member often drawing from her own experiences, and is co-hosted by Mike Rinder, a former Church of Scientology International senior executive. Both Remini and Rinder are heavily critical of the CoS, and focus the documentary on interviews with former CoS members or families claiming to have lost contact with relatives via disconnection. Remini's celebrity status has helped draw further attention towards the show, and she frequently makes use of social networking website Twitter as a platform to promote the series online.

The internet: Promotion, resources and Project Chanology

The use of the internet by the CoS is predominantly as a promotional tool for Scientology, its beliefs and practices. In addition to advertisement campaigns, such as the aforementioned Super Bowl television commercial, Scientology has begun to use social networking to reach non-Scientologists. For example, Twitter has become a forum for discussion for many topics for different religious groups, in addition to secular communities, allowing like-minded individuals to come together to discuss shared interests (Stout 2012: 81). The CoS Twitter page (@Scientology) has almost 100,000 followers (as of 2020), and regularly posts links to YouTube videos that demonstrate the benefits Scientology has had for its adherents.

In addition to the CoS' use of the internet as a method of promotion, online communication has also become a tool for critics of Scientology. Critics who have publicly expressed their opposition to the CoS and its practices have often organized to voice their views on the movement online, notably the Cult Awareness Network (Shupe 2009: 273). In his work on the impact of the internet on social movement/countermovement theory, Peckham (1998) focuses on the struggles between the CoS and online communities regarding the distribution of their confidential writing. Noting the degree of freedom of speech online, Peckham argues that the internet is used as a tool by Scientology's critics to discredit its beliefs amongst non-Scientologists, particularly through the leaking of the CoS' confidential Operating Thetan documents which 'likely would seem outrageous to anyone not prepared by years of indoctrination [within the CoS]' (1998: 329–30; see also Rothstein 2009: 367).

In an attempt to respond to this criticism and the threat of losing converts, Peckham observes that the CoS competes with its internet critics for 'virtual resources' (1998: 320). He divides virtual resources into two categories; the most valuable for anti-Scientologists is anonymity. The second resource is bandwidth, which has now become known online as the 'total amount of information space available in a particular forum' (1998: 322). In an attempt to gain dominance in online presence, the CoS began to make forum posts promoting the validity of Scientology, particularly on 'alt.religion.scientology', a highly popular anti-Scientology forum in the late 1990s. This became a competition between the CoS and their critics for bandwidth on the forums, with the CoS attempting to drown out the criticisms of critics of Scientology with 'pro-Scientology postings' (1998: 335). In addition to trying to swamp the voices of their critics, the CoS soon pursued legal action against online critics, including their notable lawsuit against Grady Ward for posting confidential Scientologist documents online (Urban 2006: 381).

Arguably the most highly publicized online clash between anti-Scientologists and the CoS is that of 'Anonymous' – 'a decentralised Internet-based group of "hacktivists"' (Robertson 2016: 311). Anonymous are renowned for their viral videos and their use of Guy Fawkes masks to maintain anonymity, based on the graphic novel and film *V for Vendetta* (Robertson 2016: 312). They are a non-hierarchical community of nameless members, and are 'less a coherent movement than a sort of complex, shifting and anarchic collective' (Urban 2016: 292). Anonymous launches campaigns that usually adopt a moral agenda, typically targeting major organizations, corporations and figures (Robertson 2016: 311). On 21 January 2008, Anonymous turned their attention towards the CoS with a YouTube video titled 'Message to Scientology' (Anonymous 2008):

> Hello leaders of Scientology. We are Anonymous. Over the years, we have been watching you – your campaigns of misinformation, your suppression of dissent, your litigious nature. . . . The extent of your malign influence over those who have come to trust you as leaders has been made clear to us. Anonymous has therefore decided that your organization should be destroyed. For the good of your followers, for the good of mankind, and for our own enjoyment, we shall proceed to expel you from the Internet, and systematically dismantle the Church of Scientology in its present form. We recognize you as a serious opponent, and do not expect our campaign to be completed in a short time frame. However, you will not prevail. . . . Your choice of methods, your hypocrisy, and the general lawlessness of your organization have sounded its death knell. You have nowhere to hide, because we are everywhere. You have no recourse in attack, because for

each of us that falls, ten more will take his place.... Knowledge is free. We are Anonymous. We are Legion. We do not forgive. We do not forget. Expect us. (Anonymous, cited in Ruskell and Lewis 2016: 330)

This message, delivered by a monotone automated voice, is described by Ruskell and Lewis as Anonymous' 'declaration of war' (2016: 330) against the CoS, beginning what became known as Project Chanology, relating to Anonymous' origin from the online bulletin-board '4chan'. Soon thereafter, numerous online attacks were launched against the CoS, such as the 'distributed denial of service' attack, which involved the use of an enormous number of 'zombie computers' to overload the servers of Scientology websites, causing them to crash and resulting in the CoS having to take their websites offline for a short period of time (Urban 2016: 293).

Project Chanology has not been limited to the internet, however, with Anonymous members organizing protests at the locations of various CoS Orgs worldwide. These protests involve Anonymous members, donning their Guy Fawkes masks, gathering at Orgs with a range of 'signs bearing slogans such as "Religion is free: Scientology is neither" and "Google 'Fair Game'"' (Urban 2016). Urban (2016: 293–4) suggests that the greatest impact Anonymous has had against the CoS is its publicizing of the Xenu mythology and distribution of the leaked OT III documents online, thus loosening the CoS' control of its esoteric elements. This '"radical democracy" of the Internet' (Ruskell and Lewis 2016: 331) has resulted in a new social environment for the CoS, in which previous methods of countering critics (particularly legal lawsuits) are ineffective in preventing information from being leaked online (Cusack 2012: 312). Indeed, Anonymous is a foe unlike any the CoS has encountered in its history, precisely because of its lack of hierarchical structure or identifiable leaders through its origin as an online community (Ruskell and Lewis 2016: 331). However, it is interesting that, as Robertson notes, 'Anonymous do not seem aware of the irony that they are attempting to silence Scientology in the name of free speech.... It is as though they are arguing that religious freedom is a good thing – just as long as it is a "real religion"' (2016: 312).

Wider popular culture

Much of Scientology's presence in the media and popular culture consists of controversial depictions of the practice and organization of the CoS. Television coverage of the CoS has often led to controversial documentaries on the movement, which have typically focused on the perceived 'cult' aspect of

Scientology (such as intimidating behaviour, greed and brainwashing). These documentaries, however, usually focus their attention on the CoS, while paying little attention to the Free Zone. However, one of the more distinctive Scientology documentaries on British television, *Scientologists at War* (2013), focused upon the clash between Marty Rathbun and the CoS. Similar to *My Scientology Movie* (2015), *Scientologists at War* documents how Rathbun claims to have been harassed by CoS members, however, it also briefly depicts his life as a Free Zone Scientologist, and how others now practise Hubbard's teachings away from the CoS. The documentary briefly details how an Israeli Scientology mission has recently become an independent Scientologist group that claims to have grown since its separation from the CoS, to the extent that former members of the mission have returned (*Scientologists at War* 2013). Furthermore, *Scientologists at War* demonstrates how Rathbun practises Scientology independently and offers his auditing services to those who wish to hire him. It is worth noting, however, that the documentary ends with a narrator explaining that while he still practises auditing, Rathbun no longer identifies himself as a Scientologist. This rather vague statement opens questions including why Rathbun no longer identifies as a Scientologist, and whether those who practise auditing without the label of 'Scientology' should be considered as Scientologists in a scholarly study. However, *Scientologists at War* remains a rare example of Free Zone practices being included in a television documentary.

Scientology does not only feature on television as a documentary topic – beyond the exposure of the Xenu documents online, the mythology has also been parodied in various forms of comedy. Perhaps the most notable comedic take on the Xenu mythology is in *Trapped in the Closet*, an episode of the American animated television series, *South Park* (*South Park: Trapped in the Closet* 2005). The episode is highly derisive of Scientology, with its depiction of the Xenu mythology being the most striking example of this. During the episode, one of the show's main protagonists, Stan, is encouraged to join Scientology and is introduced to its beliefs and practices. This includes a lengthy account of the Xenu mythology, which is depicted to viewers both visually and with a narration. Stan is told that human suffering originates from an incident involving the ruler of a galactic federation, the 'evil Lord Xenu'. He is also told that, in an attempt to solve the galaxy's overpopulation crisis, Xenu froze various alien life forms and disposed of them in volcanoes on Earth. Once the souls of the aliens were released from their bodies, they were captured and brainwashed by Xenu by being fed images of figures including Jesus Christ and the Buddha. Once this was complete, the souls were released into the world believing a false reality as a result of their brainwashing. This entire account is accompanied by 'THIS IS WHAT SCIENTOLOGISTS ACTUALLY BELIEVE' displayed on-screen (*South Park: Trapped in the Closet* 2005, emphasis in original).

In addition to its ridicule of Scientologist beliefs, *South Park* heavily criticizes the CoS for the fees it charges for its services, claiming that the institution is merely a scam, as opposed to a 'legitimate' religion. The fictional president of the CoS asks Stan, one of the show's main characters, if he 'actually believe[s] this crap', and informs him that Scientology is a 'scam on a global scale', resulting in the beliefs and practices of Scientology serving as methods of convincing Scientologists to part with their money (*South Park: Trapped in the Closet* 2005).

Scientology has also become a feature of theatrical performances, making the subject of Scientologist belief and practice the focus of their narrative. A notable example of this is *Squeeze My Cans* (Schekelberg 2017), a one-person show, written and performed by former Scientologist Cathy Schekelberg. The performance, which involves Schekelberg telling the story of her experiences as a Scientologist, drives its narrative through intermittent performances of auditing sessions and makes heavy use of Scientologist terminology and depictions of its practices. The title '*Squeeze My Cans*' is in itself a wry double entendre based on how Scientologists are expected to squeeze the 'cans' of an E-Meter to calibrate the device ahead of an auditing session. Throughout the course of the performance, Schekelberg re-enacts several of her own auditing sessions, which she presents as particularly intrusive on details of her personal life, alongside on-screen animations of the E-Meter reacting to her responses. The performance is highly critical of Scientology, highlighting the fees Schekelberg attests to have spent on CoS services, and her eventual departure from the CoS.

These accounts demonstrate that the CoS has experienced a turbulent relationship with the media throughout its history. Its methods of responding to criticisms have often added to its controversy, and despite its attempts to silence media critics, Scientology remains a popular topic in the media.

Concluding remarks

During its relatively short history, Scientology has experienced both a varied and turbulent past. At the centre of Scientology is its founder, L. Ron Hubbard. His biography is illuminating for a number of reasons. It allows us to chart his trajectory towards becoming the founder of the CoS. Between his interests in psychotherapy and the human mind, in addition to his near-death experience and fascination with Eastern religiosity, Hubbard combined a number of his personal influences in his spiritual technology. While the CoS presents itself as the only true form of Scientology, the emergence of different Scientologies has resulted in debate amongst different self-identified Scientologists as to what constitutes 'true' Scientology. Initially led by Captain Bill Robertson, the Free Zone has become an umbrella category for all practices of Scientology outside the CoS. Despite condemnation from the CoS for committing the act of squirrelling, Free Zone groups and communities have continued to emerge in recent decades, insisting that the practice of Scientology is possible outside institutional Scientologist structures.

3

Auditing and the 'tech'
The basics

The focal point of this research is the auditing process. Best summarized as a form of Scientologist counselling that promises physical and spiritual liberation, auditing is at the centre of all Scientologies, and is the practice upon which Hubbard founded the Church of Scientology (CoS). Free Zone Scientology, as this work will demonstrate, is best understood by considering how auditing is practised and comprehended by everyday Freezoners. This involves a thorough and in-depth exploration of various aspects of auditing throughout this book. To assist this analysis, this chapter provides an introductory account of the auditing process by examining Hubbard's 'tech', Dianetic theory and the hybridity of auditing as a combination of religious and secular-scientific elements.

The tech and Scientologist nomenclature

Conducting a study of Scientology can be a daunting and difficult task for those new to the subject. Such difficulties are perhaps best demonstrated through the vast amount of L. Ron Hubbard's Scientological theories, and specialized nomenclature scholars must familiarize themselves with. To enhance clarity, Appendix B contains a list of key terms in the study of Scientology and their definitions.

At the centre of Hubbard's writing and lectures is a spiritual technology – frequently referred to as the 'tech' – a series of theories, practices and beliefs he devised from the early Dianetic movement until his death in 1986. When Scientologists refer to the tech, they are most often speaking about the auditing process. Publicly established by Hubbard in *Dianetics: The Modern Science of Mental Health* (*DMSMH*), auditing aims to remove mental neuroses from the human mind. A typical auditing session is conducted through question and answer exercises between a trained auditor and a client. The client, known as the Preclear, is believed to suffer from the presence of engrams, Hubbard's term for the traces of neuroses and anxieties in the human mind (Melton 2000: 25–6). Through the question and answer method, an auditor is able to target negative past events and experiences that have become embedded in the Preclear's mind in an attempt to remove the harmful effects of the engram.

It is important to note that, despite the religious angle that is now associated with auditing, the process notionally remains rooted in scientific theory. Scientology acknowledges the benefits of various therapies and religious practices, yet maintains that Scientology is the only theory truly capable of understanding the complexities of the human mind due to its simultaneous treatment of the spiritual self (Whitehead 1987: 125–6). Moreover, Hubbard suggested that, prior to the publication of *DMSMH*, the psychology of the human mind was primarily based on theoretical speculation. He argued that 'the various axioms [of Dianetics] are not assumptions or theories – the case of past ideas about the mind – but are laws which can be subjected to the most vigorous laboratory and clinical tests' (Hubbard [1950] 2007b: ii).

Although auditing is the focal point of the tech, it is in fact one process amongst a large volume of theories and practices devised by Hubbard. In its *What Is Scientology?* guidebook, the CoS defines Hubbard's tech accordingly:

> The importance of *application* in Scientology comes from the fact that L. Ron Hubbard developed as part of the religion an actual technology that enables one to use his discoveries to better oneself and others. *Technology* means the methods of application of the principles of something, as opposed to the mere knowledge of the thing itself. And, using L. Ron Hubbard's technology, applying the methods, one can heighten his abilities and lead a better, more fulfilling life. . . . Many technologies are extant today, technologies to build bridges and technologies to fire rockets into space. But with the work of L. Ron Hubbard, for the first time there exists a proven, workable technology to improve the functions of the mind and rehabilitate the potential of the spirit. (The Church of Scientology International 1998: 81, emphasis in original)

In addition to the theories mentioned earlier, Scientology makes use of technological, physical devices to assist with its practice. Accordingly, it is important to keep in mind that the term 'tech' is used in Scientology interchangeably for its specialized devices, theories and practices pertaining to Scientologist praxis.

Study tech: Scientologist pedagogy

When discussing auditing and Dianetic theory, it would be remiss to not mention Study Tech, Hubbard's pedagogical 'tech' that is used to train auditors. Study Tech is worthy of note for two particular reasons. First, it is a method used in the training of professional auditors and by Scientologists beginning their initial studies of Hubbard's work. Second, many Scientologists, especially within the CoS, encourage scholars to adopt the methods of Study Tech when researching Hubbard's written work. Driven by his concerns with the education system of the 1970s, Hubbard developed Study Tech in an attempt to improve students' literacy ability to learn, believing it to be a 'breakthrough educational technology capable of turning schools into institutions of unprecedented learning excellence' (The Church of Scientology International 1998: 424).

Study Tech is presented by the CoS as the perfect pedagogical method, capable of not only improving the academic grades of school children but also advancing their reading levels. The main purpose of the method is to overcome what Hubbard outlined as the three barriers to study. These are believed to be issues that can prevent one from effectively learning any subject. The first barrier is 'absence of mass' (Hubbard 2001: 5), which concerns physical objects (mass) and the theories and ideas behind subjects. Hubbard argued that one could study physical objects such as a tractor thoroughly through textbooks, but if one has never seen the mass (in this case – the tractor), then their understanding would be extremely limited despite much theoretical study. The second barrier, 'too steep a gradient' (Hubbard 2001: 13), concerns beginning the study of a subject at the suitable level, before working towards more complicated and difficult subjects that can be more easily understood with a less steep gradient. The final barrier, believed to be the most important, is 'the misunderstood word' (Hubbard 2001: 14). Hubbard argued that if one misunderstands a word when studying, then this misunderstanding will compromise the student's entire study, as they will not fully grasp the subject. For example, if one was to read a page and not entirely understand what one read, then one must have encountered a word one had no definition for. This is hugely important in the practice of Scientology, emphasized by the 'Important Note' that begins each latest edition of Hubbard's works, including *DMSMH*:

> In reading this book, be very certain you never go past a word you do not fully understand. The only reason a person gives up a study or becomes confused or unable to learn is because he or she has gone past a word that is not understood. (Hubbard [1950] 2007b: (first page, no page number))

The main method of countering this issue is 'word clearing', a procedure that involves immediately consulting a dictionary or glossary when encountering a word that is not understood, after which the student can return to their reading and continue from that word (Hubbard 2001: 23). By addressing these three barriers, Hubbard argued that it would be possible to learn far more effectively and quickly.

The CoS emphasizes that Study Tech can be used by Scientologists and non-Scientologists alike. For example, during my fieldwork I was encouraged to read Hubbard's work in chronological order by CoS members, in line with the Study Tech method of approaching a study at a suitable gradient. This involved reading the 'Basic Books', published between the years of 1948 and 1956, which encompass Hubbard's teachings concerning the auditing practice and Scientologist theories.[1] My conversations with CoS members highlighted the belief that the entire core of the Scientologist belief system can be found within 'the Basics'. Hubbard's subsequent works expand upon or explain concepts in more basic terms, and are often compilations of Hubbard's bulletins to practitioners and staff members during his time as the leader of the CoS. Anyone beginning a study of Scientologist practice, whether as a scholar or Scientologist practitioner, is encouraged to read Hubbard's work in the order in which they were published, allowing them to digest his ideas in the same order as they were developed.

In addition to its perceived benefits for non-Scientologists, the use of Study Tech is of crucial importance to the successful execution of the auditing process. Study Tech is viewed as being important for Preclears to effectively approach their auditing sessions. Additionally, it is the method used to rigorously train the CoS' professional auditors, aiming to assist them in comprehending the answers they are given by Preclears during auditing (Harley and Kieffer 2009: 193). Auditors are expected to conduct their sessions according to the guidelines of the CoS, ensuring what the CoS views as a standard application of Hubbard's tech in every Org worldwide. This perception of the necessity of the application of the tech in methods believed to be 'true' to Hubbard's intentions causes divisions across Scientologies, particularly in the division between the institutional CoS and the Free Zone.

Dianetic theory: Developing the tech

The tech is most commonly associated with Hubbard's Dianetic theory and the ways in which it is utilized through the auditing process. The basic premise of Dianetics and the auditing process is allowing the trained auditor to remove engrams from the 'engrams bank', a part of the brain defined by Hubbard as the 'reactive mind' (Harley and Kieffer 2009: 185). Hubbard's original work outlined his ideas on the influence of engrams and 'locks' on the mind; engrams and locks are past experiences of mental trauma which are intertwined in such a way that the conscious and rational part of the brain, the analytical mind, is unable to detect them (Hubbard [1950] 2007b: 367–8). While in the reactive mind, the engram (the trauma) attaches itself to a lock (a specific incident or memory) on the Preclear's 'time track' – a timeline of the entirety of an individual's memory (Hubbard 2007b: vii). It is by recalling these locks that those audited are able to address the engrams in their reactive minds. Contemporary auditing sessions are materially distinctive through their use of the E-Meter, a specialist device that allows auditors to detect engrams on the time track (which we will discuss further in Chapter 7). The use of the E-Meter involves the Scientologist holding two metal canisters connected to the main device, causing the needle on the display unit to react to the responses given during auditing sessions.

While the auditor may initially be unable to locate an engram through a particular lock, *The Original Thesis* emphasizes the importance of the Preclear's time track, which allows the auditor to locate the engram by examining previous locks (Hubbard [1951] 2007b: 46). This is a process that is continuously repeated to locate all of the Preclear's engrams. Once Preclears have removed all traces of engrams from their reactive minds, they achieve the state of Clear, defined by Hubbard as 'the optimum individual, no longer possessed of any engrams' ([1950] 2007b: 494). In this state Clears are now free of all negative psychoses and neuroses that affect their life (Melton 2000: 25–6).

The 'self-help' element of Scientology and auditing was crucial to the early success of the Dianetic movement. Recovering from one's personal traumas and receiving potential medical benefits enticed practitioners seeking a new system of ideas and beliefs to improve their personal lives. An early executive member of the Dianetic movement, Helen Brown, described its appeal by claiming that 'people everywhere embraced it as though they had found something which they had hungered for all their lives' (cited in Urban 2011: 52).

Through *DMSMH* one encounters auditing in its original form, known as Book One auditing. Unlike the contemporary Scientologist practice of auditing which requires an E-Meter, Book One auditing establishes a standard auditing procedure that can both be conducted by trained auditors or by pairs using *DMSMH* as a guide (Harley and Kieffer 2009: 198). A cornerstone of the success of Book One auditing was the simplicity of its execution; the two Dianetic practitioners conducting an auditing session with only a copy of *DMSMH* need not be trained auditors. However, following further research by Hubbard and the development of auditing's religious angle, the process became an increasingly complex practice, with the additional use of technology such as the E-Meter to detect engrams. It is noteworthy, however, that the benefits of Book One auditing were neither devalued nor dismissed by Scientology following Hubbard's subsequent research, rather that the religious application of auditing was said to be simply faster and more effective to assist in the achievement of the state of Clear (The Church of Scientology International 1998: 168).

The hybridity of auditing: The secular-scientific and the religious

DMSMH, *The Original Thesis* and the Book One method of auditing offer an avenue for examining the initial practice of auditing, yet these publications must be considered in the context of how auditing was practised at the time; as a secular form of therapy. Hubbard himself critiqued the nature of organized and institutional religion and added that 'Dianetics is a science: as such, it has no opinion about religion, for sciences are based on natural laws, not on opinions' (Hubbard, cited in Urban 2011: 57). In contrast to these arguments, however, as the popularity of auditing grew, Hubbard incorporated several religious dynamics to the process. Ahead of the opening of the first CoS in 1954 (Lewis 2009a: 5), Hubbard published several additional works on auditing that introduced a variety of new beliefs and techniques to the practice. The notable example of *What to Audit*, currently published under the title of *Scientology: A History of Man* ([1952] 2007c), was Hubbard's breakthrough publication on the religious dynamic of auditing, introducing the concepts of theta beings (thetans) and 'MEST' (Matter, Energy, Space and Time), expanding on concepts previously explored in *Science of Survival* ([1951] 2007d). The thetan and MEST are believed to be entirely separate; the thetan is comparable to the concept of the human soul and is the 'true' self in Scientology. Transcending physical aspects of humanity, such as the body, the thetan represents the life force, spirituality and non-physical nature of humanity. In contrast, MEST represents the physical nature of the universe, including human bodies, stars and galaxies (Hubbard [1951] 2007d: 4–5). By establishing these concepts, Hubbard introduced Technique 88 – 'the process of locating the thetan . . . and the auditing of the thetan' (Hubbard [1952] 2007c: 1), positioning auditing as a process that treats the spiritual self, in addition to the human mind. Despite the comparable nature of thetans and the concept of spirits or souls, Hubbard intentionally avoided the use of these terms to avoid the 'philosophical baggage' (Chryssides 1999: 283) that they have acquired throughout history in Western culture (see also Urban 2011: 69).

Moreover, the religiosity of the auditing process extends to the notion of past lives. In *Have You Lived Before This Life?* ([1960] 1989), Hubbard drew attention to his theory that the reactive mind contains engrams from not only the current life but also a large number of the thetan's previous lives. Through providing testimonies from Preclears in the early Dianetic movement that claimed to experience 'mental image pictures' (1989: 19) of past lives experiences, Hubbard claimed that '[p]ast lives and deaths are evidently experiences, and without the techniques of Dianetics and Scientology they can be recalled in full only with great difficulty and with much determination' ([1960] 1989: 7). Accordingly, the auditing process acts as a hybrid of secular-scientific and religious methods, aiming to improve the current existence of the self by addressing engrams from the current life and all previous lives. Scientology's understanding of the existence of engrams in the reactive mind is, in essence, a mental health issue (as exemplified by the original publication of *DMSMH* as a book which addresses mental health). However, through Hubbard's work on the whole track, an individual's chronological collection of memories of past lives, Scientologists are provided with a religious explanation for sickness and suffering, a concept Freund et al. analyse through Max Weber's 'theodicies'; 'religious explanations of meaning-threatening experiences, for sickness, suffering, and death' (Freund, McGuire and Podhurst 2003: 143). Through understanding mental health anxieties as being caused by engrams, a concept given religious significance by Hubbard and Scientology, the notion of an engram acts as a theodicy for Scientologists in answering the question of suffering and offering a solution to it.

Though *DMSMH* concentrates on the attainment of Clear primarily through the self-help technique of Book One auditing, in contemporary Scientology practice the individual continues their spiritual development beyond the state of Clear through advanced auditing techniques. It is here that Scientologist practice becomes increasingly esoteric, with confidential teachings being passed on to practitioners in addition to the advanced methods of auditing they are expected to adopt. During these spiritual studies the Scientologist continues on Hubbard's 'Bridge to Total Freedom', often referred to as 'the Bridge'. The Bridge, according to the Church of Scientology International's *What Is Scientology?* guide, 'is an exact route with precise procedures providing uniformly predictable spiritual gains when correctly applied' (1998: 98–100). The Bridge is typically presented as a chart that displays each step a Scientologist takes on their journey through Scientology – beginning at the bottom as a Preclear, rising through stages to the state of Clear and then advancing through the fifteen Operating Thetan levels at the top of the Bridge (1998: 99).

The purpose of the OT levels is to allow Clears to become more spiritually independent and advance beyond their need for a physical body in the MEST universe. Through eradicating the reactive mind Clears re-familiarize themselves with their thetan's capabilities, allowing them to command both their mind and the MEST universe (Bromley 2009: 92; The Church of Scientology International 1998: 167). The execution of OT studies is done through a series of stages and steps, comparable to a baby learning to crawl before walking, allowing the Clear to be introduced to the advanced documents written by Hubbard that can allegedly only be fully comprehended once the previous levels have been mastered and understood (The Church of Scientology International 1998: 167). Clears are given the opportunity to develop their skills as auditors during their study of OT materials, including a form of solo auditing, during which they hold both E-Meter cannisters in one hand, while using their free hand to write notes and monitor the activity of the E-Meter's dials (The Church of Scientology International 1998: 167; Whitehead 1987: 144–5).

While promoting the early Dianetic movement, Hubbard sought the validation and support of mainstream psychological communities but was largely unsuccessful due to the lack of connection between his approach to the human mind and contemporary psychology. His presentations to the American Psychiatric Association and American Medical Association (AMA) resulted in both groups rejecting his Dianetic theories, dubbing auditing as 'worthless', with the AMA criticizing Hubbard's auditors for attempting to 'enter their ranks with magic bullets' (Melton 2009: 23). The Food and Drug Association (FDA) also condemned claims concerning the alleged abilities of the E-Meter to cure medical conditions through auditing (Young 1972: 325). The criticism of the device from the FDA and their subsequent legal battles with the CoS have become some of the more controversial events in the CoS' history. Accusing the CoS of falsely advertising the E-Meter and its capabilities, a legal battle between both parties ensued and resulted in a raid on the Washington Founding Church of Scientology, which involved the confiscation of all E-Meters and Scientologist literature by the FDA (Manca 2010: 5). These items were returned to the CoS at the end of the legal battle in 1969, with the American government ruling that E-Meters should only be used as religious, not medical, devices and requiring written disclaimers on each device stating that they should only be used in the 'religious arena' (Manca 2010: 5). The Judge of the trial, Gerhardt Gesell, issued the following order:

> The device should bear a prominent, clearly visible notice warning that any person using it for auditing or counselling of any kind is forbidden by law to represent that there is any medical or scientific basis for believing or asserting that the device is useful in the diagnosis, treatment or prevention of any disease. It should be noted in the warning that the device has been condemned by a United States District Court for misrepresentation and misbranding under the Food and Drug laws, that use is permitted only as part of religious activity, and that the E-Meter is not medically or scientifically capable of improving the health or bodily functions of anyone. (Gesell, cited in Carnegie Mellon University n.d.-a: online)

In addition to scepticism regarding the legitimacy of auditing as a method of psychiatric and psychotherapeutic practice, Scientology attracted further criticism in relation to the cost of auditing sessions. In their study of auditing, Harley and Kieffer (2009: 191) point to an enquiry made in 2007 by a former member of the International Association of Scientologists (IAS) about the fee for a twelve-and-a-half hours block of auditing at an Org (a Scientologist church) in Tampa, Florida, which was $4,000 (with a $3,200 discount for IAS members). Furthermore, as the Scientologist recruit progresses through the Operating Thetan levels in the CoS, the subsequent stages of auditing become more expensive, such as auditing 'above OT III [ranging] from $7,800 (per 12.5 hours at a 20 percent discount) to $64,350 (per 150 hours at a 45 percent discount)' (Urban 2011: 135).

Hubbard defended the high prices of auditing services by arguing that a service should always take place as an exchange, as to not receive something for one's services can be potentially damaging to the spiritual and physical functionality of both parties involved in the transaction (Harley and Kieffer 2009: 191). Also in defence of the fees of auditing, Bromley (1994) argued that the CoS is comparable to older and more established religions that charge for specific services, including certain Buddhist temples that set fees for temple entries and Jewish synagogues that charge for annual membership. Urban also compared the CoS' policies regarding auditing fees to that of donations in various denominations of other religions, arguing that the CoS seems 'fairly modest' (2011: 137) in comparison to the earnings of Christian televangelist empires. While the CoS does insist on a fee for all types of auditing on the Bridge, it is notable that there are Scientologist activities that are not charged, including the free personality test, which is used by the church to promote its practices and attract new converts (Rigal-Cellard 2009: 330).

Despite the lack of validation from the scientific and medical community, in addition to criticism regarding the costs of auditing, the CoS' positioning of the simultaneously scientific and religious nature of the process remains to this day, emphasizing Scientology's promise of both spiritual and physical improvements for its practitioners during their current lifetime (see Wallis 2007: 44; Wilson 1982: 131).

Concluding remarks

This chapter has aimed to provide the introductory basics to Hubbard's Dianetic tech and how it is applied through the auditing process. The tech is at the centre of Scientology; all Scientologist practices and theories devised by Hubbard combine to make his 'spiritual technology'. While this is evident in wider aspects of Scientology, such as Hubbard's Study Tech pedagogy, the term 'tech' is typically used to refer to the auditing process, Dianetic theory and the E-Meter. The auditing process, with its roots in Hubbard's fascination with the psychology of the human mind, has become a hybrid of secular-scientific and religious methods. It concentrates on both improving the mental health of the individual, in addition to providing spiritual fulfilment framed in terms of a wider philosophical universe.

Throughout this book, I highlight how the auditing process lies at the heart of the debate between Scientologies, and how the different understandings, interpretations and practices of Hubbard's work result in a fluid practice of Scientology outside the CoS, in addition to answering questions on the centrality of auditing to conceptions of the mind, body and the self amongst Scientologists within and outside the church.

4

'You are YOU *in* a body'

Negotiating the self in Scientology

The purpose of this chapter is to explore different Scientologist understandings of the self in relation to the auditing process. Throughout his leadership of the Church of Scientology (CoS), L. Ron Hubbard published extensively on the self and auditing. Accordingly, understanding the self in Scientology is essential in establishing the purposes and goals of auditing. This chapter aims to examine Hubbard's approach to the spiritual and physical development of the self through auditing, in addition to how issues such as the body and gender are positioned in both CoS and Free Zone spheres. By collating these approaches and practices, I address how the auditing process informs the Scientologist notion of the self, and the ways in which it highlights nuanced approaches to the development of both the physical and spiritual self across Scientologies.

Scientology, self-improvement and the existence of the self

The primary focus of Scientology is self-improvement. As a result, the Scientologist belief system contains very specific and detailed notions of the self. Precisely what the self is, the nature of its existence and the importance of its improvement are amongst the first aspects of Scientology to be studied by new, aspiring Scientologists. Scientology is a practice that requires dedication and effort from its adherents. Beyond the series of beliefs and ethical teachings that Scientologists learn, practitioners are expected to engage rigorously with a series of auditing practices aimed towards self-discovery and self-improvement. Through the application of Scientologist tech, Scientologists claim improvements in their day-to-day lives that will enable their true self to gain a greater control of the physical universe that surrounds them.

The Scientologist understanding of the self dominated many of my discussions with my research participants. My contacts in the CoS encouraged me to study

Scientology according to their Study Tech method to gain an understanding of basic ideas, before moving on to deeper Scientologist theories. This involved beginning with how Scientologists view the essence of humanity. They recommended *Scientology: The Fundamentals of Thought* as the ideal starting place to familiarize myself with Scientology's specialized approach to the human mind, and additionally allowed me to view a series of short films produced by the CoS to accompany *The Fundamentals of Thought*. Originally published by Hubbard in 1956, *The Fundamentals of Thought* outlines the basic principles and theories behind Scientology. This is largely concerned with the nature of the self, and its liberation from the physical universe via Scientological techniques. Hubbard's work on the self is both varied and detailed in scope. This chapter will consider Scientologist notions of the self across four categories through Hubbard's work and Free Zone Scientology:

- The 'Parts of Man'; Hubbard's theories regarding the physical and spiritual nature of the self.
- The existence of the self; Hubbard's theories on how the self interacts with, and exists in, the universe.
- Gender and sexuality in Scientology.
- The Bridge to Total Freedom; Hubbard's hierarchical guide of spiritual and self-development in Scientology, leading to the ultimate goal of spiritual liberation.

It is important to note that Hubbard's works on these theories were written while he was the leader of the institutionalized CoS. Additionally, they were written in relation to the CoS' beliefs and practices, and continue to be published by the CoS' publishing press, 'New Era'. Therefore, while the primary focus of this book is on Free Zone Scientology, it is also important to recognize the influence of Hubbard's writings within both the CoS and Free Zone. Accordingly, this overview of the self in the CoS will act as a foundation for an analysis of the self in Free Zone Scientology, allowing Free Zone attitudes towards the self to be framed in the context of Hubbard's original writings and in contrast to the CoS.

The 'Parts of Man': The thetan, the mind and the body

Theta beings

Hubbard ([1956] 2007: 65) considered there to be three 'Parts of Man' to each human individual. These are the spirit, the mind and the body. The spirit, known as a 'theta being', commonly referred to as the 'thetan', is in fact the 'true' self in Scientology. My contacts at the CoS explained that one does not 'have' a thetan, rather that they 'are' the thetan, or as Hubbard wrote; 'the thetan *is* the person. You are YOU *in* a body' ([1956] 2007: 74, emphasis in original). The thetan possesses 'no mass, no wavelength, no energy and no time or location in space' ([1956] 2007: 66), highlighting that unlike other Parts of Man, the thetan exists entirely outside the physical universe, and as such is a creator of 'things', rather than being a physical 'thing' itself ([1956] 2007: 66). The notion of the thetan reinforces the overarching purpose of Scientology, which is to free the thetan (the true self of the individual) from the confines of the physical universe.

Hubbard referred to the physical universe as the MEST universe, composing of Matter, Energy, Space and Time. The MEST universe is entirely separate to what Hubbard dubbed the theta universe, which concerns all the spiritual aspects of the universe – life, spirituality and thought. Conversely, MEST refers to all the physical elements of the universe, such as objects, stars and galaxies (Hubbard [1951] 2007d: 4–5). The theta universe could be considered the 'true' universe in Scientology, as MEST is considered a seeming reality that is fabricated by the agreement of all thetans that it exists. This agreement has tricked the thetan to associate itself with the unfulfilling environment of the MEST universe (Urban 2011: 70). The thetan is subject to decay, according to Hubbard ([1952] 2007c: 65), due to its misconceived dependence on the MEST universe, and it is this joining of the thetan and the MEST universe that causes the thetan to experience pain (Hubbard [1951] 2007d: 5). Unlike the MEST body, the thetan is believed to be capable of infinite possibilities and can be freed from the confines of the MEST universe only through Scientology's auditing process (Chryssides 1999: 283; Urban 2011: 70).

Hubbard's work on the liberation of the spiritual self from the physical universe has drawn comparisons with Buddhist practice (see Flinn 2009; Kent 1996). Indeed, Hubbard viewed the state of Clear as a more achievable goal than the Buddhist quest for Nirvana, which he considered to be a fruitless endeavour:

> The Buddhists spoke of Nirvana. . . . They had become completely overwhelmed, lacking any [E-Meters] and a map. We are Scientologists. We won't fall into the abyss. And we won't join Nirvana. We have [E-Meters] and a map. We know the rules and the way. This is the greatest adventure of all time. Clearing. . . . Nirvana is choked with the overwhelmed. . . . We are Scientologists. We have won. (Hubbard, cited in Kent 1996: 29)

With this work on the state of Clear and the interaction between theta and MEST, Hubbard claimed to have discovered how the essence of a person and their personality can be completely separated from the body. He additionally argued that humanity had convinced itself that it only consists of mind and body, writing that

> In Scientology, the spirit itself was separated from what spiritualists called the astral body and there should be no confusion between these two things. As you know that you are where you are at this moment, so you would know if you, a spirit, were detached from your mind and body. Man has not discovered this before because, lacking the technologies of Scientology, he had very little reality upon his detachment from his mind and body. (Hubbard [1956] 2007: 66)

It is therefore only through the execution of Scientologist practice that the abilities and perceptions of the thetan can be brought back to the surface. Scientology teaches that the thetan usually resides in the human skull, but it can also be found in four different locations; (i) separate from the physical body and universe; (ii) near the physical body while maintaining control of its actions; (iii) in the body itself, more specifically the skull and (iv) away from the body and unable to reach it (Hubbard [1956] 2007: 66).

The ideal location for the thetan is the second, residing near the body but knowingly taking full control. Hubbard taught that through attachment to a human body the thetan begins to associate 'beingness with mass and actions, [and] does not consider himself as having an individual identity or name' ([1956] 2007: 67). As a result, the thetan mistakes itself to be a part of the MEST universe. Scientology aims to 'exteriorize' the thetan from the human body, allowing it to reside in the second location, and freeing it from the confines of the MEST universe but remaining in full control of the body ([1956] 2007).

My informants at the CoS stated that the thetan has existed long before the physical body, and the process of self-improvement in Scientology concerns returning the thetan to its original state, free of the confines of MEST, rather than improving the thetan beyond any previous state. The entirety of the MEST universe is believed to be unnecessary for thetans to operate and communicate – all forms of physical communication, including the written word and even speech through physical bodies, are secondary to the ability of thetans to communicate independently, and without the mediation of the MEST universe. Therefore, the ultimate goal of self-development in Scientology is to allow the thetan to be unaffected by the traumas of the physical universe, while maintaining full control of the other Parts of Man, the mind and the body.

The mind

A fieldwork participant at the CoS informed me that it is an error to consider the mind and the thetan to be the same, rather the mind is a mechanism the thetan uses to control the body and communicate with the universe around it. Acting as a communication system, the mind does not only allow the thetan to communicate with MEST but also communicates information from MEST to the thetan. It is the mind that allows the thetan to receive data and impressions from MEST, and results in the thetan being able to independently conceive ideas regarding the past and future away from present stimuli (Hubbard [1956] 2007: 68). Scientology teaches that the mind is divided into three sections; the reactive mind, the analytical mind and the somatic mind.

The reactive mind is the part of the mind that is given the most attention in Scientology due to its influence on the thetan and its potentially damaging effect on the individual. Hubbard's research determined that the reactive mind operates and exists in the individual's subconscious, immediately reacting to any stimulation. This is the irrational part of the mind, involving what Hubbard described as 'little thinkingness' ([1956] 2007: 69), a lack of critical ability or reflection. Due to this irrationality, reactions to different types of trauma, pain and psychoses are subconsciously stored in the reactive mind as engrams; the traces of these neuroses (Melton 2000: 9). Scientology teaches that the mind consists of a series of mental pictures (memories), which are collectively stored as a 'time track', the chronological collection of memories of each individual (Hubbard [1951] 2007b: 181). Memories are believed in Scientology to be static accounts of events and the perceptions (such as emotions, sights and pains) associated with them. These records of memories are known as 'facsimilies', made by the reactive mind's ability to duplicate copies of both memories and the associated emotions that can be re-experienced when recalled, often in harmful ways (Hubbard 1982: 26). Due to the potentially dangerous nature of the facsimilies and their engrams, the reactive mind is the main focus of Dianetic auditing.

The facsimilies that have engrams attached to them are known as 'locks'. Hubbard uses the example of childbirth to demonstrate how an engram can cause a lock to resurface:

> Engram: At birth occurs the phrase 'no good' uttered during a moment of headache and gasping on the part of the child.
>
> Lock: At the age of seven, the mother, in a fit of rage while the child was ill with a minor malady, said that he was 'no good'.

The removal of the engram also removes, ordinarily without further attention, the lock. (Hubbard [1951] 2007b: 46)

In this example, a baby hears the phrase 'no good' during the traumatic experience of childbirth. This incident resides subconsciously as an engram in the reactive mind of the child. Accordingly, hearing the phrase 'no good' causes them to re-experience a headache. This painful memory becomes the lock, a traceable event on the individual's time track that can be recalled by the analytical mind during auditing. Identifying the location of this engram on the time track is the main purpose of Scientology's auditing technique. By removing the existence of the engram from the reactive mind, the lock itself will cease to affect the individual. A source at the CoS stated that the thetan takes its reactive mind from body to body, meaning that locks can be detected from previous lives, revealing the existence of the whole track. The lock and engram are intertwined in a way that, according to Hubbard ([1951] 2007b: 45), the analytical mind is unable to detect and locate in the reactive mind.

The analytical mind can be simply defined as the rational part of the human mind, in contrast to the irrational, reactive mind. The most distinctive feature of the analytical mind is its awareness; it is capable of making decisions and comprehending what it is doing (Hubbard [1956] 2007: 69). Hubbard wrote that the analytical mind accordingly combined 'perceptions of the immediate environment, of the *past* (via pictures) and estimations of the *future*, into conclusions which are based upon the realities of situations' (Hubbard [1956] 2007: 68, emphasis in original). The analytical mind is therefore entirely conscious, and rationally processes the data it receives from MEST, while the various types of stimuli associated with this data (including harmful neuroses) are sent to the reactive mind (Melton 2000: 26–7). As Hubbard's definition outlined, the analytical mind is the primary communicator between the thetan and the physical universe and allows the individual to knowingly make decisions and interact with the universe around it.

Most of Hubbard's research on the mind concerns itself with the reactive and analytical minds, meaning that the somatic mind is the part of the mind given the least amount of attention in Scientology, yet is very important in its influence on the behaviour of the individual. The somatic mind exists on an even deeper subconscious level than the reactive mind, containing no 'thinkingness' and only 'actingness' (Hubbard [1956] 2007: 71). It is this aspect of the mind that is believed to cause muscular and glandular impulses by the individual, based on the influence of the reactive mind, the analytical mind and the thetan itself. An individual can experience psychosomatic illnesses, pains and physical illness as a result of the mental pictures of the reactive mind (and their associated engrams) influencing the somatic mind without the knowledge of the thetan ([1956] 2007: 71).

In *DMSMH*, Hubbard wrote that the engram is the single source and cause of psychosomatic illnesses and that the removal of engrams brings 'about a state greatly superior to the current norm' ([1950] 2007b: 84). Furthermore, Hubbard claimed that the use of Dianetic auditing could prevent the development of psychosomatic illness, and even such afflictions as colds and allergies (Urban 2011: 47). Despite this, Hubbard maintained that this is a side effect of the process, and that auditing does not set out to cure medical conditions. During a recorded interview, Hubbard addressed this issue:

> When you know the basics of human existence and so forth, you can apply them in almost any sphere. For instance, [a] great many people think that Scientology does medical treatments and so forth, simply because people who are processed [audited] tend to get well and recover from certain illnesses. That's a secondary action. The person who is able, of course, is more able physically also. However, when a person turns up who is ill and so forth, we just send him to the doctor. We're not interested in treating human illness. (Hubbard, in *An Introduction to Scientology* 2006)

The curing of psychosomatic illnesses caused by the somatic mind is therefore an additional benefit of auditing, which is the removal of all engrams (and their harmful effects) from the reactive mind, described by my participants at the CoS as the removal of the reactive mind entirely. This greater level of control of the mind for the thetan, as described by Hubbard, makes the individual more able in life. The role of the mind as the communicator between the thetan and MEST makes the heightening of ability an important part of Scientology auditing.

Through his Dianetic research, Hubbard ([1956] 2007: 73) claimed that Scientology had established the field of biophysics, gaining a complete understanding of the influence of the mind on the body. Hubbard described the body as an 'animated vegetable' ([1952] 2007c: 64) that is merely guided and controlled by the human mind and spirit, and that its study and treatment is primarily the concern of the medical doctor (Hubbard [1956] 2007: 73). Yet the biophysics of the body was established by Hubbard through his discovery of electrical fields that surround the body:

> The body exists in its own space. That space is created by *anchor points* (points which are anchored in a space different to the physical universe space around a

body). The complexity of these anchor points can cause an independent series of electronic flows which can occasion much discomfort to the individual. The balance structure of the body, and even its joint action and physical characteristics, can be changed by changing this electrical field which exists at a distance from or within the body. (Hubbard [1956] 2007: 73, emphasis in original)

This results in there being four influences on the operation of the body; the three parts of the mind and the electrical fields surrounding the body. Hubbard ([1956] 2007: 74) argued that medical doctors lacked the correct understanding and definition of the mind, despite having achieved many results in treating the body through biochemical products and a knowledge of the structural body. It is only through the field of Scientology's biophysics, and its combined knowledge of mental and physical states, that the body can be successfully treated. This view of a medical benefit from engaging with Scientology is entirely contrary to Hubbard's statement that Scientology is 'not interested in treating human illness' (Hubbard, in *An Introduction to Scientology* 2006).

In contrast to Hubbard's claim in his *An Introduction to Scientology* interview that Scientology does not treat medical illnesses, many Scientologists attest to the perceived medical benefits of Scientology, resulting in success stories that continue to be used in the CoS' promotional materials to the present day. For example, the CoS runs a Dianetics website that includes success stories of auditing sessions, several of which involve medical improvements, such as the following from an individual claiming that auditing resulted in his recovering from kidney failure:

I was very ill for months in the hospital. I was under intensive care for weeks with a bleeding ulcer infection and kidney failure. My heart stopped three times. I was unconscious for over a week, and I did not want to live. The doctors were going to give up on me and stop the treatment. The nurses did not expect me to survive. My wife had a very hard time with it and she couldn't even call to see how I was doing; she had to have someone else call for her. She then received some Dianetics auditing and came to grips with it, at which point she was able to come into my room in the hospital and give me some auditing [Book One auditing]. She came in every day. I soon started becoming more aware of my environment and had a determinism [Scientologist nomenclature for determination] to survive. It made life bright enough to live. I am now recovered and would not have lived if it weren't for the technology of L. Ron Hubbard that helped us get through it. (B.G., cited in The Church of Scientology International n.d.-f)

While the focus of Scientology is on improving the state and abilities of the thetan through Dianetic auditing, the condition of the body is of great importance for the successful execution of auditing sessions, and has become the primary focus of a Scientologist practice known as the 'Purification Rundown'. This programme is, according to a participant at the CoS, the first step on the Bridge to Total Freedom, and is accordingly a form of auditing in itself.

The Purification Rundown: Church of Scientology and Free Zone perspectives

The Purification Rundown (often referred to as the 'Purification Program' or 'Purif') concerns itself with detoxification, predominantly the removal of harmful drugs from the body, ranging from medically prescribed drugs and industrial chemicals, to illegal drugs. Hubbard believed that not only were street drugs the most destructive element of modern society but claimed to discover that drugs remained in the human body for years after their consumption. Using the example of LSD, Hubbard argued that the drug remains in the system, lodging in mostly fatty tissues. This can prompt the drug to be triggered again, causing unpredictable 'trips' for the individual years after coming off the drug (Hubbard 2002: 15).

Particularly due to Hubbard's view of the attachment of drugs to fatty tissues, the Purif consists of a strict routine of exercise and a diet of nutritional foods to flush the drugs from the system. In 1977 Hubbard established the 'Sweat Program' to remove drugs (mainly LSD) from the body via sweat, but as his research developed he concluded that drug deposits from several sources were causing long-term harm to the body, and developed the Purif accordingly. The CoS not only advocates the Purif but provides exclusively designed Purification Centres in most of its centres, complete with equipment to 'do the Purif' (see Figures 4.1 and 4.2). The Purif involves exercise via running (often on a treadmill), spending periods of time in a sauna while staying hydrated and taking certain vitamins, and a nutritional programme of healthy food (Hubbard 2002: 19).

During my tours of these Purification Centres, one of my participants gave a detailed account of what the Purif entails, describing it as a form of auditing in itself. He added that standard auditing procedure with the E-Meter would not be as effective without the Purif, due to the body not functioning correctly because of the effects of chemicals and drugs. Scientologists at the beginning of their spiritual development are encouraged to undergo the Purif for a period of typically two to

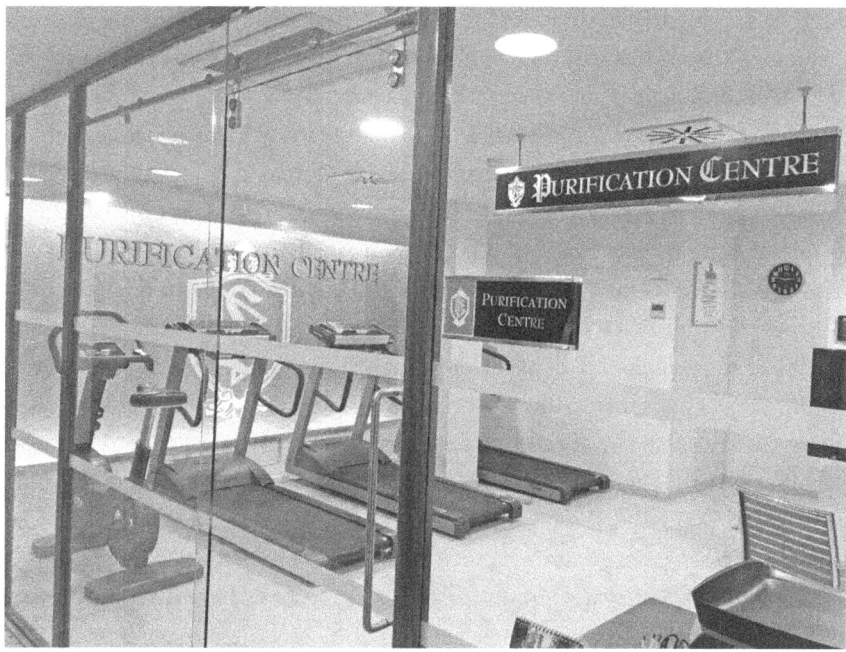

Figure 4.1 The Purification Centre at the Church of Scientology of London (photo by the author, 1 March 2017).

Figure 4.2 The treadmills at the Purification Centre in Saint Hill, East Grinstead (photo by the author, 18 April 2017).

three weeks, which involves four to five hours per day spent in the sauna, ensuring that toxins are expelled from the body. My informant explained that as with any successful auditing session, there are 'end phenomena' (E/P) when the Purif is complete, which are taken as visible signs that the Purif has been successful. For example, he recalled instances when he had seen cancer drip from the bodies of Scientologists leaving the sauna, and sunburn from previous years reappearing as its radiation is flushed away; both could be classified as E/Ps. My participant also reinforced the religiosity of the Purif, arguing that it proved the spiritual nature of humanity. He clarified this with the 'pinch test', in which an individual is pinched and asked to recall the incident. As they can still feel the pinch for a short period of time after it has taken place, the cells of the body must have a memory. These memories are passed on through life and death, meaning that previous instances of pain and drug use can be addressed through the Purif and auditing. The Purif purifies the mind and the thetan, in addition to the physical body, and is also believed to be capable of causing a rise in intelligence and mental ability.

While the body may not be considered the 'true' self by Hubbard, its treatment and improvement are important aspects of self-development in Scientology. The importance of the thetan as the true self does not negate the importance of the other Parts of Man, rather practising Scientology allows the thetan to fully control all other Parts of Man as a part of its control of the MEST universe. As noted earlier, one of the defining aspects of the Purif is the Purification Centre found in most CoS Orgs. The lack of an organizational structure in many Free Zone groups, however, immediately raises questions of how the Purif is conducted without centres dedicated purely to the Purif, in addition to Free Zone views on the Purif itself. One of my Free Zone contacts, Owen, who audits clients worldwide via online video chat methods such as Skype, explained his view of the Purif:

> As you know society and the culture changes all the time, constantly. In the 60ies and 70ies [sic] the purify and the various Drug Rundowns were created and run a lot and with great success. This was because the R/Ds [Rundowns] paralleled the clients mind and situation. Today, 40 years later, the new clients coming in (to my practice) do NOT have a history with lots of drugs, alcohol etc etc. Taking drugs is today considered a 'downer', losers [sic] game etc.... If new clients have had a few drugs like injections at dentist and like that, it is usually handled by just rehabilitating wins [successful auditing sessions] on those substances and then ordinary auditing runs very well.

Owen's view is that the Purif was created by Hubbard during a period of heavy drug use in society, and that the stigma associated with drug use today has resulted in a lesser need for their removal through the Purif. Christensen notes that 'the problem of drugs underwent a representational redescription process from the 1960s' (2016: 98), resulting in the shift of Hubbard's focus of the Purif on the contemporary issue of LSD in the 1960s, to the wider spectrum of all drugs used in wider society in 1978, including painkillers and alcohol. With the view of drugs not holding the importance they once did during Hubbard's initiation of the Purif, Owen believes that gaining 'wins' (the removal of an engram) on previous drug use is not a concern for his Preclears, yet during these auditing sessions Owen has audited several locks involving a range of different types of drugs, some of which he outlined in our email conversation:

> Drugs I have found on [auditing] cases:
>
> Street drugs: (LSD, Speed, Marihuana, Pot, Crack, etc.).
>
> Medicinal drugs: During operations, anaesthetics, local anaesthetics, at [the] dentist, in ambulances, at homevisit [sic] by doctor, pain killers, hormones (some hormones can be toxic), poisons, medicine, etc.
>
> Alcohol: all kinds.
>
> Beer: all kinds.
>
> Fumes: lighter gass [sic], glue, gasoline etc (being drunk or sniffed).
>
> Past Life drugs: anything taken in a past life.

Stating that he has 'always been able to list at least 50 drugs on almos [sic] any case who was NOT a druggie' (emphasis in original), Owen believes that residual drugs from common drugs such as alcohol and medicinal drugs are removed as a part of wider auditing sessions on other 'cases' (the instances or issue the Preclear wishes to address). Rather than encouraging the Preclear to engage with a rigorous Purification Rundown, Owen audits drug use through the standard question-and-answer auditing process, as he demonstrates:

> You rehab the number of times PC [Preclear] went release on each drug taken, just by asking:
>
> 'Did you go release on _____?'
>
> If answer is Yes and it reads:
>
> 'How many times did you go release on _____?' to F/N VGI's [Floating Needles and Very Good Indicators on the E-Meter].

This method of addressing drug use through the standard auditing procedure, rather than a dedicated Purif programme, is also adopted by Tracy – a Free Zone Scientologist – who told me that:

> The clients I have don't need the Purif and I don't deliver it here. I have several friends that do. The Purif should be for people who are trying to get residual drugs out of their system, sweating it out so to speak. Also Niacin [a vitamin commonly taken during the Purif] makes a flush, a sort of affect [*sic*] on self. That way they can know something is happening.

Like Owen, Tracy views the Purif as a procedure that is applicable only to those who are specifically trying to overcome the negative consequences of drug use, rather than the CoS' view that the Purif is a compulsory and necessary step to begin auditing sessions. Moreover, while my contact at the CoS viewed the Purif as a form of auditing, and the first step on the Bridge to Total Freedom, Tracy stated that 'the Purif is not auditing in any way. It is body handling', meaning that it is a method of improving the well-being of the body, not an auditing technique.

Much like Tracy and Owen, James also views the Purif as efficient and was fully trained in conducting the process as a CoS staff member; however, he does not make use of the Purif as an Independent Scientologist. He maintains that it is a beneficial process, stating that beyond the removal of residual drugs, 'it never failed to raise awareness and IQ in people', explaining that some were given unspecified tests before and after conducting the Purif. He also believes in the potential benefits of using Niacin in an attempt to lead a healthier lifestyle:

> I find it fascinating that the medical field is only now talking about the powers of Niacin (a key element in the Purif).

And:

> Niacin is now dispensed by the medical profession in the USA as something that reduces cholesterol or some such. I have long admired its qualities though I wouldn't advise taking it just for the sake of it.

The use of the Purif in Scientology, as demonstrated by James' approval of Niacin, is intended to not only remove residual drugs from the body but also improve the health of the individual. Owen stated that the importance of a healthy diet is 'more important to the independent auditor [than] it ever was in [the] CoS'. Taking a highly critical stance on the food served to Sea Org employees, Owen claims that 'if the Org was down-stat [performing poorly] you got rice and beans [as punishment] until the stats were up again, which could be weeks later'. Owen insisted that 'obesity is an issue with the PC [Preclear], IF the PC considers it an issue', meaning that achieving physical fitness is the decision of the Preclear, and is not, in Owen's view, an important factor in the practice of Free Zone

Scientology. James also encourages a healthy lifestyle amongst his Preclears, but similarly to Owen, views this as a recommendation, and not essential to the efficacy of auditing:

> I do recommend my clients lead a healthier lifestyle but that's in part because I worked for a time in the medical field and learned how the food industry went criminal and partly because I gained a certain suspicion of 'authorities' when in the Church.

Such responses from my Free Zone participants demonstrate that they do not view the Purif as essential to the practice of Scientology, and would rather place an emphasis on maintaining a healthy diet and lifestyle alongside auditing sessions. These views are substantially different to the importance of the Purif stressed by the CoS, particularly Tracy's statement regarding it being completely unrelated to auditing, and Owen's view that it was a process developed by Hubbard to address a problem of the time. It is notable, however, that these Freezoners are entirely independent, and do not belong to a wider, structured and regulated, Free Zone group. Thus, they lack the resources of the financially wealthy CoS to build fixed locations, such as the CoS' Orgs, to conduct Scientologist practices. To develop an understanding of the ways the Purif can be viewed in an organized Free Zone group, I discussed the topic with Hanson, a member of Ron's Org, the Free Zone Scientologist community that was established by Captain Bill Robertson in the 1980s. In the years since its establishment, Ron's Org has grown in popularity and has opened Orgs in several locations across the world, including Moscow, Switzerland, Argentina, France and Portugal (Hellesøy 2016: 450).

With these fixed locations in mind, I asked Hanson during an email conversation if he practises the Purif, and what is Ron's Org's view regarding the practice. He stated that the:

> Purif [Rundown] is certain [sic] a good thing but basically it is not really Scientology but it quite regularly necessary as people are full of drug residuals and those things can become a stop [sic]. We do not have purif centers [sic] but we deliver it.

This perspective from a Ron's Org member demonstrates some similarity to my other Free Zone participants by viewing the Purif as not being an aspect of Scientology, yet the Purif is still delivered and conducted by Ron's Org members. Hanson explained that, despite Ron's Org's numerous Orgs, the process is conducted in public saunas in the same way as in the CoS:

> We are in a public sauna. It's much cheaper than to have an own [sic] sauna and all infrastructure. And in the times I have been in the Church we did it also in public saunas. No problem.

In another similarity to my other Free Zone participants, Ron's Org encourages a healthy diet with its Preclears, yet with more rigid guidelines than my other participants:

> We recommend to eat protein rich food and vegetables etc. But it is only a recommendation. Scientology is not involving into somebodies [sic] food etc. but of course we do not accept some drinking regularly alcohol or so. But it is also not forbidden to drink sometimes alcohol [sic]. But what can we do when someone drinks sometimes really? We do not exclude him and it has no sever [sic] consequences, of course we help him/her to get rid of it, but first the subject needs to want that himself. The only consequences it has that he is no more audited.

Unlike my other Free Zone participants, Ron's Org does not simply encourage a healthy diet as a recommendation, but can deny auditing sessions to Preclears that frequently drink alcohol, reinforcing the importance of the Purif, albeit in a more relaxed fashion, in Ron's Org.

The Purification Rundown is an important practice to consider when understanding the Scientologist notion of the physical self. While the 'true' self of the Parts of Man is the spiritual thetan, the CoS views the body as an aspect of the self that can prohibit spiritual development through the presence of residual drugs, a view shared by Ron's Org. Other Freezoners, as this chapter has demonstrated, view the Purif as a potentially beneficial process, but not one that is essential to the practice of Scientology, preferring to place an emphasis on a healthy lifestyle and diet.

Hubbard's theoretical approaches to the self and auditing

Hubbard's work on the human mind and overall nature of humanity are the core of the practice of auditing and the journey of the individual on the Bridge to Total Freedom. While the Parts of Man relate specifically to the individual, namely the thetan and its operation of the body and mind in MEST, the Scientologist notion of the self is also expanded to how the individual interacts with other individuals and the world around them. These are demonstrated by a series of theories formulated by Hubbard, which apply to all aspects of life.

The cycle-of-action

Scientology teaches that its fundamental principle is the cycle-of-action. Hubbard ([1956] 2007: 21) wrote that, even from ancient texts (which he does not specify), there has been an apparent cycle-of-action that all existence is subjected to. He emphasizes the 'apparency' of this cycle, as it is 'distinct from what actually *is*' ([1956] 2007: 22, emphasis in original). This apparent cycle-of-action is outlined as:

CREATION, SURVIVAL, DESTRUCTION.

First there is *creation*.

This is then followed by *survival*.

This is followed by *destruction*. (Hubbard [1956] 2007: 22, emphasis in original)

Using the example of a child being born (creation), growing old (survival) and eventually dying (destruction), Hubbard (Hubbard [1956] 2007: 22) claimed that this apparent view of the cycle-of-action is seen as affecting all life. However, he argued that this perceived cycle-of-action's lack of ability to improve one's intelligence or well-being demonstrates its faults, and the need to define the correct cycle-of-action. Hubbard outlined the correct cycle-of-action accordingly:

CREATE, CREATE-CREATE-CREATE, CREATE-COUNTER-CREATE, NO-CREATION, NOTHINGNESS.

Create = make, manufacture, construct, postulate, bring into beingness = *Create*.

Create-Create-Create = create again continuously one moment after the next = *Survive*.

Create-Counter-Create = to create something against a creation = to create one thing and then create something else against it = *Destroy*.

No-Creation = an absence of any creation = no creative activity.

An actual cycle-of-action, then, consists of various activities, but each and every one of them is *creative*. (Hubbard [1956] 2007: 23, emphasis in original)

Expanding on this, Hubbard ([1956] 2007: 23) claimed that the concept of destruction is merely an 'apparency', and that it is in fact a creative action (create-counter-create). Using the example of the destruction of a wall as a creative action, Hubbard argued that 'there is no such thing as destruction. There is only creation against a creation' ([1956] 2007: 23). The cycle-of-action, particularly the reworked definition of destruction, is important to the Scientologist notion of self-improvement, as individuals are believed to be constantly creating, even if they don't realize that they are. Hubbard ([1956] 2007: 26) provided several examples of this, including an example of a man in employment. By being in employment, the man creates a job and sustains it by continuously working at it (create-create-

create), should the man take his job for granted and no longer creates it, he ends up not having one (moving from no-creation to nothingness). Accordingly, Hubbard ([1956] 2007: 26) explained that it is an apparency that his laziness resulted in his redundancy, but the reality is that he no longer has a job as he simply stopped creating one. These principles are at constant work in Scientology, and become integral to the improvement of the self through auditing sessions.

The three conditions of existence

The Scientologist notion of the self postulates that the individual exists through a series of three conditions, namely Beingness, Doingness and Havingness ([1956] 2007: 31–2). 'Beingness' relates to the notion of identity; such as one's name, personality and character traits. Following Beingness, an individual is able to 'do' (Doingness), by moving, creating and accomplishing. The final condition of existence allows the individual to 'have' (Havingness), by owning, possessing and taking charge of objects. It is these conditions that are believed to facilitate existence in Scientology, and are ordered by importance; beingness allows doing, and thus doing allows having ([1956] 2007: 32).

The Eight Dynamics

The cycle-of-action and three conditions of existence act as a foundation for the Eight Dynamics – a series of factors that are commonly seen as impelling humanity towards survival, determined by Hubbard as its ultimate goal in his *Excalibur* narrative (Bridge Publications 2012: 11). Described by Cusack (2009: 395) as a characterization of human destiny, the Eight Dynamics begin with more basic commands, with each command expanding further beyond the individual with each dynamic. Eventually the dynamics reach the Eighth Dynamic, the command of surviving as the 'Supreme Being', known as the 'God Dynamic' (Urban 2011: 67). The Eight Dynamics, as determined by Hubbard ([1956] 2007: 38–9), are:

1. The Self Dynamic (the First Dynamic); the drive to exist as an individual.
2. The Sex Dynamic (the Second Dynamic); the drive to exist through sexual activity. This dynamic relates to both sexual acts and the raising of children through family.
3. Group Dynamic (the Third Dynamic); the drive to exist as part of a wider community.

4. Mankind Dynamic (the Fourth Dynamic); the drive to exist as a part of the entirety of humanity, beyond certain groups.
5. Animal Dynamic (the Fifth Dynamic); the drive to exist as a part of all living things, including animals and plants.
6. Universe Dynamic (the Sixth Dynamic); the drive to exist in the MEST universe.
7. Spiritual Dynamic (the Seventh Dynamic); the drive to exist as a spirit.
8. Infinity or God Dynamic (the Eighth Dynamic); the drive to exist as infinity, or the Supreme Being.

Only the first four of these dynamics can be found in *DMSMH* (Hubbard [1950] 2007b), which was published during the secular phase of Dianetic technology. During this period of Dianetics' history, the purpose of the Four Dynamics was solely concerned with survival. Hubbard ([1950] 2007b: 42) initially saw survival as an activity concerning only the self, but soon discovered that this view did not explain the majority of human behaviours. Building upon this, Hubbard explored survival in relation to the groups surrounding the individual, the altruistic survival of humanity, and finally reached the assumption that 'behaviour could be explained by assuming [the individual] lived for sex alone' ([1950] 2007b: 42). All of these analyses proved to be unsuccessful for Hubbard as explanations of human behaviour. Hubbard concluded that 'all four of these factors, *self, sex, group* and *Mankind*' ([1950] 2007b: 42, emphasis in original) worked in tandem as the Four Dynamics serving the drive for survival.

The Four Dynamics were considered by Hubbard to be part of '[t]he earlier subject, Dianetics' ([1956] 2007: 39), but remain a part of the Eight Dynamics of Scientology. My fieldwork participants at the CoS explained that Hubbard constantly published his research as it was taking place, rather than only publishing a singular and final piece of work. The original purpose of the Four Dynamics was to explain human behaviour in relation to survival alone, but following the introduction of the more overtly 'religious' elements of Scientology, Hubbard ([1956] 2007: 39–40) taught that the development of the cycle-of-action and three conditions of existence had revealed that survival is merely an apparency, and that each dynamic is supported by the cycle-of-action and three conditions of existence. For example, Scientology teaches that individuals must master the beingness, doingness and havingness of each dynamic. Hubbard viewed the Eight Dynamics as a series of steps for the growth of the individual. Using the example of a baby being solely concerned with the First Dynamic (the self), Hubbard ([1956] 2007: 40) demonstrated that the individual goes on to grow aware of the dynamics around them. Despite insisting that no dynamic is more important than the other, successfully engaging with a particular dynamic depends entirely on successfully operating on the previous dynamic; 'a person who is incapable of operating on the Third Dynamic is incapable at once of being a part of a team and so might be said to be incapable of a social existence [the Fourth Dynamic]' ([1956] 2007). Growth within the Eight Dynamics is paramount in Scientology, and the ability to recognize and communicate within the dynamics is crucial to observe and recognize the abilities of the individual ([1956] 2007), a particularly important skill for trained auditors when auditing a Preclear.

The Tone Scale

Of additional importance to auditors, and to Scientologist communication, is the Tone Scale, a numerical scale that allows the measurement of human emotion. The Tone Scale in its seeming entirety ranges from Tone 0.0 (death) to 40.0 (Serenity of Beingness) (The Church of Scientology International n.d.-i). Yet Hubbard ([1951] 2007d: 13) wrote that the true number of levels of the Tone Scale is in fact unknown, and that there may be further levels hitherto unexplored. However, much of the use of the Tone Scale in Scientology, particularly when auditing the Preclear, concentrate on levels −3 to 4.0.

At Tone −3: A dead body that is simply MEST, distinguished from other MEST by its recent evolution through association with a theta being. Tone −1: A dead body containing some short-term living cells. Tone 0.0: Death, specifically the moment the thetan leaves the body. Tones 0.0 to 2.0: the reactive mind dominates the body, influenced by its engrams. Tones 2.0 to 4.0: the greater operation of the analytical mind. Beyond Tone 4.0: more esoteric states of mind, with the thetan gaining a greater control of the mind and body ([1951] 2007d). While the complete Tone Scale is considerable in length, Hubbard categorizes it in *DMSMH* in four zones with what he describes as 'very unprecise but nevertheless descriptive names' ([1950] 2007b: 31):

> Zone 3 is one of general happiness and well-being. Zone 2 is a level of bearable existence. Zone 1 is one of anger. Zone 0 is the zone of apathy. (Hubbard [1950] 2007b: 31)

An individual will rarely stay at the same Tone level for a prolonged period, and can be found at different locations on the Tone Scale depending on their current emotional state. Hubbard demonstrated this in *Science of Survival*, which explored the Tone Scale further, stating that '[a] person fluctuates on this scale from hour to hour and day to day. He receives good news, he goes momentarily to Tone 3.0. He receives bad news, he may sink for a moment to Tone 1.0' ([1951] 2007d: 14).

During an auditing session, a trained auditor identifies which of these levels the Preclear is currently operating. A Preclear could reside at Tone 0.07 (hopelessness) before rising to higher levels such as Tone 2.6 (disinterested) (Harley and Kieffer 2009: 199). Hubbard ([1950] 2007b: 31) argued that through confronting their engrams and locks by practising Dianetics, a Preclear could visibly rise up the Tone Scale. Indeed, an improvement in the Preclear's well-being can suggest that they have come to terms with the incident they are recalling, allowing the auditor to announce the end phenomena, confirm the Preclear's current Tone level and thus bring the auditing session to a close (Harley and Kieffer 2009: 199).

Hubbard's research determined that there were three key influences on the individual's current level on the Tone Scale. The first influence, 'accumulated entheta [a thetan influenced by MEST]' (Hubbard [1951] 2007d: 14), concerns how greatly the thetan is encumbered by its engrams and locks that prevent it from developing through irrational fears. Second, 'amount of theta' ([1951] 2007d: 14) concerns the volume of theta. As terror is also fear with great volume, an individual with a small level of theta could be deeply troubled by a small number of engrams, while a large volume of theta could allow an individual encumbered with an enormous number of engrams to successfully live a productive life. Finally, the 'ratio between the analytical mind and the reactive mind' ([1951] 2007d: 15), concerns the individual Tone levels of the reactive and analytical minds, which create an overall average Tone level. An auditor conducting Scientology processing (Hubbard's term for the execution of auditing and Dianetic technology) seeks to remove the engrams from entheta. This is the primary purpose of auditing; as Hubbard ([1951] 2007d) wrote, an auditor is seeking to raise the individual's tone, not cure their medical conditions.

The ARC Triangle

The bases of the Tone Scale are the notions of Affinity, Reality and Communication (Hubbard [1956] 2007: 47). These notions are depicted in Scientology through the ARC Triangle, a triangular diagram that represents the 'common denominator to all of life's activities' ([1956] 2007: 45). The basic purpose of the triangle is to demonstrate the relationship and interdependency of Affinity, Reality and

Communication upon one another. Affinity is concerned with the notion of feeling and emotions, including (but not exclusive to) love or anger towards other individuals. The Scientologist notion of affinity is intertwined with the Tone Scale, which measures the level of affinity towards other individuals or small groups (Hubbard [1951] 2007d: 63). Expanding on this, Hubbard ([1951] 2007d: 63) explained that the suppression of affinity can cause an individual to take on a habitual affinity towards others, which can be extended to whole groups, including the entirety of humanity, allowing the affinity of entire groups to be measured on the Tone Scale. The Tone Scale of Affinity descends from Tone 4.0 to 0.5, specifically Tone 4.0 (love and friendliness); Tone 3.0 (tolerance); Tone 2.5 (neglect); Tone 2.0 (antagonism); Tone 1.5 (hatred); Tone 1.0 (fear); Tone 0.5 (grief) ([1951] 2007d: 64–5).

The second part of the ARC Triangle, Communication, concerns more than simply the exchange of information and ideas. To communicate in Scientology additionally includes experiencing 'perceptics', Hubbard's specialized term for perceptions ([1951] 2007d: 640). This form of perception involves perceiving entities in both the MEST and theta universe, ranging from basic senses such as the olfactory sense, to perceptions of body positions of individuals with their immediate environment ([1951] 2007d: 68). Hubbard taught that Communication is the most important corner of the ARC Triangle, being the 'solvent for all things' ([1956] 2007: 47).

Reality, the third corner of the ARC Triangle, concerns apparency and the reality of that which is agreed to be real in the physical universe (Hubbard [1951] 2007d: 71; [1956] 2007: 47). Expanding on this, Hubbard ([1951] 2007d: 71–2) acknowledged that a philosophic challenge is raised by the consideration of whether something is 'real', but stated that there can be a universal agreement of what is real in the physical universe. Through the example of two individuals agreeing on the existence of a table, Hubbard stated that a third individual that claimed the table to be a black cat could be deemed insane, demonstrating the 'agreed-upon conception of the physical universe' ([1951] 2007d: 72).

In Scientology, Affinity, Reality and Communication depend on one another when explaining human attitudes and behaviours. The interdependency of the three, hence the purpose of the triangular diagram, was explained by Hubbard accordingly:

> The interrelationship of the triangle becomes apparent at once when one asks, 'Have you ever tried to talk to an angry man?'. Without a high degree of liking and without some basis of agreement, there is no *communication*. Without communication and some basis of emotional response, there can be no *reality*.

> Without some basis for agreement and communication, there can be no *affinity*. Thus we call these three things a *triangle*. Unless we have two corners of a triangle, there cannot be a third corner. Desiring any corner of the triangle, one must include the other two. (Hubbard [1956] 2007: 47, emphasis in original)

The ARC Triangle becomes a tool in Scientologist communication, as two individuals must be on the same level of affinity for communication to be understood by the person for whom it is intended, as demonstrated by Hubbard's example of the angry man. Hence the combination of Affinity, Reality and Communication as ARC becomes 'understanding'.

Beyond being a tool for Scientologist communication, however, the understanding of the Tone Scale and the ARC Triangle is integral to the training of a professional auditor. A disturbance in the ARC, known as an ARC Break (such as an emotional upset), can prevent the Preclear from being 'in-session', and not give the auditing session their full attention. To rectify this issue, auditing sessions often begin with the auditor asking, 'do you have an ARC break?' Should the E-Meter 'read' once the Preclear has responded, the auditor will proceed to ask questions about the emotional upset in an attempt rectify the break, allowing the auditing session to successfully begin (Free Zone Earth n.d.-a; Harley and Kieffer 2009: 201).

Gender: The sexless thetan?

When examining Hubbard's writing on the nature of the self, it is immediately noticeable that Hubbard made use of androcentric language, referring to both the self (and humanity as a whole) as 'Man' or 'Mankind', and adopted male pronouns throughout his work. He also displays heteronormative assumptions throughout his writing. Heteronormativity is described by Kristen Schilt and Laurel Westbrook as 'the suite of cultural, legal, and institutional practices that maintain normative assumptions that there are two and only two genders, that gender reflects biological sex, and that only sexual attraction between these "opposite" genders is natural or acceptable' (2009: 441). This understanding of a 'social norm' of heterosexuality and specific gender binaries ties in with Susan Palmer's (1994: 4) understanding of the nuclear family: an assumed family structure based on patriarchy and male dominance. The concept of heteronormativity cannot simply be confined to the relationship between heterosexuality and gender binaries, as 'racism, socioeconomic inequalities, and the colonial gaze are dependent upon ideas about normal bodies, identifications, and sex practices' (Ward and Schneider 2009: 438). Hubbard's writing suggests a heteronormative inflection to Scientology, with the dominance of androcentric language and attitudes in his work.

This use of androcentric and heteronormative language is not limited to Hubbard however, and is used by the CoS to the present day, particularly in its literature and promotional materials. This is especially notable in the 'Creed of Scientology', frequently shown in Scientology promotional films, which demonstrates the Scientologist belief in the fundamental importance of human rights. These rights are all explained with the use of male pronouns, as this extract demonstrates:

> We of the Church believe that all men of whatever race, color [*sic*] or creed were created with equal rights. That all men have inalienable rights to their own religious practices and their performance. That all men have inalienable rights to their own lives. That all men have inalienable rights to their sanity. That all men have inalienable rights to their own defense [*sic*]. That all men have inalienable rights to conceive, choose, assist or support their own organizations, churches and governments. That all men have inalienable rights to think freely, to talk freely, to write freely their own opinions and to counter or utter or write upon the opinions of others. (The Church of Scientology International n.d. d: online)

It is clear that while these rights are written in a gender-specific fashion, they are deemed by the CoS to be applicable for all humanity. Maja Pellikaan-Engel highlights the potentially dangerous consequences of the terms 'Man' and 'Mankind':

> The word 'mankind' can mean: the entire human race, as well as the male sex alone. It is comparable to the plural 'homines', 'hommes', or 'men', all of which can refer to females and males, as well as to males only. The two senses of these expressions have led to tragic misunderstandings throughout history. In the French Revolution, for example, women fought side by side with men to bring about equal rights for *all* men, the *whole* of mankind, or *tous* les hommes; but in actuality, the female and male soldiers in that battle were fighting towards the same in words only. So when the philosopher Olympe de Gouges demanded equal rights for women, the reply she received was the guillotine. (Pellikaan-Engel 1998: 237–8, emphasis in original)

It is because of examples such as these, Pellikaan-Engel (1998: 238) argues, that feminists have avoided such discriminatory language, promoting the use of gender-neutral terms, such as 'humankind', in contemporary times. With this in mind, Hubbard is often viewed as 'a child of his age' (Patheos n.d.: online), but on the other hand, these contemporary examples from Scientologist literature suggests the normativity of a male perspective or subject-position under which women and other gendered voices can be positioned.

Yet, while both leaders of the CoS since its emergence in the 1950s have been male, there is no rule or guideline in Scientology that would prohibit a woman from progressing as a staff member of the CoS (Patheos n.d.: online). For example, the CoS allows both men and women to become ministers due to their perception of all humanity as sexless spiritual beings (The Church of Scientology International n.d.-k). It is this understanding of a sexless thetan that results in Palmer's categorization of Scientology as a 'sex unity' NRM; a movement which views the notion of sex/gender as entirely superfluous, a 'false identity obscuring the immortal, sexless spirit' (1994: 10; see also Dawson 2006: 138).

During my fieldwork at the CoS, I was able to meet both male and female staff members of various levels of authority, and the CoS' website states that 'Scientology is a meritocracy. There are no "glass ceiling" limitations based on race, gender, ethnicity or similar criteria for individuals who serve as ministers or as executives in the Church's ecclesiastical management' (The Church of Scientology International n.d.-k: online). The CoS' approach to gender in both spiritual and organizational contexts has additionally been promoted by STAND (Scientologists Taking Action Against Discrimination), their campaign against religious discrimination and bigotry (Thomas 2017b). In a STAND blog post entitled 'Gender Schmender', a female CoS member writes that all staff positions in the CoS are open to men and women, and states that as 'a fairly new religion, Scientology is in a position of not having to carry on any tired old gender traditions. Scientology addresses YOU, a spiritual being, and the gender of the body is rather inconsequential' (Butz 2018: online, emphasis in original). This belief in the sexless thetan presents no barrier or advantage to being a specific gender when advancing on the Bridge to Total Freedom and receiving auditing sessions (Patheos n.d.), further exemplifying Scientology's status as a sex unity movement.

In their study of gender demographics in Scientology, Lewis and Tøllefsen (2014) make use of statistics from New Zealand, Australia, Canada and the UK to report that men are the dominant gender in Scientology in each Anglophone nation, providing gender statistics from government censuses conducted in 2001. While census data can be a limited method of gauging religiosity (or religious adherence) amongst nations, they are illuminating data in themselves, giving scholars a glimpse of how individuals self-identify. While examining the numbers of self-identified Scientologists from Anglophone censuses, Lewis and Tøllefsen

(2014: 134) observe that there is no obvious explanation for the dominance of men in these statistics, a contrast to a common observation that religion appeals more to women than men, such as Puttick's claim that 'women have always been the biggest "consumers of religion"' (1997: 1). When sharing these statistics with former Scientologists, Lewis and Tøllefsen (2014: 137) received three distinct responses; some dismissed the evidence that Scientologists are predominantly men; others claimed that the statistics are irrelevant due to the sexless nature of the thetan, the true self; while others made gender stereotypical statements claiming that women would be attracted to more 'emotional' religions such as Christianity, while men would be attracted to more 'intellectual' religions such as Scientology. Lewis and Tøllefsen (2014) found none of these responses to be satisfactory.

In an attempt to postulate a reason for the dominant number of male Scientologists, Lewis and Tøllefsen (see also Tøllefsen and Lewis 2016) turn to the notion of geek culture. The contemporary use of the term 'geek', as understood by Lewis and Tøllefsen (2014: 138) , relates to individuals who are typically male, possess low social skills, a proficiency in working with technology and interests in aspects of popular culture, including fantasy and science fiction – notably, the 'Trekkies' (the large community of fans of the *Star Trek* franchise). They observe that there are several aspects of Scientology that could appeal to geek culture, particularly the overlaps between Scientology and science fiction. It is impossible to ignore Hubbard's history as a writer of science fiction, and while critics of Scientology use this to argue that the religion is no more 'real' than Hubbard's science fiction writings, Lewis and Tøllefsen (2014) note Bainbridge's view of Scientology's science fiction roots as one of its strengths: 'the science fiction subculture does not remember Hubbard fondly, but it gave him a deep reservoir of alternative culture from which to draw in creating his new scientific and technological religion' (Bainbridge 1987: 67). Indeed, as I previously discussed in Chapter 2, Hubbard's first publicly available writing on his Dianetic theory was in *Astounding Science Fiction* magazine, allowing Hubbard's ideas to make a 'sociological rather than ideological' (Lewis and Tøllefsen 2014: 138) connection with the science fiction community.

The example of the geek community's association with science fiction presents one aspect of a 'number of different overlapping male-majority milieu which, when taken together, might constitute a substantial source of male recruits to Scientology' (2014: 139). Lewis and Tøllefsen observe that the ability of a number of subcultures, including the science fiction community and groups interested in UFOs to typically attract men can somewhat explain the dominance of male numbers in Scientology, making it possible to categorize 'Scientology as a geek-friendly [and thereby male-friendly] religion' (2014).

While Lewis and Tøllefsen (2014) acknowledge that not all Scientologists are geeks, this postulation for the predominantly male membership of Scientology can be problematic. It is true that Hubbard achieved popularity in the 1940s through his pulp fiction works, and that publishing his work in *Astounding Science Fiction* magazine led to the early popularity of Dianetic theory amongst the science fiction community. However, the association with science fiction in the early 1950s is of little use when discussing the census statistics of 2001, particularly as there is little evidence to suggest that Hubbard's science fiction works have resonated or gained a notable following with today's geek community. Contemporary geek culture is commonly associated with online video gaming (such as *World of Warcraft*), role-playing games (such as *Dungeons & Dragons*) and highly successful science fiction film and television franchises (such as *Star Trek* and *Star Wars*). It would seem that the disparity between men and women in Scientology cannot be explained solely in terms of its relationship with popular culture.

The dominance of men identifying as Scientologists, coupled with the heteronormativity of Hubbard's writing, has resulted in the issue of sexism being raised by anti-Scientologists. *The Village Voice*, a website that has published several articles criticizing the CoS, posted a series of extracts from earlier editions of Hubbard's *Scientology: A New Slant on Life* (originally published in 1965), in a chapter titled 'A Woman's Creativity', to depict Hubbard as a misogynist:

> A society in which women are taught *anything but* the management of a family, the care of men, and the creation of the future generation is a society which is on its way out. . . . The historian can peg the point where a society begins its sharpest decline at the instant when women begin to take part, on an equal footing with men, in political and business affairs, since this means that the men are decadent and the women are no longer women. This is not a sermon on the role or position of women; it is a statement of bald and basic fact. (Hubbard, cited in Scherstuhl 2010: online, emphasis in original)

Scherstuhl, the author of the article, states that 'A Woman's Creativity' was omitted from later editions of *A New Slant on Life*, and was 'replaced by more conventional self-help claptrap' (2010: online), much of which he speculates was not written by Hubbard. Hubbard's concern for women 'no longer [being] women' (Hubbard, cited in Scherstuhl 2010: online) is reminiscent of the archetypical understanding of the nuclear family, in which the role of women is not in the public workplace, but in the household (Palmer 1994: 5).

Further to the controversies regarding Hubbard's writing on women are his attitudes towards the gay community. Current editions of *DMSMH*, republished by the CoS through their *Golden Age of Knowledge* initiative in 2007, continue to contain Hubbard's definition of sexual perverts to include 'homosexuality, lesbianism, sexual sadism, etc.' ([1950] 2007b: 125). Hubbard additionally stated that a member of the gay community is physically ill and is therefore 'very far from culpable for his condition, but he is also so far from normal and so extremely dangerous to society that the tolerance of perversion is as thoroughly bad for society as punishment for it' ([1950] 2007b: 126). Such statements from Hubbard, particularly his use of the word 'normal' when describing heterosexuality, demonstrates a considerable heteronormative attitude towards society that is not only limited to his use of male pronouns and gender-specific language.

Don Jolly (2016: 411) argues that sexuality and Hubbard's aforementioned Second Dynamic of existence (concerning sex, reproduction and the family unit) lies at the heart of narratives by several prominent ex-Scientologists. Throughout his study, Jolly considers Paul Haggis' rejection of the CoS' 'institutionalized homophobia' (2016: 414), Kate Bornstein's exploration of gender fluidity through the understanding of a sexless thetan, and Jenna Miscavige-Hill's 'inability to express the feminine' (2016: 416) during her time in the Sea Org. Using these examples, he argues that 'sexuality is an attractive method by which those who leave the CoS can explain their actions in a context open to interpretation and understanding by western culture at large' (2016: 419). Haggis' narrative is of particular interest due to his accusation of homophobia being directed towards the institutionalized CoS, not typical Scientologist practitioners; he states that 'there has been a hidden anti-gay sentiment in the Church for a long time. . . . [However] the great majority of Scientologists I know are good people who are genuinely interested in improving conditions on this planet and helping others' (Haggis, cited in 2016: 414). When I posed the question of sexuality to Free Zone Scientologists, James (an Independent Scientologist) provided a response that echoed Haggis' sentiment:

> One of my clients outside the Church is a gay man and I have zero issue with it. There was zero issue with it in the Church too. [In] the 70s [*sic*] in London one of my Church colleagues was bi-sexual and another was gay. At some point it [became] a problem but that is coincident with the rise of David Miscavige.

Much like Haggis' highly publicized narrative, James claims to have not encountered homophobia amongst practising Scientologists, both in his time as a member of the CoS and the Free Zone, and points to a homophobia within the institutionalized CoS under the leadership of David Miscavige. James' perspective highlights a prominent distinction amongst Freezoners regarding the CoS under Hubbard and the CoS under Miscavige, and how the CoS under Hubbard is frequently viewed as being more progressive. It is notable, however, that James' response did not mention Hubbard's problematic writing on gender and sexuality, limiting the criticism of homophobia in the CoS to the direction it has taken under Miscavige.

Additionally suggesting an institutionalized homophobia in the CoS, Freezoner Owen told me that he witnessed the CoS 'handle' (address with auditing) members of the gay community 'when they did not want that handling themselves'. In his professional capacity as a Free Zone auditor, Owen has audited LGBT Preclears, but states that their sexuality or gender only becomes part of the auditing session if the Preclear wishes to 'handle' it. When I questioned him on transgender people during an email conversation, Owen expressed a belief in the genderless thetan of Scientology that could be categorized under Palmer's (1994: 10) sex unity typology, but believes that 'personality traits' of different genders can influence the behaviours of Preclears during auditing sessions:

> Ideally there should be no difference, but fact is that there is a great difference. Not so much connected with gender, but a lot connected with wether [*sic*] the person is mostly playing out (dramatizing) his masculine or feminine personality traits. . . . If he is not in balance but polarized, then the person who is mostly dramatizing the feminine (creative) side tends more to be able to develop the spiritual side (which has NO gender). The person who is mostly playing out his maskuline [*sic*] sides wants more to be in control have things in check [*sic*] which is more on the physical plane and therefore does not develop [spiritual] vertues [*sic*] much, as long as he stays in the maskuline [*sic*] side.

This statement displays Owen's view of how stereotypical characteristics are prominent in each gender. He claims that during his auditing sessions he has experienced feminine personalities more capable of spiritual development from what he describes as a 'creative side', while masculine personalities remain rooted in physical realities due to their insistence on control. In an attempt to counter the influences of gender on auditing sessions, and thus allow the Preclear to focus on the spiritual self, Owen works with a process he described as 'balancing', which aims to '[polarize] integrity parts and [get] them back in balance'.

On face value, the issue of gender and sexuality does not initially seem a particularly notable factor when examining Scientologist notions of the self.

Both the CoS and Free Zone serve as an example of Palmer's sex unity typology of NRMs, emphasizing the sexless and genderless nature of the thetan, the 'true' self. However, upon closer inspection, both gender and sexuality have been complicated and controversial issues in the history of Scientology. Hubbard's use of male pronouns, and unenlightened writing on homosexuality and women in his written work, suggests a heteronormative world view that is still adopted by the CoS to the present day. Issues involving sexuality have been dominant factors in ex-member narratives in Scientology, while my Free Zone participants point towards a homophobic attitude in the institutional CoS, particularly under David Miscavige. These factors culminate in a contested understanding of gender: the true self in Scientology, the spiritual thetan, is understood to be genderless through Hubbard's philosophical writing and cosmology, yet the application of this belief does not overcome a dominant heteronormativity in the CoS, where gender and sexuality continues to play a part in its community.

The Bridge to Total Freedom: Preclear, Clear and Operating Thetan

'The Bridge'

In line with the Study Tech method of reading Hubbard's work in chronological order, Scientologists will approach the auditing process as a journey through a series of hierarchal spiritual states attained through specific procedures dictated by Hubbard along a linear, chronological track. These are found in the Bridge to Total Freedom, typically presented by the CoS as a chart, which documents all the stages a Scientologist aims to traverse during their engagement with Hubbard's tech. Many of my research participants referred to their experiences of Scientology as a 'journey', with an implication that there is an ultimate goal and destination for their study of Hubbard's texts and work. This is immediately apparent in the importance of the Bridge. Reinforcing Scientology's status as a World Affirming movement (Wallis 2007: 44), in addition to recalling Wilson's (1982: 131) characterization of NRMs as offering its followers a this-worldly salvation through fast methods, the Bridge is a progressive system that promises salvation to Scientologists in the current lifetime (Bromley 2009: 92).

The Bridge is divided into two sections, displaying two journeys beginning at the bottom and finishing at the top. The left side, 'Training', is for the development of trained auditors amongst the CoS' staff, beginning with their initial training and rising through each Classification in order. The second, 'Processing', concerns the development of a Scientologist on their journey from Preclear to Clear, and subsequently on to the Operating Thetan (OT) levels. Progression on these sections is not mutually exclusive, however, with Hubbard encouraging Scientologists to traverse both sides of the Bridge (Westbrook 2019: 30). Yet Westbrook observes that most of his fieldwork participants in the CoS 'either received high levels of auditing or high levels of auditor training (including administrative/staff training), but usually not both' (2015: 315).

For most Scientologists, particularly those who are not staff members at the CoS, their practice primarily concentrates on the Processing side of the Bridge. Each step of their journey on the Bridge will involve a specific type of auditing, both with a trained auditor and individually through solo auditing, allowing them to advance to the next step once certain requirements have been met (Christensen 2009: 111). Furthermore, through progressing along the Bridge, the Scientologist is trained in auditing others, 'and from that time forward spends at least a minimal amount of time assisting those just beginning their training' (Melton 2000: 30). Despite the rigorously structured nature of the Bridge, previous research (Westbrook 2015: 314) has demonstrated that there are no estimations for the period of time a Scientologist can take when advancing between levels.

The CoS encourages its members to engage with Hubbard's literature chronologically, and the initial auditing sessions leading to the state of Clear involve texts that are publicly available. However, once the state of Clear has been achieved, many of the instructions, readings and information that accompany the esoteric Operating Thetan levels are confidentially held by the CoS, and Scientologists 'doing' the OT levels are required to maintain the confidentiality of these details and documents.

The Preclear

Everyone, when initially engaging with Scientology, begins as a Preclear: someone who has yet to achieve the state of Clear. A Preclear is an individual who is affected by the irrationality of the reactive mind and their engrams, and can impulsively react to different senses through the influence of the engrams on their somatic mind. The purpose of auditing for the Preclear, as explored in Chapter 3, is to clear these engrams and the reactive mind, granting the Preclear a greater control of the analytical mind (Hubbard [1951] 2007b: 19; Melton 2000: 9).

All Preclears begin at the bottom of the Bridge to Total Freedom, with the aim of rising from the bottom to the very top, reinforcing the notion of a journey. Beginning with the Purif, the Preclear will prepare themselves for the journey to Clear by removing toxins from the body, before moving on to the more 'traditional' form of auditing, with use of an E-Meter and a trained auditor. Westbrook (2019: 34) argues, based on his extensive fieldwork with practising Scientologists, that most CoS members (at least 90 per cent by his estimations) are Preclears, and have not yet reached the state of Clear. While half of his formal interviewees were Clear or above – a circumstance he cites as being due to his interviewees being selected by the CoS – he draws his conclusion from his encounters with 'a preponderance of Preclears' (2019: 35) during his general fieldwork. This led him to the conclusion that most CoS members are in the early stages of their progression on the Bridge.

During the Preclear's journey to Clear, he or she is led by an auditor through a series of questions and answers that strictly adhere to Hubbard's Auditor's Code, a set of guidelines that all auditors must follow to successfully audit a Preclear (Hubbard [1950] 2007b: 217). It is the Code, according to my conversations with CoS staff members at Saint Hill, which demonstrates the division between the practice of auditing and psychology/psychotherapy. They stated that counsellors and psychologists would often advise on and evaluate the situations of their patients, which is specifically against the Auditor's Code – Scientology auditors are not permitted to advise the Preclear on how to live their lives or address certain situations; their goal is to remove the engrams. As of June 1980, according to the CoS website (The Church of Scientology International n.d.-a), the Auditor's Code has been updated to cover all the responsibilities of the auditor in line with the religious development of Dianetics, including the use of the E-Meters during auditing. Through frequently attending auditing sessions, it is taught that the Preclear will begin to progress towards the state of Clear by traversing the Bridge through removing their engrams.

Clear

Once the Preclear has removed all engrams from their reactive mind through auditing, they will eventually achieve the state of Clear. Beyond being free of the harmful effects of engrams and the reactive mind, a Clear is believed to experience a range of additional abilities, including heightened intelligence and a resistance to psychosomatic illness, allowing the Clear to advance more successfully through life (Urban 2011: 47). In *DMSMH*, Hubbard wrote that a 'Clear can be tested for any and all psychoses, neuroses, compulsions and repressions ... and can be examined for any autogenic (self-generated) diseases referred to as psychosomatic ills' (Hubbard [1950] 2007b: 13). These claims lead Urban (2011: 48) to argue that the state of Clear is an empty signifier, a vague concept given great meaning; a state that is almost universally attractive due to its wide range of benefits. In addition to the removal of mental neuroses and heightened intelligence, Hubbard also claimed that Clears do not suffer from bodily illness, including colds and allergies (2011). The state of Clear was the ultimate goal of Hubbard's original Dianetic theory, and remains a highly important and sought-after state in Scientology. However, through introducing the more overtly 'religious' elements to Scientology, Hubbard revealed a further series of hierarchical levels based on spirituality and cosmology, known as the OT levels. Using the example of a baby learning to crawl before walking, the CoS believes that the previous stages of the Bridge must be completed before the Clear can truly understand the next level of spiritual study (The Church of Scientology International 1998: 167).

Operating Thetan

Following the attainment of Clear, and the eradication of the engrams in the reactive mind, the Bridge continues through fifteen OT levels. These levels reside at the top of the Bridge, and allow the Clear to restore the full abilities of their thetan, unhindered by the MEST universe, and become 'wholly oneself' (The Church of Scientology International 1998: 167). It is here that Scientologists reach the ultimate goal of Scientology – spiritual independence, with the thetan overcoming the mind and body. This is a process that my fieldwork participants at the CoS described as often being faster than the journey from Preclear to Clear. Now that the Scientologist has achieved control of the analytical mind, they are able to undertake an independent method of auditing known as 'solo auditing' (Whitehead 1987: 128). To ensure the success of this process, the Clear is required to complete a series of training programmes and courses before they are permitted to begin the OT levels (Free Zone Earth n.d.-b).

Each level of OT is kept confidential until the previous level has been completed by the Clear/OT. Due to the confidential nature of the OT levels, much of their content is shrouded in secrecy, although alleged aspects of these stages have been leaked into the public domain via online sources (Rothstein 2009: 371). The Bridge itself explicitly states that OT IX–XV are currently not available to any Scientologists, while the other levels remain confidential until the Clear or OT has reached the required stage in their spiritual development to study them. According to one of my participants at the CoS, OT XV is the highest known level of Operating Thetan achievable, and the materials required for the study of OT IX–XV were prepared by Hubbard prior to his death. However, they also added that the reason OT VIII is the highest level currently available to practising Scientologists is simply because the later levels have not yet been achieved by any of the world's most advanced Scientologists. During my fieldwork, I was told that the erasing of the reactive mind and its engrams does not mean that there is no longer any need for auditing. The Clear still has a mind to audit, thus prompting them to continue along the Bridge through the OT levels. Through these levels, Scientologists address current and new problems that may arise in their lives, along with improving the lives of others. The OT levels are believed to create a greater level of awareness of the surrounding universe, and (on a basic level) help a Scientologist with everyday issues. The highest level achievable at the Saint Hill Org in the UK is OT V, while OT VI and VII are achievable at Flag in Clearwater, Florida, the CoS' worldwide headquarters. Finally, OT VIII, introduced in 1988, is currently exclusive to the *Freewinds* – the Sea Org vessel (Rathbun 2011).

Despite the presence of hierarchical levels in the spiritual development of Scientologists, my participants considered there to be no class system in the CoS based on one's levels. However, attaining the state of Clear and progression through the subsequent OT levels are highly desirable achievements in Scientology. This distinction of achievement and spiritual capabilities in Scientology creates a class system based on Max Weber's notion of 'status honor [*sic*]' ([1948] 1991a: 186). Weber's typology involves a distinction between what is typically viewed as a purely economical class system on the one hand, and status groups on the other. While these two categories can overlap, status groups act as communities that are bound by the estimation of social honour. This is particularly apparent in the Sea Org, an elite organization composing of 'the most dedicated Scientologists in the world – individuals who have dedicated their lives to the service of their religion' (The Church of Scientology International 1998: 542). Indeed, as demonstrated in Weber's work on routinized charisma, the founder of an NRM (following their death) is likely to be replaced by administrative structures – particularly through staff, organizational rules and 'above all, officials' (Weber [1948] 1991b: 297). This is especially apparent through the presence of the Sea Org, which employs staff that have traversed both the Training and Processing sides of the Bridge to the upper OT levels. Thus, Sea Org staff hold the authority and the ability to deliver the most advanced OT levels to practitioners, particularly in the Flag Land Base in Clearwater (Westbrook 2019: 30), which I shall return to in Chapter 6.

Operating Thetan III, body thetans and solo auditing

As I have previously outlined in Chapter 1 of this book, Scientologists within the CoS are alleged to be given confidential papers concerning the Xenu mythology upon reaching OT III, detailing the true origin of theta beings' existence on Earth. Copies of these documents, in Hubbard's own handwriting, can be easily accessed online, despite the CoS' many attempts to have them removed (WikiLeaks n.d.-a). Beyond the difficulty in deciphering Hubbard's handwriting, the documents can be confusing and complicated to digest, and, as Rothstein observes, 'could mean something only to devoted Scientologists and the very patient scholar' (2009: 367). During my conversations on the OT levels with CoS members, it was reinforced that they remain confidential simply due to the prior Scientology training required to understand them, drawing back to Hubbard's Study Tech approach of learning and progression on the Bridge. These documents have been the topic of scholarly analysis however, notably Rothstein's (2009) content analysis and Urban's (2017) examination of the history and secrecy surrounding OT III. Furthermore, the publication of confidential documents returns to the issue of Urban's 'ethical and epistemological double bind of secrecy' (2017: 15): the challenge of ethically engaging with leaked texts from new religions and minority movements. Urban suggests a workable method around this issue:

> While I do not think there is any easy way out of this ethical/epistemological double bind, I would suggest there are some alternative strategies for dealing with it. In the case of Scientology's advanced OT materials, at least, I suggest that we shift our gaze away from the *content* of the secret . . . and instead focus on the more visible *forms and strategies* through which secret knowledge is revealed and concealed. (Urban 2017: 15, emphasis in original)

I find Urban's recommendation to be the most appropriate approach. Accordingly, I do not intend to place a great emphasis on the content of the OT III documents and the Xenu narrative in this analysis. Rather, during the course of conducting fieldwork interviews, I was led to consider the implications and influences the documents have on the practice of auditing in the advanced stages of Scientology, particularly in Free Zone Scientologies. The fluid nature of Scientologies outside the CoS, particularly for those who practise an individualized form Scientology that is unrestricted by organizational rules, resulted in some of my fieldwork participants choosing to discuss their experiences and practices at the OT levels at their own discretion. With this in mind, it is necessary to bring attention to the basic beliefs derived from the OT III documents, and the ways in which they can be interpreted, used or even discarded in the nuanced methods of Free Zone auditing.

The most notable aspect of OT III is the notion of 'body thetans'. These are 'little traumatized Beings [sic] who have battened [secured] onto the bodies of their healthier fellows and who must be audited by the latter to the point where they can disengage' (Whitehead 1987: 185). The OT III documents, 'according to several ex-Scientologists' reports, handwritten copies of Hubbard's own notes, and court testimonies' (Urban 2006: 37), state that these body thetans are the spirits of an enormous number of individuals from the seventy-six planets of a Galactic Federation led by Xenu seventy-five million years ago. In an attempt to solve an overpopulation crisis, Xenu is said to have frozen individuals and brought them to Teegeeack (Earth), deposited them around volcanoes and subsequently destroyed them by detonating hydrogen bombs. The spirits of these individuals continued to exist on Earth, became forced into clusters, and subsequently attached themselves to living creatures (Rothstein 2009: 373; Urban 2006: 371).

As a result, the OT III documents are believed to reveal to Scientologists that each human is not simply a thetan attached to a physical body in the MEST universe, as they have previously learned in Hubbard's works, but that the body is additionally attached to a number of other thetans that need to be audited (Rothstein 2009: 373). This revelation, as Whitehead observes, can come 'as something of a shock even to sophisticated Scientologists, because they have become accustomed to the dominant flavor [sic] of the belief system which emphasizes the isolated autonomy of the free thetan' (1987: 185). Each being is additionally believed to have been subjected to 'implants' by Xenu, intended to kill each individual (through diseases such as pneumonia) that attempts to uncover the origin of their existence. These implants, however, are believed to be counteracted by auditing at OT III (Rothstein 2009: 380; Urban 2006: 371). Through the culmination of these events, each body thetan is alleged to suffer from the traumatic events of Incidents I and II. Incident I concerns the very beginning of the time track; the moment all thetans arrived in the MEST universe. Incident II concerns the Xenu narrative, specifically the destruction of the beings on Teegeeack and the implants placed by Xenu (Carnegie Mellon University n.d.-b).

Ex-Scientologist, and prominent online anti-Scientology campaigner, Chris Shelton (2015: 181–2), writes that the clustering of thetans causes confusion, resulting in each thetan being unable to distinguish their own thoughts and identities. Body thetans 'are often asleep or unconscious' (Shelton 2015: 184), but occasionally awaken and respond to the world around them, causing confusion to the thetan of the individual controlling the body. Bound by a common negative experience, clusters of thousands of body thetans can be attached to each individual. After reading the leaked OT materials as an ex-member, Shelton explains that

> Through the solo auditing procedure of OT III, one sits silently in a room by oneself with an E-Meter setup, and telepathically contacts each of these body thetans... and one-by-one releases them from this immobilized state so they can go off and have their own independent lives again. This is done by running each body thetan one contacts through the entirety of Incident 2 and then Incident 1 [*sic*]. This releases them. This is all done silently with no verbal commands necessary. (Shelton 2015: 185)

By conducting solo auditing at OT III, Scientologists aim to 'run' Incident I and II, 'going over a memory or following an auditing procedure' (Carnegie Mellon University n.d.-b: online), to remove their presence from each body thetan. In the leaked OT III documents, Hubbard writes that running Incidents I and II on each body thetan is a 'long job, requiring care, patience and good auditing. You are running beings. They respond like any preclear [*sic*]' (Hubbard, cited in Rothstein 2009: 373). Beyond its use at OT III, solo auditing becomes a significant practice for Scientologists progressing throughout the entirety of the OT levels, and requires a far more independent approach on behalf of the Scientologist. To assist in this, solo auditors are assigned Solo Case Supervisors to ensure that they are correctly conducting their sessions. Using the same method as the Preclear version of auditing, all rudiments and preparation checks, including abiding to the Auditor's Code, are observed throughout the sessions, however, this time the Clears are responsible for these themselves. Solo auditing continues to be conducted through a series of questions and answers, but in silence, with the solo auditor operating the E-Meter independently (a technique I will explore further in Chapter 6) (Free Zone Earth n.d.-b; Whitehead 1987: 128). Despite the silent nature of solo auditing, it is reported that the process continues the command and response method of standard auditing practice, and aims to reach the end phenomena (visible signs of a successful auditing session) at the conclusion of the session (Free Zone Earth n.d.-b).

OT III has become arguably the most controversial aspect of the Scientology belief system, a situation intensified by the guarded nature with which the CoS protects the documents. While the Xenu narrative has become a popular method of ridiculing Scientology in popular culture, most notably in *South Park* (*South Park: Trapped in the Closet* 2005), it is not taken lightly in Scientology, which positions the narrative as a scientific fact (Rothstein 2009: 378). Rothstein argues that

> The intellectual weakness of the text, and the absurd claim that it should be scientific, is overpowered by the urge to honor [sic] Hubbard as the greatest individual that ever lived. In effect the myth adds to the hagiographic construction and maintenance of Hubbard as savior [sic]. (Rothstein 2009: 378)

Despite the emphasis on presenting all of Hubbard's written work as possessing scriptural authority (Rothstein 2009: 378), Shelton (2015: 179) explains that the Xenu mythology and the content of its narrative are, for Scientologists, the least important aspects of OT III. Accordingly, while the narrative is presented as fact, its main purpose to Scientologists is the revelation of the presence of additional thetans attached to the body, and the auditing methods necessary to remove them.

The Bridge to Total Freedom and Operating Thetan in Free Zone Scientology

Hubbard's work on the Bridge and OT levels was written during his leadership of the CoS, through which he revealed his work and trained auditors to administer the tech according to his specifications. Yet through the Scientology schisms that have emerged, particularly from the 1980s onwards, the Bridge is used and understood as a model for Scientologist development in movements in which Hubbard was not involved. This has allowed for a degree of interpretation amongst Free Zone Scientologies regarding the importance of certain stages of the Bridge, and particularly OT III.

While most Free Zone groups are very fluid in nature, often prompting individuals to practise and alter Scientology to their preferred methods (which I will discuss further in the next chapter). Ron's Org is the most notable example of an organizational schism of Scientology, establishing its own guidelines and principles to the understanding and application of the tech. During my interview with Hanson, a member of Ron's Org, he explained that Ron's Org audits practitioners across the entirety of the Bridge, from Preclear to OT. Yet, during our interview, Hanson stated that Ron's Org has altered the structure of the Bridge based on the research of the movement's founder, Captain Bill Robertson:

> You have now today [sic] the grades first and then you have Dianetics. And we changed that back, actually. Put Dianetics again before the grades, not after. And what is also different to us, I mean not [what the CoS calls] OT V, VI, VII; we call it Excalibur. And that also differs a little bit because Captain Bill studied that very, very thoroughly, because there were some things which were not really working and that then became Excalibur.

In addition to the amendments based on the research of Robertson, Hanson claimed that the CoS has altered the application of the OT levels since the passing of Hubbard, which Ron's Org seeks to avoid. During our discussions of the development of the self, Hanson made no reference to body thetans, but spoke of auditing as the personal development of the thetan as the true self:

> You mentioned your thetan, you know, actually this changes into 'I know this is me', you know? . . . Before Scientology, of course, I was young [and] a lifetime for me was extremely long. You can bet that 2000 years ago Jesus was born, and [that is] a huge amount of time, you know? Today I consider that . . . in the worst case [it] is just twenty lifetimes or hundred years, and it's not that long ago. . . . I'm a spiritual being and I mean, of course, this body I have will pass away inevitably. And then I just get a new body and continue but I will not die. I know I'm immortal. This is what I know. This is really what I got an absolutely certain in that [sic]. And I don't fear death in any . . . I mean, I [would not] like to die in two years with pain, but death by itself, now I don't fear that at all.

Drawing on Hubbard's ([1960] 1989) work on reincarnation and past lives in Scientology, Hanson speaks of the thetan as an immortal spiritual entity that inhabits bodies in the physical universe, which are simply vessels for the thetan's interaction with the MEST universe. My interviews with other Scientologists in the Free Zone were, for the most part, not with members of institutional groups such as Ron's Org, but rather individuals who have established their own auditing groups or provide their auditing services as independent auditors. Tracy, who runs an independent Free Zone group, audits Scientologists across the entirety of the Bridge, yet places an emphasis on the achievement of the state of Clear. During an email conversation, she expressed her view that

> Auditing is for the Preclear. We sort him out. . . . Auditing is there to increase his ability and certainty in life. It is to free him from fixed emotions and restore his power of choice. . . . Part of what makes our therapy work is that we help the

person sort out what is body, what is mind, and what is himself, as a spiritual being, and not mis-assign things. Only truth can bring about a betterment in condition, and if he thinks its [sic] his body when it is really something in his mind he can't get better until he knows which is which. Panic attacks are a great example of that, [a] person gets a panic attack, thinks he [sic] dying (body) goes to hospital and [finds there is] nothing wrong with him. Something caused his adrenaline to spike, he adds to it with his own created fear and the whole thing escalates out of hand.

Tracy's practice of auditing is rooted in the self-help angle found in Dianetics, as an attempt to assist the Scientologist to engage with their life in the physical world. During our contact, she reinforced the importance of understanding the true nature of the self to be the thetan, not the physical body. Another independent auditor I interviewed, Owen, shares Tracy's view of the thetan as the true self, but does not concern himself with the Bridge when auditing Preclears. Viewing Clear as the ultimate goal in Scientology, he explained that:

I don't even use the term 'Clear'. I look at what people want to be handled. I had a guy a couple of weeks ago – he's a musician – and he plays flute in the Queen's Guard. But he wanted to do more with his music. So, I made a programme to help him handle his music – we finished the programme on Friday and on Tuesday he came and told me he's got two new jobs. One in an amateur orchestra and another in a Fire Brigade orchestra. This is what I like to do. I like to help people who want to improve things and do new things. We work on it until they can do it. 'Clear' or 'OT' or whatever, I don't care – call it what you want.

Placing an emphasis on self-improvement, Owen focuses his auditing practice on assisting his clients with challenges they face in life, rather than the rigid guidelines of the Bridge. Displaying the variety of auditing methods outside the CoS, Jeff, an independent spiritual counsellor, practises a form of auditing that concentrates purely on the notion of body thetans, and their removal from the physical body. Since leaving the CoS, Jeff has established his own spiritual counselling group in which he aims to free his clients from the spirits they believe to be affecting their lives. He has noticeably moved away from much of Scientology's specialized terminology, viewing the sessions he provides his clients as spiritual counselling, and describing body thetans as spirits. Much of this stems from his disagreement with Hubbard's proposed methods of removing body thetans from the body:

The OT levels, which you have probably read about, are the only real area where Ron Hubbard started dealing with themes other than the person and stuff. Ron's position from the beginning is: you are a being, and you have a body. Okay. It's a nice simple model, and if that was true processing [auditing] would be a lot easier and simpler. The problem is that there is an infinite number of discarnate beings around. Many more than have bodies. And I've discovered this over the years and I've got a lot of ways of proving it. . . . On the OT levels [is] the first time a person, a Scientologist, gets the story that 'gee, there's things called body thetans that permeate your body and they affect you'. The story was to get rid of them.

Describing solo auditing in Scientology as 'creating an invisible hand and scraping [body thetans] off', Jeff views Hubbard's methods to be harmful to the spiritual beings associated with the individual being audited:

> Interestingly enough, in the early '50s Ron said there are beings, and you treat them just like Preclears. . . . And he said 'you use ARC, and you use the Auditor's Code, and you know, you talk to them just like a Preclear, that's what I do'. But shortly after that Ron had a bad experience with some of these beings, and he wrote 'they just chatter, ignore them'. You see? Until, finally, he got into the OT level kind of stuff. And then he said 'drive them out' basically. Get rid of all of them. It definitely had gone from being a conversational auditing kind of thing to 'drive them out by any means possible'. Which means it's like an adversarial situation, and if you've ever had any kind of counselling, any kind at all, you'll know that an adversarial counsellor does not produce desirable results in whoever they're dealing with. It's like the counsellor saying 'you're shit, get out of here'. Or whatever. And that's the whole OT levels.

In his own method of freeing his clients from spiritual beings, Jeff claims to conduct sessions in which he has conversations with spirits in a calm and sensitive approach. This way, Jeff believes that the spirits can be helped with their own problems:

> Anyway, so over the years I became more conversive with what spirits were doing, and I had conversations, well, my counselling was more getting in comm [Scientologist nomenclature for effective communication] with the spirit asking them what they were stuck in. What incident they were stuck in. Instead of trying to do a brute force – 'who are you, what are you, who were you before?', and sort of try to get them out. I just talked to them, find out who they were. . . . 'Oh, okay, you died in a car crash. How did you get there? What did you do? What you failed to do to cause that?'. And they would sort of wake up and come to present time, and I would send them off – 'Hey, have you ever been to Florida? No? Okay, why don't you go down check the beaches out, they're nice down there'. Basically, [I am] relocating spiritual beings that were affecting the person.

> Very simple sort of approach. So, everything I did was based on what I was learning from the beings.... I run weekly meetings in my local town.... They're free, and I advertise them as – 'you come, and you will talk to any spirit that you care to converse with. I'll ask them any questions you want.' And I keep the groups small so that it isn't a mass congregation. I've done a couple of talks in a local library, but the whole point [of] my practice now is training people to talk to spirits themselves. Because, if you are being bothered by spirits, if you have doubts, things you know, they usually impinge on you.

Using Hubbard's work on OT III as a foundation, Jeff practises a form of spiritual counselling that he does not define as auditing, but is informed by his experience as an auditor in the CoS. Of all my fieldwork participants, Jeff was the one that distanced himself the most from Scientologist nomenclature and identity, demonstrating how auditing methods can be applied in a wide range of spaces. A dominant number of my interviews with Freezoners reinforced the notion of the 'true' self as a spiritual being, however, with the Bridge being altered or interpreted depending on the personal view of the individual.

Concluding remarks

By examining L. Ron Hubbard's theoretical background to Scientologist practice, this chapter has demonstrated that the Scientologist notion of the self not only is a part of the Scientologist belief system but also lies at the centre of the practice of Scientology. All practices conducted by Scientologists lead to the eventual goal of spiritual fulfilment, a process that involves constant developing of the self. This requires Scientologists to engage with the practice of auditing, but also the study of a wide range of specialized literature written by Hubbard. Through these writings, they develop an understanding of the self through the 'Parts of Man', which divides the individual into three categories; the thetan, the mind and the body. The core principle of the Parts of Man is that the 'true' self of the individual is the thetan, while the body and mind are only aspects of the physical MEST universe. Through engagement with Hubbard's Dianetic technology, it is believed that the thetan's spiritual power can be restored through progression on the Bridge to Total Freedom, giving it full control over the mind and body, leading the individual to a more successful life.

Through progressing the Bridge, experienced and advanced Scientologists familiarize themselves with Hubbard's esoteric writings during the OT levels. Until this point, progression in Scientology concentrates purely on the development of the individual, specifically the thetan. According to leaked documents, testimonies from former CoS members, and my interviews with Free Zone Scientologists, OT III reveals the presence of body thetans attached to the individual's body in clusters. At this point, the auditing process (now conducted as a solo procedure) becomes a process that continues to liberate the thetan from the MEST universe, in addition to the removal of other thetans from the body that can impact the individual in negative ways.

Despite the goal of restoring the thetan's abilities and granting it control of the MEST universe, and the view of the mind and body as being a part of that MEST universe, much of Hubbard's work concerns the physical body, and how its development plays a part in the development of the thetan. Hubbard's writing makes considerable use of heteronormative and androcentric language, and suggests a specific idea of normalcy in Scientology that continue to be published in contemporary and revised editions of *DMSMH* (Hubbard [1950] 2007b). Any mention of Hubbard's writing on this topic remained absent in my conversations with Freezoners, who don't consider homosexuality to be an issue to be addressed in auditing. Some participants view the CoS as institutionally homophobic, however, with the notable example of James's claim that the homophobia of the CoS is a recent development under the leadership of David Miscavige, not Hubbard.

In addition to the understandings of the physical self in terms of gender and sexuality, my fieldwork has demonstrated the considerable importance of the Purification Rundown in the CoS, a specialized programme that specifically treats the body, through the removal of residual drug substances and exercise, in an attempt to prepare the body for auditing sessions. My participants at the CoS view the Purif as essential to being able to develop the thetan, and as a form of auditing in itself due to its location at the beginning of the Bridge. Yet my work with Freezoners has suggested a more relaxed interpretation of the Purif, particularly amongst independent Freezoners who do not belong to a wider Free Zone group, who view the Purif as potentially beneficial but something a Scientologist can pursue additionally if they wish, not as an essential part of Scientology. My conversation with a Ron's Org member also presented an understanding of the Purif as 'not really Scientology', albeit a very important process nonetheless. The Purif in Ron's Org is conducted in saunas, and Preclears are expected to live healthy lifestyles in order to continue with the auditing sessions, specifically avoiding frequent consumption of alcohol. Ron's Org is a movement defined by its adherence to the tech as specifically created by Hubbard, making his work on the Purif important to the execution of Scientologist tech.

In her work on women in new religions, Palmer (1994: 10) categorized Scientology under her 'sex unity' typology of NRM, a movement that does not place a considerable emphasis on gender, or even the physical nature of the self. As a result, due to the Scientologist belief in the true nature of the self as being the spirit, the thetan is seen as genderless. While this is an accurate view of the Scientologist understanding of the true self in the spiritual thetan, this chapter has demonstrated that much of Scientology, both in the CoS and Free Zone, nonetheless considers the development of the body to be important to its practice. Achieving complete independence for the thetan from the MEST universe is the main goal of Scientology, yet the process of attaining this involves the regulation of the body. In addition, Scientologists claim to have achieved physical and medical benefits through engaging with Hubbard's tech.

Part II

Fluidity and boundaries

5

Authenticity and innovation
The 'true tech' and 'mistakes by Hubbard'

This chapter explores discourses of authenticity and innovation in the contemporary practice of auditing, and the ways in which different Scientologist groups and individuals attempt to control the tech in establishing their vision of a 'true' Scientology. Drawing from my fieldwork with both the Church of Scientology (CoS) and Free Zone, I consider the divisions between Scientologies that claim an authentic practice of Scientology by drawing legitimacy from L. Ron Hubbard's work on the one hand, and fluid forms of Scientology in the Free Zone that adapt or innovate the tech on the other. By exploring these dynamics and different approaches to auditing, this chapter addresses how auditing is practised and understood in contemporary forms of Scientology. It goes on to argue that these differences are at the heart of Free Zone Scientology, directly influencing the emergence of different types of Free Zone Scientologies, which in turn results in the production of boundaries based on interpretations of the application of Hubbard's tech.

The discourse of authenticity and innovation

Contemporary auditing, across the several forms of Scientologies I encountered during my research, is closely tied with the issue of authenticity and innovation. Through being the initial developer of the auditing process, L. Ron Hubbard is frequently seen as the ultimate authority on the application of what is known as the tech. Despite having published extensively on the topic, precisely what lay behind Hubbard's belief system and the auditing process is highly contested between different Scientologies and individual Scientologists. Recent decades have demonstrated a number of Scientologist groups, distinct and separate from the CoS, laying claim to a 'true' interpretation of the tech. These groups, as Hellesøy demonstrates, 'go back to the authority of Hubbard's own texts to legitimize their authority' (2016: 460).

This discourse of authenticity creates a debate on the interpretation of Hubbard's work, with several Scientologies, most notably the CoS and Ron's Org, attempting to use Hubbard's writings to assert their claims as a legitimate form of Scientology. Indeed, as Lewis has observed, 'the conflict between CoS and non-CoS Scientologists boils to competing assertions about legitimacy' (2016: 477). With this in mind, the concept of 'Free Zone Scientology' could be simply viewed as a movement united in opposition to the CoS; however, the data I gathered in my research provides evidence of a category that encompasses fluid practices and debates regarding issues of authenticity and innovation. Precisely how the tech works, and how auditing should be practised, is a contested issue in the Free Zone itself, resulting in auditing becoming far more nuanced than it may at first appear. Accordingly, divisions have emerged in Scientologies outside the CoS, creating boundaries between categories such as 'Free Zone' (associated with Captain Bill Robertson) and 'Independent Scientology', as this chapter will demonstrate.

The varied application of auditing has developed, in part, due to a number of Free Zone Scientologists practising a very individualized form of Scientology, choosing to innovate or adapt the tech in methods that they deem to be effective. These differences in the application of the tech create divisions between Scientologist groups based on the classically 'religious' themes of orthodoxy and heterodoxy. More specifically, they centre on the attempts of the CoS to define the work of Hubbard, and their criticism of squirrels that heretically apply the tech outside the CoS (Gregg and Chryssides 2017: 26; Lewis 2016: 477). However, the notion of squirrelling is not limited to criticism of the Free Zone from the CoS, with several Scientologist groups and individuals viewing both the CoS and other Free Zone groups as squirrelling through practising a distorted version of auditing, or innovating the process to suit their methods.

The authority of L. Ron Hubbard: The 'source' of the tech

At the centre of many New Religious Movements (NRMs) resides the charismatic leader who attracts adoration and devotion from their followers (Barker 1992: 13; 2014: 241). Hubbard, as the leader of Scientology, is no different. His work, teachings and personality lie at the core of Scientology. A striking aspect of my fieldwork in the CoS is the use of formal titles to address Hubbard in conversation, including 'Mr Hubbard' and 'LRH'. Despite these formalities, CoS members often refer to Hubbard as 'Ron' as an expression of endearment.[1] The most notable term for Hubbard is 'Source', reinforcing Hubbard's role in Scientology as the source of all spiritual and philosophical knowledge (Atack n.d.; Westbrook 2016a: 30), an ability that established his status as the undisputed leader of Scientology.

Previous scholarship on the notion of charisma has tended to focus on charismatic leaders in terms of the devotion they inspire from followers (Barker 1992: 13) and the level of authority they derive from this dedication (Weber [1948] 1991c: 246–7). In this analysis, however, I establish how the charisma of Hubbard continues to influence contemporary forms of auditing since his death. The death of a charismatic leader is often framed through Weber's ([1948] 1991b: 297) routinization of charisma, which posits that the teachings and practices of the leader become routinized through administrative procedures. For example, Wessinger (2012: 87) demonstrates how charismatic authority has become institutionalized through forms of religious office. Indeed, Lewis (2016: 479) draws from Weber's routinization of charisma to demonstrate how the contemporary CoS establishes itself as a 'traditional' form of Scientology. However, Free Zone understandings of Hubbard somewhat nuance the scholarly theories surrounding charisma. Weber's prediction of routinization is certainly applicable to the CoS, and the ways in which it lays claim to the 'true' Hubbard through institutional bodies. I argue, however, that this approach only accounts for one facet of contemporary Scientology. With an increasing number of Scientologists practising in the Free Zone, organizational structures and boundaries have broken down, leading to the emergence of fluid Scientologies. The unregulated nature of Free Zone Scientologies offers a contrast to Weber's theory of routinization, with many Scientologists practising an 'individualized' form of Scientology – rejecting the need for organizational staff, such as the CoS' ministers, and often choosing to reject an orthodoxy of belief in Scientology by innovating Hubbard's practices and belief system.

The ways in which many Free Zone Scientologists move away from routinized manifestations of Hubbard's charisma points towards Wessinger's (2012: 88) description of loss of charisma, wherein a charismatic leader may lose authority amongst their followers. A number of my fieldwork participants, as this chapter will demonstrate, voice concern regarding certain aspects of Hubbard's work, with some even describing what they perceive as errors in his approaches to Scientology. These Freezoners continue to hold Hubbard in high regard but have distanced themselves from the level of devotion encouraged by the CoS, demonstrating Hubbard's lack of authority in certain Free Zone spaces. The category of 'Free Zone Scientology' illustrates a nuanced picture, however, with other groups and individuals rejecting those that have moved away from the strict application of Scientology according to Hubbard's work. This discourse of authenticity and innovation is closely linked with Hubbard's charisma, specifically the contrast between Freezoners who insist on devotion to Hubbard on the one hand, and those who reject his authority on the other, thus challenging previous scholarly conceptions of charismatic leaders, particularly theories of routinization and devotion.

Hubbard is seen by the CoS (and many Scientologists in the Free Zone) as being infallible, and his teachings and practices are accepted and strictly adhered to without question. Despite this devotion from Scientologists, however, Hubbard is neither seen as a god nor a divine prophet; rather, he is presented by the CoS as possessing extraordinary talent, intelligence and moral integrity. The events of Hubbard's life are celebrated in CoS literature and information centres, which often include interactive booths featuring information displays and videos on Hubbard's life, career and achievements.

Through viewing the hagiographic narrative of Hubbard's life as a source of inspiration, Scientologists often seek to emulate his spiritual progress and achievements. Drawing on his interviews with members of the CoS, Westbrook observes a similarity between Hubbard and Bodhisattva figures. He argues that, by encouraging Scientologists to follow his own journey on the Bridge to Total Freedom, 'Hubbard is popularly considered among Scientologists as a Buddhistic figure and indeed the Metteyya [sic]' (2016a: 30). My experience of CoS members expressing a personal connection with Hubbard is echoed in Westbrook's fieldwork:

> As a result, Scientologists often refer to Hubbard with the familial 'Ron', and several interviewees referred to him as a personal friend. This was most noticeably the case for members who knew and worked with him, but I also encountered this sentiment among parishioners who had no personal acquaintance whatsoever. (Westbrook 2016a: 30)

Westbrook's research points to a deep affection for Hubbard amongst Scientologists, particularly CoS members. Corresponding to Westbrook's account, CoS members I have met discussed their views of Hubbard in similar terms, with a particular gratitude towards him for providing the tech they believe to have improved their lives. For example, one staff member at the CoS of London described how her life was transformed by completing Hubbard's introductory Scientology courses and expressed a deep gratitude towards him for his work. These testimonies demonstrate a view of Hubbard as a spiritual figure and teacher, not a divine being. However, there are other ways in which Hubbard is both viewed and presented by Scientologists that demonstrate supernatural elements. This is particularly apparent in the public announcement of Hubbard's death in 1986. According to a death certificate signed by his personal physician, Hubbard died due to a stroke (Lindsay 1986: 29). Yet the public announcement of his death, made by David Miscavige to a gathering of Scientologists, does not explicitly state that Hubbard had died, but rather that he had moved on to another state of existence to continue his research:

> He has now moved on to his next level of OT [Operating Thetan] research. This level is beyond anything any of us have ever imagined. This level is in fact done in an exterior state, meaning that it is done completely exterior from the body. At this level of OT, the body is nothing more than an impediment and encumbrance to any further gain as an OT. Thus, at 20:00 hours, Friday the 24th of January, AD [After Dianetics] 36, L. Ron Hubbard discarded the body he had used in this lifetime for 74 years, 10 months, and 11 days. The body he had used to habilitate his existence in this MEST universe, had ceased to be useful, and in fact had become an impediment to the work he now must do out of its confines. (Miscavige [1986] 2013)

Miscavige's statement is striking in a number of ways. While Scientologists will often use the Gregorian calendar, it is not uncommon for landmark events in Scientology's history to be dated in years 'After Dianetics'. By establishing a calendar system that draws a line between periods of history in which *Dianetics: The Modern Science of Mental Health* (*DMSMH*) did not exist, and contemporary time in which it does, the CoS demonstrates its view of the enormous importance of the publication of *DMSMH* for humanity. In itself, this draws back to the Scientologist view of Hubbard as Source, with the use of the After Dianetics dating system reinforcing the importance of his writing in human history. Of additional importance is Miscavige's allusion to Hubbard developing the tech without the body. As I argued in Chapter 4, the belief that the body is a vessel for the 'true' self is one of the fundamental aspects of Scientology, yet the description of Hubbard's choosing to discard the body as a method of researching further aspects of OT suggests that his death was of a different nature to most others. Miscavige went on to say:

> I can understand that many of you are probably experiencing the effects of a secondary [an emotional upset caused by grief], however it is important that

you can put this into the proper perspective. LRH defines a body in the *Tech Dictionary* as 'an identifying form, or non-identifying form, to facilitate the control of, the communication of and with, and the havingness of the thetan in his existence in the MEST universe. The body is a physical object, it is not the being himself.' The being we knew as L. Ron Hubbard still exists. However, the body he had could no longer serve his purposes. This decision was one made at complete cause [choice] by L. Ron Hubbard. Although you may feel grief, understand that he did not, and does not now. He has simply moved on to his next step. (Miscavige [1986] 2013)

Further to Hubbard working on OT research without the use of the body, Miscavige's statement claims that Hubbard's discarding of the body was entirely intentional; he did not die, but simply chose to leave the body to be able to work on his research further. Of additional interest when considering the CoS' view of Hubbard's death are the replicas of his office that can be found in Orgs across the world (see Figure 5.1). These offices, designed as a tribute to the founder of Scientology, contain 'a collection of Hubbard's books, a desk with writing instruments, and a picture of Hubbard' (Melton 2009: 29). Melton suggests that the offices are designed 'as if one day [Hubbard] may walk into the building and

Figure 5.1 L. Ron Hubbard's Office at the Church of Scientology of London (photo by the author, 1 March 2017).

need a place to continue his work' (Melton 2009: 29), yet a Scientologist I met at the CoS dismissed such ideas of a 'resurrection' for Hubbard, stating that the offices are simply a mark of respect for the founder.

Miscavige's statement also raises the question of whether the CoS views Hubbard's theory and teaching as still in development to the present day, and whether their practices will change based upon this assumption. There seems to be no evidence of this amongst ordinary Scientologists, however. As I have previously explained, my participants at the CoS stated that all of Hubbard's theories and teachings can be found in his 'Basic Books' (the Basics), published between the years of 1948 and 1956. While there was no mention from my participants regarding any posthumous work from Hubbard, his authority and teachings remain central to the CoS to the present day.

In addition to the Basic Books and extended writing on the auditing tech, Hubbard wrote a vast volume of work that is adhered to by Scientologists, such as his teachings on morality, life improvement and education. As Urban (2011: 131) observes, the CoS consists of a variety of large organizational bodies, all of which draw authority through Hubbard. For example, the CoS is managed by WISE (World Institute of Scientology Enterprises), a business management methodology created by Hubbard. WISE is an entity that presides over a Scientologist technology that is believed to be an effective tool for organizing all businesses, both secular and religious (WISE International n.d.). With Hubbard's authority influencing the CoS both administratively and in its practice, it is clear that his role as 'Source' dominates almost all aspects of the CoS, a characteristic that has endured to the present day.

The alleged disappearance and death of L. Ron Hubbard

The whereabouts of Hubbard following his withdrawal from public life in the early 1980s was a contributing factor to Captain Bill Robertson's departure from the CoS and establishment of the Free Zone and Ron's Org. This withdrawal was intended for Hubbard to concentrate on his research and writing, and also involved his resignation from the leadership role in the CoS. This resulted in the establishment of the Church of Scientology International to coordinate CoS affairs (Rigal-Cellard 2009: 326). Despite the official account of Hubbard's death stating that he died on 24 January 1986 (The Church of Scientology International n.d.-c), the final years of Hubbard's life have become the subject of various conspiracy theories.

Robertson had become convinced that government agents, with the intention of seizing Hubbard's tech from practising Scientologists, had infiltrated the CoS. Claiming to have had orders from Hubbard to 'start the game anew outside' (Ron's Org Committee n.d.-b) should such an event occur, Robertson urged Scientologists leaving the CoS to protect Hubbard's books, lectures and tapes to preserve the purity of the tech (see also Hellesøy 2013). His concerns regarding Hubbard's whereabouts in the 1980s had a considerable influence on Ron's Org, within which there is considerable debate regarding the correct date of Hubbard's death. When I posed the question to a Ron's Org member, Hanson, he stated that 'you can ask me, but you cannot ask Ron's Org. Even in Ron's Org there is not a common agreement on when he passed away.' Citing a period of time in 1972 during which he claims Hubbard 'disappeared', Hanson states that much of the CoS' activity made him suspicious as to whether Hubbard was still alive:

> And then end of '72 he disappeared, obviously for 10 months, nobody knows anything about it. But the biggest, biggest change is, you know, L. Ron Hubbard was talking so very much, there's so many tapes in which he spoke. And after [1972] there is not a single one, there is only one tape I [was] able to get, but this is a piece of strange tape. This is not a lecture really, this is rather a conversation with his doctor or whatever he was. It was very strange. You cannot really [tell], [because of] bad quality, if it's really LRH or not. Could be, yes. But this is very difficult.... Obviously, the management found out that the people start to doubt if LRH was around or not, and they released some messages by L. Ron Hubbard, he spoke, and we listened to that and we said 'this is the old man? No, that's not his voice.'... So we don't know what happened after '72. Maybe he passed away. Maybe he was just broken. Maybe he had some other illness, or strokes. They say in '75 he had a stroke, and in '78 he had a stroke, but there was no proof that LRH was really around as we knew him before.... I hardly can answer. For me it's a real big blank what really happened with LRH.

These disputes regarding where Hubbard was, or whether he was even alive, present several problems for Free Zone Scientologists attempting to identify which of Hubbard's works released by the CoS are to be considered legitimate, and as a result which auditing theories, techniques and methods are truly the work of Hubbard. Hanson stated that Ron's Org is 'very critical of all the stuff [published from] '73 and later', and accordingly Ron's Org uses the 1969 edition of *DMSMH* to ensure it follows what it views as an authentic practice of auditing according to Hubbard's work.

James, an Independent Scientologist, rejects the notion that later works by Hubbard were fabricated by the CoS, claiming that he knew 'a great many people who, working under Hubbard, developed Scientology further from the late '70s up until when he died in 1986'. However, several earlier former members of the CoS seem more inclined to agree that Hubbard was not present during the early 1980s. Owen left the CoS in 1982 following its management's threat to declare him a Suppressive Person for arguing that Hubbard had ceased any involvement with the CoS:

> My answer was, almost verbatim, 'I don't know what it is, but if Ron was here running the show, everyone would be well paid, well [rested], and well fed. Since that's not the case, there must be something wrong with the management.' And that was it. That was enough – being dissatisfied with the management. The next day I was called in with the C/S [Case Supervisor], and she said 'I've got enough here to declare you a Suppressive five times – but since you are so up there [presented with awards by Hubbard], you can just go to the RPF [Rehabilitation Project Force].'[2] My answer was – 'I know the five reasons to put a person on the RPF, and I don't have any of those, so I'm not going on the RPF.' She then told me I could leave and that was it.

Owen remains unsure what had become of Hubbard by 1982. Prior to this he completed a variety of 'LRH Missions' – objectives specifically given to him by Hubbard. He believes that Hubbard's presence was very much felt in the commands and the organization at the time, but after 1982 that presence was gone; he states, 'I don't know where he was. I don't know if he was dead or alive. I know nothing. I could just feel that he was not behind the scenes anymore.' Alternatively, Tracy does not believe that some of Hubbard's later works are fabricated by the CoS, but notes that some works were republished by the 'LRH Library' with minor alterations that are clear to those familiar with Hubbard's writing:

> They started publishing the LRH Library to handle the copyright limitations. I'm not sure of the year, probably even before 1986. They have changed some words to be politically correct, like 'chink', and left out two paragraphs in the *History of Man*, (truthfully the paragraphs were more like an afterthought than necessary) dropped off all the applause and introductions on some tapes, destroyed the history by removing initials of those who helped him with the HCOB's [Hubbard Communications Office Bulletins], removed names of people who were declared suppressive [sic] like David Mayo [a former influential member of the CoS], even Mary Sue Hubbard [Hubbard's wife] is barely mentioned anywhere.

Furthermore, Tracy does not believe that Hubbard died before 1986, but provides a different account of the narrative of his death:

> People instinctively knew something was wrong. There are wild stories like he was put on ice and even dead for years. The truth as I heard it was Miscavige and Dr Denk [Hubbard's personal doctor] took LRH in the motorhome with them when they went to Las Vegas (possibly Reno) to gamble. When they came back LRH was dead. So they rushed back to Gold [Gold Base – a CoS base in Los Angeles] and covered up that he had died while they were gambling. Dr Denk mentioned that it felt strange to have a dead man in the back when they were driving back. This came from Dr Denk via one friend who told a friend of mine who told me. I think it is the most accurate statement.

Believing the announced date of Hubbard's death to be correct, Tracy does not concern herself with the legitimacy of Hubbard's writing during his lifetime, determining that the illegitimate alterations to Hubbard's work were introduced by the CoS after his death in 1986. However, this is not as straightforward for other Scientologists, including Chris (an Independent Scientologist), who firmly believes that the CoS fabricated works by Hubbard, stating that many later editions of Hubbard's works have been amended in a 'non-LRH' way:

> After Ron's death, everything is suspect, though Ron could have directed items to be issued which were only ready after he died. Since David Miscavige was the primary agent for these alterations, and since we have a rough idea of when he came to occupy various posts, we know when he became able to alter LRH tech and policy. So that would be a starting point. I'd say at least [five] years before LRH died.

These contrasting accounts of Hubbard's death and the questions they raise about the authenticity of certain writings from the 1970s and 1980s has had a direct impact on auditing in the Free Zone. The lack of agreed date for Hubbard's death results in scepticism from some Free Zone Scientologists regarding the legitimacy of certain publications credited to Hubbard by the CoS, resulting in a discourse of authenticity on which publications should be used in Scientologist practice.

David Miscavige: The contemporary leader of the Church of Scientology

In the years following his announcement of Hubbard's death, David Miscavige became the Chairman of the Board of the Religious Technology Center, continuing as leader of the CoS to the present day (Urban 2011: 131). Notably, Miscavige's role is not one that was previously held by Hubbard. Miscavige does not conduct his own Scientological research, rather his role is seen as acting as an administrative leader of the CoS and preserving Hubbard's tech through the Religious Technology Center. Acting as an entity separate from the CoS, the Religious Technology Center 'holds the ultimate ecclesiastical authority regarding the standard and pure application of L. Ron Hubbard's religious technologies' (Religious Technology Center n.d.: online). This use of the term 'ecclesiastical', an explicitly religious term, is a strong statement from the CoS regarding its religious authority, particularly in drawing a line between the purism of the CoS and the heterodoxy of the squirrels. The establishment of the Religious Technology Center in 1982 recalls Weber's notion of the routinized charisma of office, which replaces the movement's charismatic leader following their passing (Stark 2007: 264; Weber [1948] 1991b: 297). Accordingly, Hubbard's role as a charismatic leader has been transferred to the Religious Technology Center – the charismatic office that aims to authorize a particular interpretation of Hubbard's writings and regulate the application of his teachings. Additionally, Lewis also draws from Weber's theory of routinized charisma to argue that 'the Church of Scientology's legitimation strategy has narrowed to focus almost exclusively on its claim to what has become – both in form and in effect – traditional authority' (2016: 480). Miscavige's leadership of the CoS is legitimized through the authority of the Religious Technology Center, allowing him to launch new CoS initiatives and re-publications of Hubbard's writings.

During his time as chairman of the board, Miscavige has led the CoS through a number of milestones, most notably the CoS' victory in what has become known as 'The War' – the CoS' long-running legal battle with the Internal Revenue Service (IRS) for tax exemption. Following a lengthy campaign by the CoS, involving a turbulent relationship with the IRS, Miscavige announced that

> On October first, 1993, at 8:37 p.m. Eastern Standard Time, the IRS issued letters recognizing Scientology and every one of its organizations as fully tax exempt! The war is over! Now your first question is probably – what exactly does this mean? My answer is: everything. The magnitude of this is greater than you may imagine. (Miscavige, cited in Urban 2011: 173)

As Urban remarks, securing tax-exempt status 'was *everything* and perhaps the most important thing the Church had fought for over the last two decades' (Urban 2011: 173, emphasis in original). It was more than a financial victory – it was a public recognition of Scientology's status as a 'legitimate' religion in the United States, and is arguably the foundation of the CoS' contemporary campaign against religious discrimination in the form of 'Scientologists Taking Action Against Discrimination' (STAND) (Thomas 2017b). Through leading the CoS to its victory in 'The War', a conflict that began during Hubbard's leadership of the CoS, Miscavige solidified his role as the leader of the CoS by completing Hubbard's mission.

As the first and thus far only leader of the CoS following the founder, Miscavige's leadership has not been without its controversies, both within various Scientologist communities and the wider public sphere. Contemporary media exposés of the CoS frequently feature critical portrayals of Miscavige, such as the allegations from Marty Rathbun in *My Scientology Movie* (2015) that he physically beats his staff, and a series in the *St. Petersburg Times* in 2009 which claimed he 'forced [CoS] executives to play a brutal, all-night game of musical chairs to the tune of Queen's "Bohemian Rhapsody"' (Urban 2011: 6). Furthermore, re-publications of Hubbard's work and new CoS initiatives launched by Miscavige have resulted in a degree of rebellion in the CoS, with several of my fieldwork participants in the Free Zone leaving the CoS during his leadership, voicing concerns regarding alterations made to Hubbard's tech. This discourse has resulted in some Free Zone Scientologists drawing a distinction between the CoS as led by Hubbard and 'Miscavology', which they view as distorted application of the tech (Schorey 2016: 353).

The distinction between Hubbard's CoS and 'Miscavology' is of significance to the wider debate on the auditing process in contemporary Scientologies. On the one hand, many Free Zone Scientologists, thought of as 'squirrels' by the CoS, accuse the CoS of changing Hubbard's tech. Yet on the other, in establishing the Religious Technology Center as an organization that aims to preserve the tech in the way it believes Hubbard intended, the CoS lays claim to a truly 'authentic' auditing practice, frequently referred to (particularly by the CoS) as 'Standard Tech'.

Standard Tech debate

Standard Tech refers to the application of the tech precisely as Hubbard intended it to be practised in his written work. This encompasses the entirety of Hubbard's tech, including the auditing process. Practising Scientology precisely according to Standard Tech is a prominent aspect of the CoS, whose adherence to Standard Tech has been compared previously to Christian dogma (Bainbridge 2009).

Noting that Hubbard's perceived infallibility is preserved in his teachings, Flinn argues this 'doctrine of standardness in technical application guarantees the form of the teaching in Scientology' (2009: 217). However, precisely what Standard Tech means is a disputed issue across different Scientologies. Some Free Zone groups and individuals do not place much importance on Standard Tech, and encourage innovation. Other forms of Scientology, including the CoS and prominent Free Zone groups, however, insist on strict application of auditing procedures according to their perception of Standard Tech.

The CoS maintains that the Bridge to Total Freedom can only be traversed through the precise application of Standard Tech – particularly Dianetics and Scientology. The intention of keeping these practices in complete accordance with the works of Hubbard has resulted in many Scientologist terms and concepts, including Dianetics and Scientology, becoming copyrighted trademarks (Westbrook 2019: 32). This is seen by the CoS as more than simply protecting their application of Dianetics and Scientology in business terms, but also a validation of their claim to Standard Tech. To demonstrate this, at the CoS' 1982 'US Mission Holders Conference' in San Francisco, CoS Attorney Larry Heller compared the tech to the 'Coca Cola' brand, using it as an example of how CoS aims to provide a product that consumers can expect to be of a certain quality. Moreover, he explained the importance of trademarks and copyrights to the authenticity of the tech:

> Those trademarks, just like the Coca-Cola trademarks, represents a symbol which assures the public of a certain quality of service which they are going to receive if they purchase something or receive services under that trademark. . . . All of the Scientology/Dianetics trademarks were previously owned by L. Ron Hubbard. L. Ron Hubbard has donated the vast majority of those to a corporation which some of you have probably heard of, by the name of Religious Technology Center. In donating those trademarks, L. Ron Hubbard imposed the duty on Religious Technology Center (RTC) of assuring that the source of those trademarks, the technology that those trademarks represent, are given and disseminated to the public in the way that he formulated those trademarks. It's what you know as being on Source, applying tech. (Sea Organization Executive Directive 2104 1984: 1–2)

By laying claim to 'true' Standard Tech through legal trademarks formulated and owned by Hubbard himself, the CoS claims to offer identical application of the tech across Orgs worldwide, thus attempting to ensure that all practitioners receive authentic Standard Tech. My interviews with Free Zone Scientologists created a blurred perception of Standard Tech, however, with some participants simply stating that it is impossible to know precisely what constitutes 'Standard Tech', while others claim that the CoS has altered Hubbard's work, thus undermining the authenticity of Standard Tech. Ron's Org serves as the most notable example of this, marking its 'legitimacy by portraying [itself] as adhering to true Scientology, in contrast to the CoS, which is teaching a false, altered version' (Hellesøy 2016: 456).

Ron's Org outlines one of its goals as 'making sure that Standard Tech as per LRH and CBR [Captain Bill Robertson] is available for everybody and will continue to be available in the future and is applied throughout the world' (Ron's Org Committee n.d.-a: online). Unlike this confident assertion of Standard Tech, however, Hanson from Ron's Org expressed apprehension towards giving a definition of Standard Tech in our interview, believing it to be too difficult a question to answer. Citing the various changes made by Hubbard to the tech throughout his leadership of the CoS, including the re-publication of *DMSMH* (known as *New Era Dianetics*) in 1978, Hanson asked, 'what is now "standard"? [Laughs] Nobody knows.' Demonstrating contested nature of Standard Tech, spiritual counsellor (and former CoS member) Jeff stated that the category constantly changed and evolved during Hubbard's research on Scientology:

> There is no Standard Tech, somebody may have told you this, but Standard Tech was what Ron Hubbard said at that moment. He said there is only one Standard Tech. He said this in '50-'52. In the '70s there was three or four different versions of Standard Tech. In other words, Standard Tech was whatever Ron realized he was writing [at the time]. You can see the iterations of Standard Tech. So that if you were a practising auditor as I was, you found that you were really working with this whole bunch of technology that had bandages on [laughs].

My interviews with Hanson and Jeff highlight that throughout the history of Scientology, the tech and methods of conducting auditing sessions have altered. This is partly due to Hubbard's research methods, in which he continued to develop Dianetic theory while acting as leader of the CoS. Through this additional research, Hubbard implemented changes in practice that resulted in several methods of auditing during his lifetime. The efficacy of these methods continues to cause divisions and debates in Scientologies to this day. Following Hubbard's death, however, the notion of Standard Tech has been a source of controversy in both the CoS and Free Zone communities. This has created a diverse range of contemporary forms of auditing, with some groups claiming to be true to Hubbard's source, and others innovating the tech by adopting new auditing techniques and methods.

Contemporary auditing and Standard Tech in the Church of Scientology

A prominent aspect of Free Zone Scientology is how it distances its application of auditing from that of the CoS, often viewing CoS' auditing practices as a distorted version of Hubbard's original teaching (as exemplified by the criticism of 'Miscavology'). However, the ways in which auditing is promoted through new initiatives by the CoS are also indicative of the CoS' attempt to maintain its control of the tech and position itself as 'true Scientology' in response to the 'squirrelling' Freezoners. Following Hubbard's death in 1986, CoS practices and programmes have developed under the supervision of the RTC, with an emphasis on remaining true to the perceived vision of Hubbard. Applying the tech in the precise manner Hubbard intended has been the focal point of two major projects undertaken by the CoS since Hubbard's death – the *Golden Age of Knowledge* and *Golden Age of Tech Phase II*. These projects were intended to revolutionize all CoS Orgs to provide Standard Tech at the same consistent level. To achieve this, the CoS aimed to return to the original intentions of Hubbard's work through the re-publication of his texts and distribution of high-quality audio recordings of Hubbard's lectures.

The project that became known as the *Golden Age of Knowledge* aimed to compile a complete and definitive account of Hubbard's work on Scientology (The Church of Scientology International n.d.-e). The *Golden Age of Knowledge* is presented by the CoS as being an extraordinarily large and challenging endeavour, comprising some twenty-five years of researching, recovering and verifying Hubbard's work in both written and recorded formats (Bridge Publications n.d.). This project, according to the CoS, demonstrated that whole sections of the Basic Books were omitted from the previous editions due to printing or publishing errors, meaning that 'no matter how carefully those books were studied – words cleared, concepts demonstrated – full conceptual understanding was impossible' (Bridge Publications n.d.: online).

The *Golden Age of Knowledge* initiative spanned four years from 2005 to 2009, beginning with the launch of Hubbard's 'Congress Lectures' (his announcements on research breakthroughs and developments), to the reissued and restored Basic Books, and finally Hubbard's 'Advanced Clinical Course Lectures', comprising '500 written issues chronicling the day-to-day record of L. Ron Hubbard's path of discovery in Dianetics and Scientology' (The Church of Scientology International n.d.-e: online). The *Golden Age of Knowledge* is described by the CoS as being 'the most monumental achievement in the history of the religion –

completion of the 25-year program to recover, verify and restore the Scripture of the Scientology religion' (The Church of Scientology International n.d.-e: online, emphasis in original).

Following a lengthy process of gathering, editing and remastering audio recordings of Hubbard's lectures on the latest developments of his research, the CoS released the Congress Lectures as the first part of the *Golden Age of Knowledge* in 2005 (The Church of Scientology International n.d.-e: online, emphasis in original). Scientology, as one CoS member told me, was not revealed by Hubbard in a singular work, nor was the entirety of its complex beliefs and practices revealed in the establishment of the CoS in the early 1950s. Throughout his lifetime, Hubbard would continue to develop the tech by continuing his research. Following a publication on his recent research, Hubbard would conduct lectures in which he would explore the theories of his publication further. My participants explained that audio recordings of these lectures are now distributed by the CoS on CDs alongside their respective Basic Book, allowing CoS members to engage with Hubbard's written work and the subsequent development of his ideas through spoken lectures.

In the second stage of the *Golden Age of Knowledge*, the Basics were republished and 'fully restored' (The Church of Scientology International n.d. e: online) according to the CoS' view of Hubbard's original intentions. Specific details on the changes made to Hubbard's work in the re-publication of the Basics are sparse in CoS literature; however, I was able to gain clarification from my conversations with CoS members. One CoS practitioner described how previous editions of Hubbard's work contained certain errors. He explained that these errors were not made by Hubbard, rather they were minor errors caused by issues such as printing, or by transcribers writing from Hubbard's Dictaphone recordings. Such issues were believed to potentially hinder the process of traversing the Bridge, meaning that the process is now considered more efficient through reading the revised Basics.

Other CoS members spoke of how engaging with the republished Basics has improved their understanding of Scientology. For example, a CoS practitioner recalled the challenge of understanding many of Hubbard's specialized jargon, frequently referred to by my participants as 'Scientologese', during her earlier years as a Scientologist. This, she stated, was rectified by the glossaries included in all re-publications of the Basics. An additional CoS member added that older editions of Hubbard's work were problematic for study due to various interferences in the publication process that were responsible for distorting Hubbard's texts. For example, a large amount of Hubbard's work was dictated on a Dictaphone, causing potential issues for typists who may misspell or replace words due to their lack of fluency in Scientologese. Due to the discourse of adherence to the precise application of Hubbard's work in the CoS, my participant remarked that previous editions of *DMSMH* and other works clearly showed positive results, but not as effectively or as quickly as it could be.

Following the release of the Congress Lectures and Basic Books, Miscavige concluded the *Golden Age of Knowledge* in 2009 through the announcement of Hubbard's Advanced Clinical Course Lectures. These lectures, which focus on teaching auditors how to apply the tech, complete the CoS' vision of 'the long-hoped-for goal of *total* knowledge' (The Church of Scientology International n.d.-e: online, emphasis in original), as it believes Hubbard intended it.

Through releasing this collection of Hubbard's books and accompanying lectures, the CoS claims not only to present a complete collection of Hubbard's work but also to present the work precisely as Hubbard had intended, and the 'true' method of applying the tech (The Church of Scientology International n.d.-e: online). This was clear at the CoS' 'OT Summit' event in June 2007, when David Miscavige launched the restored Basic Books by presenting testimonies from practising Scientologists who have already engaged with the *Golden Age of Knowledge*. These accounts highlight the various ways that the *Golden Age of Knowledge* is a significant step in the CoS. For example, initial testimonies speak of the improved knowledge Scientologists can now have of Hubbard's work:

> The whole thing is crystal clear in one picture.
>
> . . .
>
> They're everything – and the entire Bridge wraps around these Basics. This *is* Dianetics and Scientology.
>
> . . .
>
> You have like a knowledge, you have like an encyclopaedic concept of Dianetics and Scientology.
>
> . . .
>
> It's not even that I know it. I *am* it. (The Golden Age of Knowledge 2008: online, emphasis in original)

Other testimonies highlight that the CoS not only perceives the *Golden Age of Knowledge* as an improvement in the accessibility of Hubbard's tech but also that this presentation of his republished work represents his true intention:

> You're going on Ron's journey. You're following Ron's footsteps and he's telling you his discoveries.
>
> . . .

> You're going up a mountain to the peak, and you're cutting through the trail. And you're with LRH cutting through the trail all the way up.
>
> . . .
>
> The comm [communication] is so real, even, sometimes he says, 'I'm talking to you', and you're like, 'Oh, yes, you're talking to me'.
>
> . . .
>
> And he'd be talking and you'd be like, 'Oh, that's what's going to be next'. And then that would be the next sentence and I'd be like, 'How did I know that?'. And I knew it because of what I'd studied. (The Golden Age of Knowledge 2008: online)

The final testimonies from Miscavige's presentation focus on the spiritual importance of Hubbard's work, and the influence of the *Golden Age of Knowledge* in controlling the MEST universe:

> And at one point I'm sitting there reading, and I realized, 'oh my god, I'm reading this book outside my body!'
>
> . . .
>
> I was exterior most of the time.
>
> . . .
>
> I've gone exterior on these lectures.
>
> . . .
>
> It's like – BANG! You're out. You know you're out. And you ain't [sic] going anywhere but to the stars. (The Golden Age of Knowledge 2008: online, emphasis in original)

The process of 'going exterior' in Scientology, the outer-body experience of one's thetan leaving one's MEST body, is normally associated with the OT levels that are explored after reaching the state of Clear. Yet with the introduction of the *Golden Age of Knowledge*, the CoS positions this experience as being possible through engagement with Hubbard's Basic Books and lectures, highlighting its belief in the *Golden Age of Knowledge* as being the authentic tech according to Hubbard.

Following the completion of the *Golden Age of Knowledge* in 2009, the CoS launched the *Golden Age of Tech Phase II* (often referred to as the *Golden Age of Tech*), in an attempt to distribute the changes to the tech in the *Golden Age of Knowledge* as standard practice in CoS Orgs worldwide. At the celebratory launch of the *Golden Age of Tech* in 2013 at Clearwater, Florida, Miscavige described this latest initiative in Scientologist practice as a 'turning point' for Scientology, stating that 'by the time this weekend is over, it is going to be a whole new world.

You have arrived at a turning point – a turning point that guarantees our future into eternity' (cited in The Church of Scientology International n.d.-b: online). This ceremony was coupled with the opening of the CoS' Flag Building at its 'Flag Land Base' in Clearwater. The Scientology Flag Land Base acts as the CoS' world headquarters and comprises several buildings across Clearwater that provide Scientology services. It is at the new Flag Building that Scientologists can fully access the *Golden Age of Tech*, which includes the 'Super Power' programme and the 'Cause Resurgence Rundown', a series of procedures that aim to heighten spiritual awareness, which I shall discuss further in Chapter 6. Despite emerging decades after Hubbard's death, the CoS promotes the *Golden Age of Tech* as a result of a comprehensive study of the entirety of Hubbard's work on Scientologist tech, claiming that it is a fulfilment of his vision, and that 'all of [the CoS'] work was predicated upon the mission that the material can never be lost or altered' (The Church of Scientology International n.d.-b: online).

As a CoS staff member explained during my time at the Church of Scientology of London, the *Golden Age of Tech* is the distribution of Standard Tech across all Scientology Churches, Missions and Orgs worldwide. With this control of Hubbard's work, and the application of what it views as the most effective and authentic form of auditing available, the CoS is able to use the tech as a method of establishing the boundaries between itself and the 'squirrels' of the Free Zone.

The Free Zone and the Golden Age of Knowledge and Tech

It became clear throughout my fieldwork that preserving the sanctity and authenticity of auditing, according to Hubbard's work, is an important goal for many Scientologies. Through establishing the *Golden Age of Knowledge* and the *Golden Age of Tech*, the CoS has made an assertion of providing auditing to practitioners precisely as Hubbard intended. It is perhaps unsurprising that many Freezoners I interviewed, due to their opposition to the CoS, are critical of the *Golden Age* initiatives. For example, James believes that the *Golden Age of Tech* adopts a flawed approach to auditing:

> But there are huge problems with the *Golden Age of Tech*, real problems, apart from the drilling, drilling, drilling, practice, practice, practice aspect. Hubbard strived for many, many years, decades, to make training as streamlined as possible. . . . He felt that the fastest he got somebody equipped in the chair and actually confronting another person and helping them the faster you would learn. The *Golden Age of Tech* has slowed that process down almost to a complete

stop, it basically means there's prerequisites, prerequisites, prerequisites, to a point – like the E-Meter is just an aid, it's not the be all and end all, there are many, many more aspects of counselling, but you spend forever trying to learn about what the E-Meter is and how to use it, it just stops the whole training cycle.

Echoing James's concern regarding the skills of auditors trained through the *Golden Age of Tech*, Hanson (a Ron's Org member) rejects the claim of the CoS that the initiative is entirely based upon Hubbard's intention for the tech:

> That is actually one of the reasons we left the Church. Because we already then observed that there's changes in the technology we couldn't agree [*sic*]. . . . So what is G*olden Age of Tech Phase II* and *Phase I* and so on? . . . I don't know where [David Miscavige] has that from, but I don't consider that [to be] any Standard Tech [devised by] L. Ron Hubbard [*sic*]. Of course, it contains some elements, but what we can tell you frankly and openly those people coming from the Church quite regularly have problems to audit the basic stuff they should audit. And many, many auditors never made it. And that is an indicator by itself that they can't learn it.

Moving the focus of the *Golden Age* initiatives to the re-publication of Hubbard's works, Independent Scientologist Chris is highly critical of the Basic Books, believing that the tech must be kept purely in line with Hubbard's original vision:

> 'The Basics' were new edits of all the early books and lectures. These edits have been compared to older edits and found to have dropped, added and altered technology. Ron was adamant that unnecessary courses and such not be added to the line-up, so as not to lengthen the runway for any given course or rundown.

Through this process of editing Hubbard's primary Scientologist writings, Lewis argues that the CoS has attempted to emphasize its religiosity, 'which comes at the cost of deemphasizing its status as a science' (2016: 477). To demonstrate this, Lewis (2016: 477) compares alterations between the original 1956 and republished 2007 editions of Hubbard's *The Fundamentals of Thought*, in which there has been a shift to a more overtly 'religious' narrative in the latest edition, particularly the several instances when the word 'science' has been omitted from the text. Such alterations demonstrate that Hubbard's work has been amended since his death, resulting in a reversal of the squirrel dynamic – with Free Zone communities accusing the CoS of squirrelling (2016: 477). This shift is also demonstrated in my discussions on the *Golden Age of Tech* with Eric, an Independent Scientologist who views the CoS as being the true squirrels:

> I know of [the *Golden Age of Tech*], it is more bullshit from Miscavige (when talking about Miscavige, you tend to become injurious because the guy is totally

wicked and crazy). These changes are not in the LRH vision of auditing. They have two purposes – money, and [to] make auditing heavier [and] longer. The Independent field will never consider including it in its practice. The Independents are loyal to LRH tech because it works wonderfully and gives results.

A prominent theme when discussing the *Golden Age of Tech* with Freezoners is the influence of David Miscavige in his role as the leader of the CoS. Several of my fieldwork participants seem to view two different versions of CoS – the CoS under Hubbard, and the CoS under Miscavige. Tracy, as a former acquaintance of Hubbard's, seems to view Miscavige's leadership of the CoS as detrimental to the tech:

> In our Advance Clinical Course in 1958 [Hubbard] explained the Frankenstein Monster Effect, and when he did I could see it applied to his creation of the Church. He knew it would eventually go down the dwindling spiral. Eventually the creator of a machine (the CoS is a type of machine, set up like a factory to move Preclears though the lines as fast as possible and spit them out at the other end as a 'product') puts the machine on automatic and it eventually breaks down. I'm sure he expected it.

These changes to the way the tech is applied in the CoS, and the frequent opposition to it from the Free Zone, are a dominant aspect of how Free Zone communities operate. However, it would be an error to assume that the notion of a 'common enemy' is a unifying factor in the Free Zone. Divisions between Scientologies outside the institutional CoS demonstrate how different perspectives on Hubbard's authority and authentic tech make the Free Zone a highly nuanced category. At the heart of these divisions lies the debate on what constitutes as Standard Tech, and whether strict adherence to Standard Tech is necessary for the application of Hubbard's ideas.

Free Zone auditing and application of the tech

My conversations with Free Zone participants highlight how the level of authority assigned to Hubbard has a direct influence on the methods with which Free Zone Scientologists conduct their auditing sessions. Coupled with the issue of Hubbard's authority in how the tech should be applied is the presence of innovation in certain Free Zone Scientologies. Certain Free Zone groups, particularly individuals that practise auditing independently, encourage innovating Hubbard's tech in ways that they deem to be beneficial. These changes include alterations to the methods of conducting auditing, amending or disregarding Hubbard's rigid guidelines for auditing procedures, or even developing new types of E-Meters. Through such innovation, some Scientologists move beyond the Standard Tech debate, creating a fluid environment in which they are free to conduct auditing sessions without the hierarchical guidelines of an institutional body.

As the central ritual of Scientology, the auditing process has come to be viewed as a religious practice that draws from scientific and religious discourses. This straddling of boundaries between science and religion, particularly Hubbard's initial rejection of religious elements to auditing, creates a variety of attitudes towards auditing in the Free Zone and subsequently impacts Free Zone views of the religiosity of Scientology. During my interview with Tracy, a Free Zone Scientologist and member of the early Dianetic movement, she recalled her initial mixed feelings towards the transition of the Dianetic movement to Scientology:

> I don't know how others felt when Scientology became a Church in N.J. [New Jersey] in 1952 or 1953. I know I was shocked when he said all auditors were now Ministers. I was an escapee from various Christian religions my mother had forced upon me every Sunday and the last thing I wanted to be in this world was a Minister. I did some soul searching. I did understand the necessity for it, as Dianetics was not accepted by [the scientific community in] the United States. You couldn't get a license to practice [sic] unless you had a psychology degree. . . . I could understand how it could be categorized under religion, but I didn't like it. Originally we were taught that there was no category for Scientology, that it superseded anything we had on this planet, and that all other things could be understood better through the use of Scientology, not the other way around. So it was a step down to be a religion. I don't know of any rebellion though. It was accepted as far as I know.

Despite this initial mixed response, Tracy now believes the auditing process blurs the boundaries between science and religion:

> That's a tough one. It is both. Not a religious practice as commonly thought of, we don't pray to God or bend down to Allah. We used not to have any of the artifacts [sic] associated with religion, but LRH eventually came up with black garb like the Catholic Church has and a post for a Minister. But in the sense that we deal with the spiritual nature of man to free him from his own lies and the effect of lies from others we are on the road to truth, and I believe that is a religious pursuit. Besides, we have all the weirdnesses [sic] of religion, with the Xenu story, which probably makes as much sense to the un-indoctrinated as the Virgin Mary does to

those who do not believe. But the tech is extremely scientific in nature. You apply it correctly, and PC [Preclear] gets better within his own estimation.

Coupling her view of Scientology as a mixture of scientific and religious practices, Tracy stated that she could perform marriage ceremonies at her Free Zone group, but has chosen to focus her attention on auditing. Her group has, however, previously sent a member to perform a 'last rites sort of session' for a dying Free Zone Scientologist. This simply involved him confessing to sins and being given forgiveness. This ritual does not, however, fit with Scientologist discourse, demonstrating the ways in which the fluid environment of Free Zone Scientology can allow for practices that extend beyond what would typically be considered 'Scientologist practice'. Despite this, Tracy views the primary and most important aspect of Scientology to be the auditing process. Similarly, Independent Scientologist and auditor, James, focuses his Scientologist practice on developing the self through auditing and learning how to audit others. He explained that Independent Scientology 'is really only about auditing and training'. Despite attending rituals and gatherings, such as weddings, during his early years as an Independent Scientologist, he felt that these were more social events, stating that 'there isn't a lot of ritual to do with Scientology'. Clarifying this, he argued that 'any ritual the Church of Scientology says we have is really just a "legal rudiment" – meaning it was something we did to justify our position as a legal religion'.

Ron's Org member, Hanson, agrees with the notion of the central role of auditing, describing it as 'the highest art in Scientology'. Yet he views auditing as the culmination of Hubbard's work on philosophy, the self and spirituality – which he views as justification for considering Scientology to be a religion:

> I would say it is religion. It is a term by itself. It took me many, many years to understand that Scientology is a religion. But when I understood it is a religion then I have to say, sorry, now this sounds very arrogant, that Scientology is more a religion than any other religion. But it took me many years to understand that. And it is certainly a religion, but on the other hand religion has such a bad reputation, that you do not position yourself as a religion. . . . LRH always said it is a science, but it's difficult to duplicate that and understand. I consider it as definitely applied religious philosophy, I would say that fits best for me. An applied religious philosophy which is bringing about health and happiness and abilities and so on.

Unlike these nuanced approaches to auditing as a religious or scientific procedure, Independent Scientologist Eric stated in a written response to my questions that 'Scientology has become a religion ONLY for [financial] reasons. Auditing is a self-help practice which has nothing to do with religion. It is really a scientific procedure.' Despite not viewing Scientology and auditing as religious, Eric maintains his adherence to Hubbard's work and is unwilling to develop his own version of the tech.

For some Scientologists outside the institutionalized CoS, however, the lack of organizational guidelines (or a hierarchy of staff) has presented an opportunity for conducting auditing sessions using methods that they personally deem to be effective. During my interview with Owen, an independent auditor, he rejected the need for the E-Meter, a device that is usually synonymous with auditing:

> I don't use the E-Meter. All of Scientology in the '50s was researched and discovered without the E-Meter. An E-Meter is, in my opinion, something that Ron invented in order to be able to train people who couldn't 'think' with the tech, those that needed a tool in order to get involved in the PC's reactive mind. [Without the E-Meter] you can have a greater presence, and greater range of questions.

Drawing from Hubbard's early research before the E-Meter became a feature of auditing sessions, Owen believes that the E-Meter is a non-essential device. Furthermore, Owen conducts his auditing sessions via Skype, an online voice chat system. In doing this, Owen strays from one of the most distinctive aspects of auditing: that it physically takes place in one room between the auditor and the person being audited, typically sitting directly opposite one another. Despite his initial reservations regarding this method, Owen now finds it to be the most effective way of auditing his clients, allowing him to expand his client base across countries including Australia, America and Germany.

The Free Zone acts as a fluid, and often unregulated, environment. Accordingly, how professional auditors in the Free Zone are trained is a concern for some Freezoners. James stated during our interview, however, that training to audit outside the CoS is not a daunting task, as the CoS provides the basics required, and all auditors simply refine their abilities by learning further techniques:

> I learned all the foundations within the Church, so what I learned outside the Church was additions to what I already learned. But even [for] someone learning from scratch outside the Church . . . from what I can see the Free Zone is the biggest leader in that. I don't think it's too different. You still learn the basics of communications, you still learn the fundamentals of the E-Meter, and you still learn the fundamentals of spiritual counselling. The *Golden Age of Tech* changed the whole game in the Church anyway, they don't operate the same way as they used to. So you could probably say that, as far as training goes, the Free Zone and other groups outside probably train people better than the Church does.

Holding the view that it is entirely possible for an individual to learn how to audit outside the CoS, James encourages Independent Scientologists to work on some of their development alone, such as reading Hubbard's *Self Analysis* ([1951] 1983). Serving as an example of the fluid nature of Scientology outside the CoS, James has no objections to Scientologists altering the tech, believing that Hubbard encouraged highly trained auditors to develop their own tech. Despite this, he does not develop his own interpretation of the tech, arguing that Hubbard's tech is 'as good as it's going to get'.

Ron's Org similarly claims to apply Scientology according to Hubbard's methods before Captain Bill Robertson's departure from the CoS; Hanson explained that Ron's Org auditors are trained in a similar fashion to CoS auditors from the 1970s. This is a rejection of contemporary CoS training of auditors through the *Golden Age of Tech*, which he views as being too lengthy and ineffective:

> We train them actually very similar, I would say, to the time of the '70s. We have, of course the text changed a little bit in the years, but they're very, very close to this time. So, a person comes in and he studies those stuff, relatively fast, he's studying maybe two weeks and then we send him in-session and – if you want to make an auditor then he has to apply it. He has to audit it. You don't make an auditor by making him study five years. It's a lot of theory and he'll have no idea what to do with it. And you are absolutely confused at the end, so better give him simple things to start with, to study, and to apply it. That is our approach.

On a much smaller scale than Ron's Org, Tracy runs a Free Zone Scientology group from her home and has additionally worked with auditors from Ron's Org and other independent auditors. At her practice, Tracy delivers auditing to one Preclear at a time (due to small staffing numbers) but occasionally encourages her students to conduct auditing sessions. She is highly trained in auditing, creates auditing programmes for her auditors to follow in their personal training, and estimates that her practice averages on assisting one practitioner to reach Clear per year. Tracy views her delivery of the tech as being in accordance with Hubbard's work, and does not develop her own tech.

'Squirrelling' amongst the 'squirrels': Boundaries in Free Zone Scientology

As I have previously observed, the opposition towards the CoS from many Free Zone communities and individuals could present an image of Free Zone

Scientology as a unified movement. However, when considering the construction of Hubbard's authority on the various forms of auditing in the Free Zone, it becomes clear that the nuanced nature of auditing has a direct influence on Free Zone boundaries. While there are earlier examples of Independent Scientologist groups being established, most notably 'Dianology' in the 1960s (Cusack 2016: 489), the first major Scientologist schism occurred in the early 1980s, during which half the membership of the CoS is alleged to have left (the anti-Scientologist journalist, Tony Ortega, suggests approximately over ten thousand Scientologists) (Lewis 2016: 468; Ortega 2013a). While there is little evidence to substantiate this significant number, the attention surrounding the early 1980s schism (both within Free Zone spaces and anti-Scientology journalism) is indicative of its significance. This initial schism was led by Captain Bill Robertson, Hubbard's close personal friend and former high-ranking CoS staff member. Despite 'Free Zone' becoming a term synonymous with all Scientologists outside the CoS, Robertson's Free Zone and Ron's Org as a result, has become known as a distinct branch of Scientology with its own set of beliefs.

Following his departure from the CoS, Robertson conducted his own research, expanding Hubbard's cosmological work on the OT levels, in line with communications allegedly received from extra-terrestrials, including telepathic conversations with Elron Elray, believed to be the spirit of Hubbard (Gregg and Thomas 2019: 354; Ortega 2013a). Despite the emphasis in Ron's Org on the notion of 'Standard Tech', these alleged extra-terrestrial communications suggest that Ron's Org are able to innovate the tech, a process that is legitimized through the direct communication with Hubbard in the form of Elron Elray. However, there is no significant evidence to suggest that Ron's Org has developed any aspects of the tech since the death of Robertson. This emphasis on Robertson's role in Scientology, particularly legitimized by his close relationship with Hubbard, distinguishes Robertson's 'Free Zone' from other types of Free Zone Scientology.

Lewis (2016: 468) notes that this schism during the 1980s is one of two major movements that defected from the CoS, with the second being in the early twenty-first century. James was able to clarify the division between these two movements. As a former CoS member who falls into Lewis' second category, James considers himself an 'Independent Scientologist' (or 'Indie'), and views the Free Zone as an older community with different views:

> [The Free Zone is] a particular group . . . that left the Church much earlier than I did and had some ideological differences. Not necessarily a great many, but it's sort of stuck in the 70s and 80s in terms of what Scientology is. They basically

believe that Hubbard didn't do any development after maybe around 1980 – that it was somebody else. I worked for the Church for 30 years, so I happened to know a great many people who, working under Hubbard, developed Scientology further from the late 70s up until when he died in 1986. So I know for a fact that some of their beliefs – I have no problem with them having those beliefs, and I have no argument with them, they're free to do whatever they want – but I happen to know that some of those things I think are incorrect from my point of view, based on my knowledge. . . . Sometimes insider knowledge. Many of these guys also never worked for the Church, they were members and they were, let's say, ecclesiastical members and some of them were even trained inside Scientology but they didn't necessarily work inside Scientology or worked at the highest levels of Scientology, so they've just got certain differences. But I'm not against the Free Zone, I'm just not a Free Zone member.

James, using his experience as a CoS staff member, rejects the theories regarding Hubbard's lack of involvement with Scientologist tech since the early 1980s, stating that the Free Zone practices are a dated form of Scientology. While he does not consider members of the 1980s Free Zone movement to be squirrelling, his remarks point to boundaries between Scientologies outside the CoS based upon the interpretation of Hubbard's work. Furthermore, my interviews suggest that the use of the term 'Independent' to describe Scientologists outside the CoS is a more recent phenomenon, as Chris, an Independent Scientologist, stated:

I prefer the term 'Field' or 'Independent Field'. 'Free Zone' has come to be a tainted term, since the Free Zone contains a lot of people who are 'squirrelling' [sic] (practicing non-standard Scientology) and/or highly critical of the Founder. Apparently, 'Free Zone' used to be a more neutral term, but that was before I came to be part of the Independent Field.

Chris' statement brings the discussion back to the overarching debate in auditing practice – the division between groups that lay claim to a 'true' Scientology and the squirrels. Notably, the term 'squirrelling' is typically associated with its use by the CoS to categorize those practising 'incorrect' forms of auditing outside the CoS, yet during my conversations with Free Zone Scientologists I frequently noticed the term being used to describe both the CoS and its auditing practices. However, in a contrast to the popular view of the Free Zone as a group united in direct opposition to the CoS, Chris' argument demonstrates that non-CoS Scientologists can accuse one another of squirrelling, depending on their interpretation of Hubbard's work, and the legitimacy of innovating his tech. Linking back to his criticism of Scientologists who innovate Hubbard's tech, Chris outlines what he views as two factions in the 'Independent Field', drawing a distinction between the purist Scientologists who seek to preserve Hubbard's tech, and the squirrelling of innovators:

> Consider the 'Field' as having two factions, more or less. There are the people who are 'with-LRH'. And the people who are not. The 'with-LRH' people are often the most trained and educated in the subject. They insist on precision of application of the Technology, and adherence to the policies laid down by Ron in relation to the Technology. The other people do not run 'standard' Scientology. They mix it up with other things or think they have some better idea than Ron about this or that. They are frequently critical of Ron, whereas the 'with-LRH' crowd treat him with deep respect and gratitude for all he did. . . . It's also worth understanding that those of us who are 'with-LRH' consider that the Church as currently constituted has long since ceased to practice [sic] 'standard' Scientology. In fact most of those who aren't 'with-LRH' will say the same thing. This isn't a questionable point. It isn't like the Catholics and Lutherans, which have the same Bible, but virtually different religions. It is a matter of, 'This bulletin of X date, entitled Y, dictates Z'. And we know for a fact that the Church does not follow it or has significantly deviated from it. 'What is Scientology' is a very narrow thing, and very precisely laid out by what LRH wrote and said. There is little or no room for 'interpretation'.

Chris, as we have previously observed, believes that the term 'Free Zone' has become 'tainted'. In his view, this is due to a large proportion of Free Zone Scientologists choosing to develop auditing tech and methods in their own field. He views any Free Zone Scientologist that alters the tech to be 'not-with LRH', and views deviation from 'standard' Scientology to be an error, as Scientology is precisely structured by Hubbard's work. Despite believing that the CoS has 'ceased to practice "standard" Scientology', Chris is in agreement with their view of Hubbard as 'Source', suggesting a view of the founder and creator of auditing to be infallible, thus negating any need for further innovation in the field:

> There's no need to 'develop' anything. All the needed technology is already in place from LRH. And LRH had the whole track . . . behind him. I don't. So I'd just screw it up, most likely. And no one else knew as much as LRH did about the whole track of research, from earliest days up to 1986. If you didn't spend all that time working on this technology, you sure don't have the skill to extend or alter it.

This is a direct contrast to the view of James, who believes that Hubbard encouraged Scientologists to innovate the tech:

> I'm sure some will say 'we have the one true tech' because I have heard such claims, but they are false. The real difference is in the atmosphere and spirit in

which it is delivered in the indie field, much less draconian, much less emphasis on having to donate endless sums of money, disconnect from nay-sayers etc. Hubbard wrote a prodigious amount of auditing material so some independents pick and choose what time period to follow. Some believe anything after 1979 is bogus but that is simply not true. Others believe that Captain Bill Robertson had a posthumous line to Hubbard and that Hubbard dictated new materials to him. I beg to differ. Robertson was a trained auditor himself and has simply continued and developed new materials, but if he doesn't say they are Hubbard's then they won't be followed, which is crazy because Hubbard encouraged highly trained people to develop new tech.

James cites Robertson as an example of how auditing can be developed in the Free Zone, albeit dismissing the claims of his telepathic communications with the spirit of Hubbard. Despite this approval of developing the tech in the independent field, James does not develop his own tech as he views Hubbard's work 'as good as it's going to get'. This exemplifies how those who develop their own tech (or encourage it) do not reject the importance of Hubbard's work. Owen, who was personally acquainted with Hubbard during his time in the Sea Org, perceives himself as adhering to Hubbard's intentions while adjusting the tech to suit his auditing methods:

> In some aspects I am [with LRH] and in some aspects I am not. It depends on what you're talking about – a lot of the tech is very valuable, and after spending 40,000 hours in the chair I know that you can create results. But on other aspects I am not with him – he got confused. The whole disconnection thing doesn't add up with the principle that communication solves everything. 'In doubt: communicate' – that's what LRH said, but then they started disconnecting. These two things don't add up.

It is important to remember that not all Free Zone Scientologists who left the CoS during the early 1980s view a firm boundary between the Freezoners of the 1980s and 'Independents' of the twenty-first century. For example, Tracy is a former CoS member who left during the period of Robertson's establishment of the Free Zone, yet considers herself to be both Free Zone and Independent. However, she makes a distinction between 'Independent' and 'Indie' Scientologists:

> I can also call myself an Independent Scientologist, but the 'Indies' are mostly more recent defectees [*sic*] and have had a somewhat different experience in the Church and in the application of the technology. Most Freezoners use the original tech and eye the later tech that was issued by the [CoS] as possibly altered.

By drawing distinctions between different Scientologies based on the application of the tech, Tracy is exemplifying the ways in which boundaries are made through the control of Hubbard's tech. She additionally stated that the divisions within the Free Zone were not as simple as Chris suggests:

> This is difficult to answer because there are many different types of groups in the Free Zone. 1) With LRH but only through 1972, consider later tech squirrel. 2) With LRH but expand beyond such as Ron's Orgs and the former Knowledgism. Have additional processes of their own. 3) The 'Indies' who consider any Freezoner squirrel. (Amusing since they are in the Free Zone the minute they leave the Church of Scientology – all a matter of terminology). 4) Those who set up Scientology and called it something else to avoid attacks by the Church of Scientology.... 5) I use all LRH tech and also can do some Ron's Org tech. Not many of us in the US can. 6) Real squirrels, people who had a little training and really don't know what they are doing and screw up people.... Odd thing, Indies think all of the Free Zone is squirrel, but some of the RTC [Religious Technology Center] training and methodology they were trained in is squirrel. Example, a needle on the E-Meter has to float back and forth three times before it was a floating needle, a David Miscavige special. False squirrel datum. I'm for anyone or anything that improves self-determinism and frees up stuck emotional points. Even psychologists can sometimes help someone.

This statement from Tracy contains a number of assertions and accusations that are central to the production of boundaries between Scientologies, additionally demonstrating the centrality of the auditing process in the debate of orthodox authenticity as against heterodox innovation. Much like other Free Zone groups, she accuses Miscavige's CoS of squirrelling, particularly the new training methods and auditing techniques implemented by the RTC. These accusations exemplify the reversal of the squirrelling dynamic between the CoS and Free Zone, yet Tracy also displays how the control of Hubbard's 'true' tech continues to cause boundary disputes within the Free Zone. Observing that recent some Independent Scientology communities, or 'Indies', accuse the 'Free Zone' of the 1980s of squirrelling, Tracy wryly notes that the Independent Scientologist community are part of the wider Free Zone umbrella by practising Scientology outside the CoS, and are therefore squirrels according to Hubbard's (1965a: 6) original squirrelling policy. However, Tracy goes on to make an accusation of squirrelling herself, claiming that Freezoners who alter the tech with little knowledge of auditing and Hubbard's work are squirrels. These statements indicate how boundaries can be made and broken across Scientologies based on interpretations of auditing.

During my interview with Owen, he spoke of how he left the CoS in the early 1980s and worked closely with Captain Bill Robertson in piloting his new materials in the Free Zone. However, Owen does not dedicate much thought to the issue of divisions in the Free Zone, but is simply more focused on getting good results from auditing:

> You have your clients and you work in the Independent Field. But you don't need to stress 'I'm Free Zone!'. People are more concerned with what they're delivering, from what I can see.

This relaxed approach to boundaries is also shared by James. Despite categorizing himself as an Independent Scientologist or Indie, he will describe himself as a Buddhist to outsiders, due to his view of the auditing process as an adapted form of Buddhist practice:

> So, if somebody asks me in the street what I believe I say I'm a Buddhist. I don't have to say the word 'Scientologist' as really it is Buddhism. We believe in reincarnation, we believe in karma – Scientology has something very similar to karma. And even Hubbard said in many lectures that the problem with Buddhism for him (and I have to agree) is that sitting on a mountaintop didn't really do much for most people. A small percentage might reach a higher plane, but most people get cold and lose weight – that's all that happens. All that Scientology really does is the auditing side of things, which builds a way of going from a lower awareness level to a higher awareness level. They're spiritual techniques that basically don't require you to go and live in a cave. A lot more rituals have been added that are not fundamental to its beliefs, like Buddhism.

James's view of Scientologist practice is reminiscent of Flinn's analysis of Scientology as a technological form of Buddhism, in which he argued that Scientology's Buddhistic characteristics are 'an investment of technology itself with symbolic power that gives meaning to the believer's existence' (2009: 221). Through his use of Scientologist tech and devices, while drawing inspiration from Buddhist practice, James breaks down boundaries in the umbrella category of Free Zone Scientology, choosing instead to promote a fluidity in auditing methods.

It is important to note that while distinctions between the CoS under L. Ron Hubbard and CoS under David Miscavige are often alluded to by Free Zone Scientologists, Hubbard is not universally viewed as a perfect being in the independent community. James mentioned in a survey interview that there 'were mistakes [made] by Hubbard' in Scientology policy, while Owen shares an anecdote he heard regarding Hubbard's introduction of the 'religion angle':

> Ray Kemp was a Scientologist in 1951/52 who lived next door to Ron. This is his story to me; I don't know how much is true: At one point Ron asked him 'how do I get tax exemption?', and Ray said 'make a Church' – and that I have known all this time. It's so right to me, this religious business is just in order to get tax exemption.

Owen views Scientology as a self-help philosophy rather than a religion. His view on the roots of Scientology's religious status is in stark contrast to the CoS' presentation of Hubbard as 'Source'. Despite these statements, my participants were far more positive about the CoS under Hubbard than about the CoS under Miscavige. Several of my informants view contemporary CoS tech to be less efficient than it was under Hubbard's leadership. However, by not viewing Hubbard as infallible, Owen and James are open to a fluidity in the ways auditing can be practised. This is an attitude that is in direct conflict with Scientologists who emphasize the preservation of Hubbard's original ideas. During my interview with Eric, he drew a distinction between himself as an Independent Scientologist who promotes the sanctity of Hubbard's work, and what he views as the innovation of the Free Zone:

> I am an Independent Scientologist; I am faithful to the teachings and technology of LRH. . . . The Free Zone is a bunch of 'anything' – good but weird people who do not respect the technology and try to develop it. I am 100% faithful to LRH.

Eric's firm attitude towards applying Hubbard's tech precisely according to his writings, and criticism of those who choose to innovate the tech through making personal changes, not only demonstrates the divisions in Scientologies outside the CoS but the direct impact auditing has on these boundaries. Throughout my fieldwork it became increasingly evident that not only do many Scientologists outside the CoS view auditing as the main focus of Scientology but that it is the debates surrounding the interpretation of Hubbard's considerable body of writing and the Standard Tech that most often cause new Scientologies to emerge.

Concluding remarks

The role of the charismatic leader has been a considerable focus of NRM scholarship (Barker 1984; Weber [1948] 1991c). While these studies have primarily focused on the devotion of NRM practitioners to their leader, and the qualities that prompt this devotion, the current status of Scientology as an NRM in transition and transformation allows an opportunity to view first-hand how authority changes following the death of the founder. Both the contemporary activities of the institutional CoS, and the recent study of the CoS by Westbrook (2019), indicate that Hubbard remains central to its application of Scientology. Since assuming the role of leader of the CoS, David Miscavige has launched two major initiatives (the *Golden Age of Knowledge* and *Golden Age of Tech Phase II*) that have directly influenced the ways Scientologists learn about the tech, auditors are trained and auditing sessions are conducted (Gregg and Thomas 2019: 356). By promoting the *Golden Age* initiatives as the fulfilment of Hubbard's vision for Scientology, and aiming to ensure Standard Tech across all CoS Orgs, the CoS lays claim to a truly authentic practice of auditing through the authority of Hubbard. As a result, they remain firmly critical of all other Scientologists that make use of the tech outside the CoS, particularly those who squirrel by innovating the tech by moving it away from Hubbard's original methods (Gregg and Chryssides 2017: 26).

Conversely, several Free Zone groups or individuals, most notably Ron's Org, are highly critical of the practice of auditing in the CoS, particularly the *Golden Age* initiatives, which they view as not being 'true' Standard Tech. This has resulted in a reversal of the squirrelling dynamic, with the CoS becoming regarded as squirrels by Free Zone communities (Lewis 2016: 477). However, as this chapter has demonstrated, the notion of squirrelling – the accusation of deviating from Hubbard's work – has created divisions and boundaries in the Free Zone itself. This has resulted in different Scientologies laying claim to a 'correct' Standard Tech on the one hand, and, on the other, some choosing to innovate Hubbard's work based on their own practices. This has resulted in a discourse surrounding the interpretation of Hubbard's work, the notion of Standard Tech and the innovation of the tech in the Free Zone. Accordingly, auditing has become the most significant contributing factor to the emergence of new Scientologies, the boundaries between them and the ways in which they lay claim to a true understanding of Hubbard's work.

6

'Doing Scientology'

E-Meters, objects and material culture

Engaging with the auditing process in contemporary Scientology practice involves the use of distinctive material culture. This chapter addresses how the material culture of Scientology and the ways in which its use of technological devices, particularly the E-Meter, are essential to auditing in many Scientologies. I discuss how the introduction of the E-Meter transformed the practice of auditing in the transition from Dianetics to Scientology, before exploring the use of the device in auditing sessions in both the CoS and Free Zone. This discussion expands upon the previous chapter's analysis of issues of authenticity and innovation in the construction of boundaries between different types of Scientology and practitioners of auditing. Finally, I consider further material culture in Scientology, including CoS Orgs and additional technological devices that play a part in the application of auditing.

Religious objects, materials and things

The scholarly examination of a contemporary religion can be enriched by paying close attention to the physical objects, or 'things', which are used by the movement in question, and the importance that is placed upon them. Morgan (2011: 140) observes that a 'thing' is distinguished by its parts, design, shape and other characteristics that make it identifiable. Furthermore, he adds that the examination of a thing, and as a result the recognition of what it is and what it does, implies methods of classification, identification, historical narratives and moral codes. Immediately obvious examples of religious things would be votives, which are common things in the material world that are given new meaning and expectations when offered to a deity (Weinryb 2017: 98). The area of material religion can extend to any object used in a religious context. Such all-encompassing understandings of things are dependent on their social environment, and therefore can be illuminating for the study of the context in which they appear.

This examination of things marks a shift in the academic study of religions from a more 'text'-based approach. Cort (1996: 614) argues that the history of the scholarly study of religions has been dominated by textual analysis, due in no small part to the Euro-American academy's prioritizing of the written word. However, this is an approach that has been increasingly challenged in contemporary academia, particularly due to the emphasis on lived religion and the study of objects. As established in Leonard Primiano's (1995) eminent study on vernacular religion, the study of religions must emphasize its focus on the reality of everyday life for individuals and societies. This moves the discipline away from the notion of official religion as an understanding of religion as it is dictated by institutional bodies, a category Primiano finds unsatisfactory, and more towards what Graham Harvey describes as the 'lived realities' (2014: 16) of religion. By using the lens of 'lived' or 'vernacular' religion, scholars can refocus their attention towards rituals and practices involving a range of physical objects and symbols (Morgan 2014: 480). Simply put, the study of lived and material religion concerns what individuals 'do', and the objects with which they do it.

With the lived religion approach in mind, scholars can focus their studies on the creativity involved in religious practice (Bowman and Valk 2014: 15). This has resulted in recent scholarship turning its attention to 'invented' or 'hyperreal' religions, such as Jediism and Matrixism (Cusack 2010). In a critique of the text-centric approach to researching these groups, Paul-François Tremlett (2013: 11) argues that the studies of these movements would be enriched by a more materialist approach, in which religions should be viewed as nodes connecting people and objects. Tremlett's argument is especially pertinent to the wider study of New Religious Movements, particularly Scientology, which acts as a postmodern religion in which practitioners interact through rituals involving physical and technological objects. Swainson has argued that Scientology acts as a 'microcosm of neoliberalism' (2016: 202) by adopting consumerist approaches to ideas and religiosity. Accordingly, Scientology uses a 'literal interpretation of the theoretical spiritual marketplace' (Swainson 2016: 202), offering its religious goods and services through capitalist frameworks. Consequently, the religious goods offered by Scientology, specifically its objects and devices in this case, demonstrate more than simply the beliefs upon which they are based – they point towards the ways in which Scientology uses its objects, symbols and imagery to market the tech to practitioners – both within CoS and Free Zone spheres.

I have previously outlined in this book how Scientology positions the concept of L. Ron Hubbard's tech not only as his Scientological theories and methods but also as the technological objects that have become an intrinsic aspect of the auditing process across a range of Scientologies. Visual elements have also become a distinctive aspect of Scientology, particularly the CoS' use of symbols, such as the Scientology Cross.[1] Yet the material culture of Scientology goes beyond its visually distinctive appearance, and into the category of technology, offering Scientologists spiritual freedom through the methods of what it presents as a working scientific technology. It would be a great error to categorize much of Scientology's material culture as a mere by-product of its belief system, or as secondary to its written texts. Its technological devices, particularly the E-Meter, lie at the heart of Scientology, and are viewed across a significant number of Scientologies as essential in reaching the true goals of the Scientologist praxis.

'A very peculiar instrument': The E-Meter

Introduction to the E-Meter

When considering the material culture of Scientology, particularly that pertaining to the practice of auditing, it is appropriate to begin with the E-Meter, the device most commonly associated with Scientologist practice. Occasionally referred to as the 'Electrometer' or 'Hubbard Electrometer' (Hubbard 1982: 6), the E-Meter was an integral part of Hubbard's development of the 'religion angle', the process of transition to religiosity for his Dianetic technology.

Despite being introduced alongside the religious elements of auditing, Hubbard positioned the E-Meter as simultaneously scientific and religious – a distinguishing feature of contemporary Scientology. The technological nature of the device is significant in this regard, both in terms of its visual appearance and its use in auditing sessions, leading to Grünschloß's assessment of Scientology '*the* technological *religion* of a fully disenchanted industrial world' (2009: 236, emphasis in original). This approach from Grünschloß is framed in terms of the E-Meter's emphasis on spiritual healing, and how it emerged alongside a number of movements emphasizing healing above salvation in the late twentieth century, as observed by Bowman (1999). Similarly, scholarly analyses of the E-Meter (Harley and Kieffer 2009; Whitehead 1987) have concerned the role of the device in spiritual healing through technological means, specifically within the CoS. My examination of the E-Meter builds upon these studies by taking a different approach. Through adopting the method of lived religion, this account demonstrates the ways in which nuanced understandings of the E-Meter across Free Zone Scientology challenge the understanding of Scientology as a technological religion, as established by Grünschloß (2009: 236). The data I will discuss in this chapter illustrate varied Free Zone attitudes towards the E-Meter, with one respondent rejecting the need for the device altogether, and others discussing the E-Meter as useful yet non-essential. Altogether, these conversations demonstrate an accommodation of religious and secular-scientific elements in Free Zone Scientology, albeit with a greater emphasis on the secular elements of self-help and mental health. With these nuances in mind, I argue that the use of the E-Meter, in addition to various understandings of the device, contributes to the emerging boundaries and fluidity in Free Zone Scientology, building upon the previous chapter's analysis of the discourse of authenticity and innovation.

The E-Meter is a device operated by a professionally trained auditor during auditing sessions. This is connected to a pair of electrodes (known by

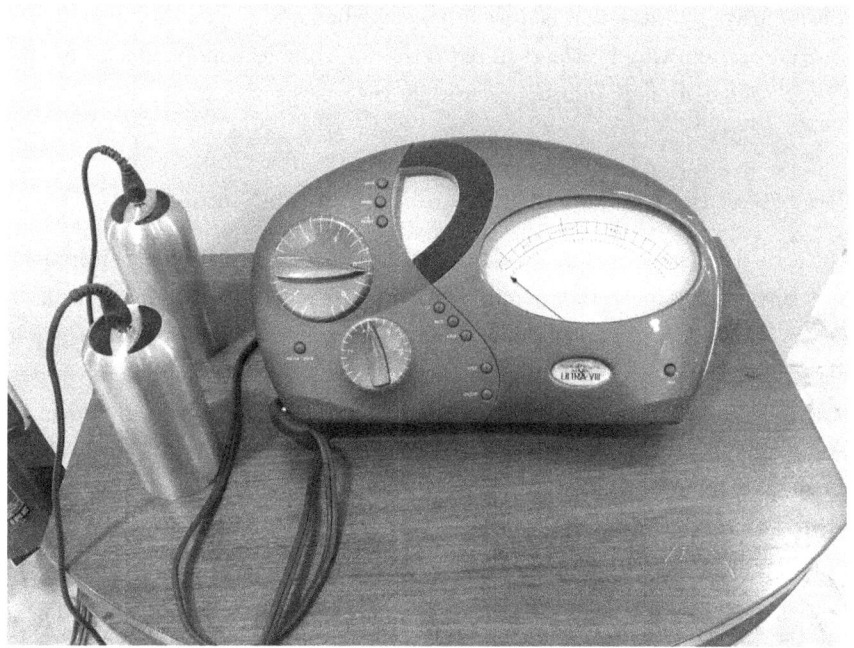

Figure 6.1 The Mark Ultra VIII E-Meter at the Church of Scientology of London (photo by the author, 1 March 2017).

Scientologists as 'tin cans'), which are held in each hand by the person being audited (either a Preclear or a Clear studying the Operating Thetan levels, the upper stages of Scientology) (Whitehead 1987: 142). The auditor will ask the Preclear a series of questions related to an incident of trauma in their life in an attempt to detect and remove the engrams from their reactive mind. During this process, the auditor will sit opposite the Preclear and privately operate the dials (particularly the tone arm dial) of the E-Meter, thereby adjusting the flow of electricity to the electrodes. Simultaneously, the auditor observes the activity of the needle's movements in reaction to the Preclear's answers and responses (Bainbridge and Stark 1980: 132). According to Hubbard, the E-Meter allows the auditor to identify where the engrams lie. As the engram exists on a subconscious level in the reactive mind, it therefore cannot be detected by the more rational analytical mind. The E-Meter is central to the attempt to detect these engrams and remove them (Harley and Kieffer 2009: 196–7).

When Hubbard published his initial research in *Dianetics: The Modern Science of Mental Health* (*DMSMH*), auditing was presented as an entirely secular practice that could be conducted by two individuals simply using a copy of *DMSMH*. This type of auditing has since become known as 'Book One auditing', and is not considered irrelevant in contemporary Scientology – rather it is a type of auditing that is now enhanced when additionally conducted with an E-Meter, allowing Preclears to reach the state of Clear more effectively (The Church of Scientology International 1998: 164).

The role of the E-Meter in the establishment of Scientology

The early development of the E-Meter dates back to the 1940s, when chiropractor and science fiction author Volney Mathison began experimenting with lie detectors. Mathison, a collaborator of Hubbard's, created a device that began to be used occasionally in auditing sessions during the early Dianetic movement (Urban 2011: 49). Following a feud between the pair in 1954, Hubbard made minor alterations to the device and presented it as the 'Hubbard E-Meter' (Urban 2011: 51; Whitehead 1987: 144). In a recorded interview, Hubbard acknowledged the similarities between the E-Meter and the lie detector, but outlined how they differ in purpose:

> [The E-Meter is] one of the most misunderstood objects that anybody had anything to do with. And the Meter simply shows where an individual is aberrated. And the lie detector, of course, is not a lie detector. It doesn't detect

lies, it only detects disagreements. You ask the fellow, 'did you murder the girl?' and he disagrees with murdering the girl. And, of course, he gets a reaction on the lie detector, and they take him out to the electric chair and electrocute him. Lie detectors are no good, but it does show that he is upset about the idea of murdering a girl. . . . Now, if you ask him why he was upset about this particular idea, you might find some relative who had been murdered, that he had completely forgotten about. And he illuminates this sector of his life and it clears. (Hubbard, in *An Introduction to Scientology* 2006)

Alongside his work on the E-Meter, Hubbard published a milestone book in the history of Scientology in 1952 – *What to Audit* (republished by the CoS as *Scientology: A History of Man*). This book outlines the more overtly 'religious' nature of auditing, establishing the concept of the thetan and its relationship with the MEST universe. *What to Audit* is intended to assist auditors in knowing what to target during auditing sessions, and goes beyond Book One auditing by making the E-Meter central to the process. During this research, Hubbard introduced Technique 88, which he described as an enormous advance over the previous understanding of auditing, allowing the process to achieve 'incredibly fast results' (Hubbard [1952] 2007c: 1). Technique 88 is executed by targeting the four following areas during auditing sessions; (i) the present or 'current' life; (ii) one's genetic or evolutionary chain; (iii) significant portions of the whole track and (iv) the whole track itself (Hubbard [1952] 2007c: 99). Coupled with the development of the religion angle, the E-Meter was an intrinsic part of the Dianetic movement's transition to Scientology. Hubbard explained this distinction accordingly:

'Dianetics' [means] 'through mind', do you see? And is in essence actually a mental study. 'Scientology' had to be broadened because it was more firmly established that Man was a spirit after that, and you couldn't go along with the same word. (Hubbard, in An Introduction to Scientology 2006)

This distinction between treating the individual as a spiritual being, not just as a physical entity, is what Hubbard claimed creates such remarkable results for Scientology's use of the E-Meter. When asked in a recorded interview if comparisons could be made between Scientology and psychoanalysis, Hubbard candidly responded:

Don't associate Scientology with such people – that's terrible, that's bad manners. That business about sex and all that sort of thing. These people in psychoanalysis, they worked on somebody for a year just to find out if they could help him, and then they charged him about £9000 for having not helped him and so forth.

> But that's psychotherapy, that's for the neurotic or the person who is insane, or something like that. That's nothing to do with Scientology. Scientology is for an able guy like you, or like me – able to function in life, able to make his own way, does his work and so forth. That's the man that should be helped. (Hubbard, in An Introduction to Scientology 2006)

In addition to its central role in contemporary auditing, the E-Meter has become one of the most recognizable objects associated with the CoS. E-Meters have not remained the same throughout the CoS' history, however, and newer models have been released and distributed amongst Scientologist Orgs worldwide. The latest and most advanced E-Meter used by the CoS is the Mark Ultra VIII, released in 2013. During my tour of the Saint Hill Manor (Hubbard's former home), I was able to view a display in Hubbard's office of several E-Meter models through Scientologist history, ranging from the early Mathison Meters (named after Volney Mathison) to the most recent E-Meters, including the Mark Ultra VIII. Unlike earlier models, the Mark Ultra VIII features the far more 'futuristic' and sleek design sported by the more recent E-Meters, alongside battery operation and a digital interface. According to a staff member at the CoS, all the E-Meters were designed by Hubbard, including those released after his death in 1986. This, he explained, is because the technology for Hubbard's later designs has only been developed in recent years. It is believed that Hubbard's level of knowledge of this advanced technology was a result of his exploration of past lives through auditing, in which he was able to access greater technology from more advanced civilizations on other planets. This belief is connected to Hubbard's esoteric cosmological works on the 'whole track' – the complete collection of memories from an individual's entire existence (including past lives) over 80 trillion years of existence that are hidden in the unconscious mind (Grünschloß 2009: 234).

Using the E-Meter

On a basic level, the E-Meter measures the galvanic skin response of the Preclear when recalling past events, prompting readings on the E-Meter (through the movement of its needle) which in theory allow the auditor to detect engrams faster and more effectively (Chryssides 2004: 385–6). However, my fieldwork participants at the CoS disagree with this. They believe that rather than measuring the galvanic skin response of the individual being audited, the E-Meter detects the mental pictures (memories) stored on the time track; the chronological collection of memories of each individual (Hubbard [1951] 2007b: 45). Through the use of the E-Meter during auditing, it is believed that the auditor will be able to detect and remove engrams more effectively.

Hubbard promoted the introduction of the E-Meter as a historic event for not only Scientology but the entirety of humanity, claiming that 'Leeuwenhoek (the inventor of the microscope) found the way only to find bacteria; the E-Meter provides the way for Man to find his freedom and to rise to social and constructive levels of which Man has never dreamed' (Hubbard 1982: 6). Hubbard considered the E-Meter to be a scientific and entirely precise device (Urban 2011: 50), but insisted that much training is needed to correctly use the E-Meter. It is essential in Scientologist practice that any trained auditor using an E-Meter should be fully trained in its use. In 1961, Hubbard recorded an auditor training lecture at Saint Hill, East Grinstead, in which he summarized his view on the efficacy the E-Meter and the importance of understanding how to use it:

> The E-Meter is a very peculiar instrument. It is absolutely accurate. But when somebody is so knuckleheaded as not to ask the right questions, of course, it apparently gives wrong answers. An E-Meter is as accurate as the auditor asks the right questions [sic]. It itself is totally accurate. But you have to find out what it is talking about, and it is not necessarily talking about what you are talking about as the auditor. But it is talking about something, and the probability is that it is very close to what you're talking about when it's talking sporadically, but not quite it. Now when you ask the right question, the E-Meter then reads highly consistently. But the near-right question reads inconsistently. So, when you get the inconsistent reads your question is not quite right as a general rule. . . . But when you ask the right question the E-Meter will then tell you by reading consistently. (Hubbard [1961] 2013: online)

This excerpt from Hubbard's lecture is illuminating in its demonstration of the sanctity of the E-Meter in Scientology. Not only does Hubbard consider the E-Meter to be infallible, and therefore incapable of giving incorrect results, he also speaks of how the device 'talks' through its needle movement. Through giving the E-Meter agency Hubbard positions the device as a subject, not an object. The E-Meter is accordingly presented as being able to communicate with the auditor, during which the auditor is expected to be able to effectively understand what information is being conveyed by the device. Accordingly, any errors made during an auditing session is down to the auditor, not the E-Meter. To this end, auditors are trained in Training Routines, a series of specialized techniques that are believed improve the communication between the auditor and the E-Meter, thus allowing the auditor to appropriately interpret the responses and emotions of the Preclear (Whitehead 1987: 135).[2]

Reading the E-Meter involves paying close attention to the movement of its needle and the way it responds to the reaction and answers of the person being audited. Hubbard (1982: 6) wrote that the electrical impulses caused by thought during the recall of a lock create an electrical resistance. This resistance is detected by the E-Meter, and is measured in terms of its 'rises' and 'falls' (see Figure 6.2) – notifying the auditor of the presence of the engram during a lock, allowing it to be detected and removed more effectively (Chryssides 1999: 385–6; Whitehead 1987: 143). The most notable physical features of the device are the needle and display interface that measures the resistance (Figure 6.2), the tone arm (Figure 6.3), and the two cans held in each hand by the person being audited (Figures 6.4 and 6.5) (Whitehead 1987: 144–5).

Using the tone arm to adjust the E-Meter's flow of electricity, the auditor will lead the Preclear through a series of commands and questions while observing the actions of the needle. The E-Meter allows the auditor to recognize when a Preclear is subconsciously withholding information in the reactive mind. This allows the auditor to use question and answer techniques to bring that information to the surface by getting the Preclear to recall the earliest events

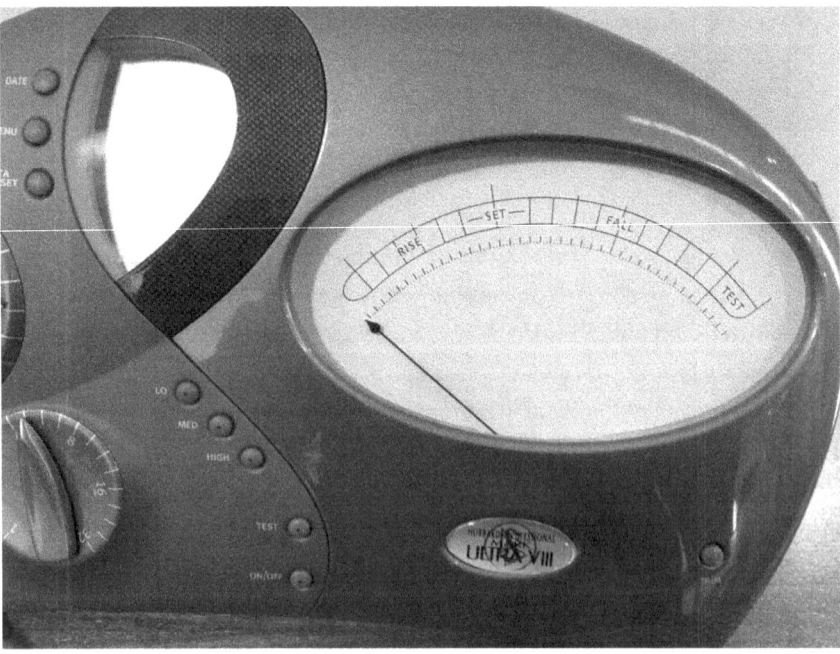

Figure 6.2 The needle and display interface of the Mark Ultra VIII E-Meter at the Church of Scientology of London (photo by the author, 1 March 2017).

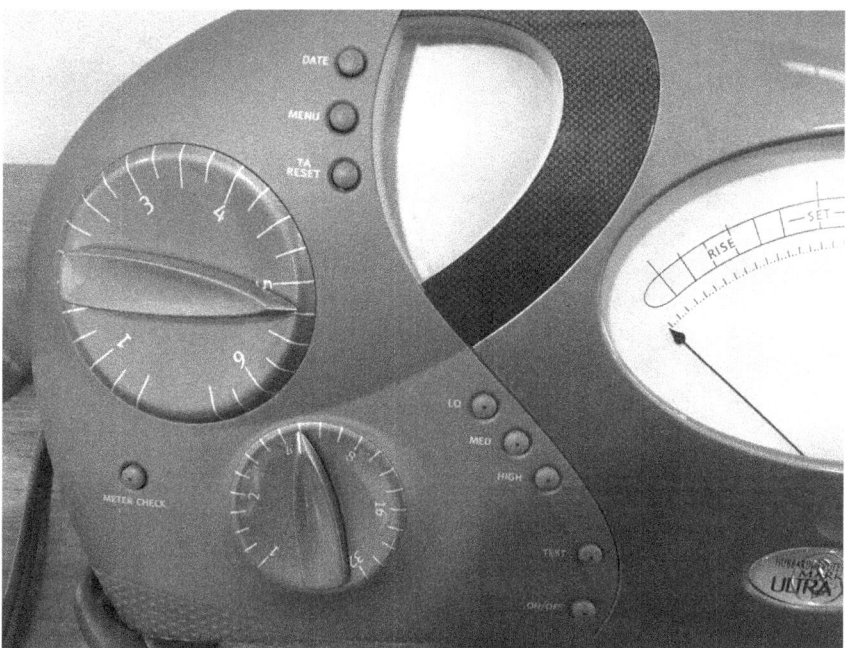

Figure 6.3 The tone arm of the Mark Ultra VIII E-Meter at the Church of Scientology of London (photo by the author, 1 March 2017).

of the trauma (the lock), thus removing the engram and causing the incident to 'flatten' (Harley and Kieffer 2009: 201). Once the questions have successfully allowed the auditor to identify the Preclear's lock, the removal of the engram is indicated by the needle remaining idle (Hubbard 1982: 58). This is known as a 'floating needle', or 'free needle' and 'F/N' (Whitehead 1987: 153). Additionally, the removal of the engram can be determined from 'good indicators' from the Preclear's behaviour (as per the Tone Scale), and a 'cognition' from the Preclear – a realization about the cause of their engram (Harley and Kieffer 2009: 200; Whitehead 1987: 153).

To demonstrate the use of the E-Meter, a staff member at the Church of Scientology of London offered me a 'stress test' (keenly observing that it was not an auditing session). The stress test was conducted on a Mark Ultra VIII E-Meter, and was intended to demonstrate how the E-Meter works and responds to the emotions of the individual. As in an auditing session, I held one canister of the E-Meter in each hand, while the staff member activated and set up the device. As he was doing this, he explained the Scientologist belief that all memories are stored in the reactive mind like a 'picture bank', allowing us to visualize them. These memories, and the engrams attached to them, carry a charge that can be

Figure 6.4 The E-Meter canister of the Mark Ultra VIII E-Meter at the Church of Scientology of London (photo by the author, 1 March 2017).

displayed by a moving needle on the E-Meter when it is brought to the surface. During this brief demonstration, I was asked questions about my life, ranging from commands such as 'think about people in your life, or your family, friends, and so on' to 'think of a previous negative experience of stress or discomfort'. Through this short exercise, I was able to see the needle on the E-Meter slightly move as I reacted to the questions.

A stress test can be seen very much as an introduction to the auditing process at a very basic level. Once Preclears begin to engage with the auditing process, they start their journeys on Hubbard's Bridge, and begin to rise through a series of structures states and levels, eventually reaching the OT levels. While the documents used during OT auditing are intended to be kept confidential (as we discussed in Chapters 1 and 4), the Bridge does detail the

Figure 6.5 Inside the E-Meter canister of the Mark Ultra VIII E-Meter at the Church of Scientology of London (photo by the author, 1 March 2017).

need for the Clear (an individual freed from any engrams) to engage with solo auditing. The E-Meter itself remains an integral part of these sessions, however, the simultaneous role of the Clear as both auditor and person being audited requires both cans to be held in one hand, using a piece of plastic or wood to separate the two. This allows the Clear to receive reads from the E-Meter, while keeping a spare hand to operate the E-Meter dials and write notes (Whitehead 1987: 144–5). As an expansion to the E-Meter, and for greater convenience for the Clear, they may also make use of a remote tone arm that connects to the E-Meter. The remote tone arm features a dial on its side, allowing the E-Meter to be operated by a hand holding both the E-Meter cans, while allowing the other hand to be entirely free to write notes.

The E-Meter in the Free Zone

As previously noted, the CoS is organized in a highly structured manner, with abidance to what it perceives is Standard Tech, the Auditor's Code and the confidential nature of the Operating Thetan levels acting as examples of the rigid control system of the CoS. The practice of Scientology away from the CoS, and thus away from a strictly organized system, can involve highly varied and different applications of Hubbard's work and the tech or material culture.

It is clear that the E-Meter has become an essential device to the auditing process in the CoS, but many of my interviews with Scientologists in the Free Zone suggest a more relaxed view regarding its application. Ron's Org member Hanson spoke of an overreliance on the E-Meter in the CoS, and considered it to be the most striking difference between Ron's Org and CoS methods of conducing auditing:

> [I was] not fully aware in the beginning [of my time in] the Church in the 80s, auditing turned into an E-Meter dependency. You were always checking for reads on the E-Meter, and actually the E-Meter said to you if you are allowed to audit something or if you are not allowed to auditing something. Which is opposite to what LRH taught as before [*sic*]. Actually, he just started to audit and used the E-Meter at the end of the action to make sure it is clean. So, the E-Meter was used to see if still the charge [engram and lock] there, is something not handled there? He says it's that way, and I can agree very much to that – he says is that auditor and the PC [Preclear], and E-Meter, are in agreement that what was audited is really now audited and finished. And if all those three elements are in agreement that it is completed then it's completed. And in the Church it's [the] opposite. I mean, I can tell you really saddening stories about PCs, you know, they are crying because they have ARC-break and upset. . . . And then the auditor is going to ask the E-Meter, 'do you have an ARC [Affinity, Reality, Communication] break?', and if the E-Meter doesn't read, he has no tools to handle that ARC break. And we [Ron's Org] just say 'hey, come on, this person is so ARC broken, handle him! Audit him!'. The E-Meter won't read at all, it can't read because this is buried under tears. So [it is a] different approach, basically.

Hanson suggests there is an overreliance on the E-Meter in the CoS that is detrimental to the auditing process, believing that the auditor's observations of the Preclear's reactions and emotions should take precedence over reading the response of the E-Meter. Similarly, Independent Scientologist James feels that the emphasis on E-Meter training in the contemporary CoS distracts auditors from the activity of auditing itself:

> The E-Meter is just an aid, it's not the be all and end all, there are many, many more aspects of counselling, but you spend forever trying to learn about what the E-Meter is and how to use it, it just stops the whole training cycle.

Another participant, Owen, audits his Preclears exclusively via Skype, and views the E-Meter to be of very little importance to auditing, particularly for auditors that are sufficiently trained in Hubbard's tech:

> An E-Meter is, in my opinion, something that Ron invented in order to be able to train people who couldn't 'think' with the tech, those that needed a tool in order to get involved in the PC's reactive mind. [Without the E-Meter] you can have a greater presence, and greater range of questions. For many years I vowed to never audit without the E-Meter or on Skype, but then I had two PCs . . . last summer who [paid for hotels], and thought 'we don't want to do this – why don't you audit us on Skype?'. So, I said if they dared try that we could give it a go. I've done it ever since – it worked perfectly, it was totally natural. People restrict themselves because they think they can't audit without an E-Meter – bullshit. Auditing works very well without an E-Meter.

Further to the debate as to the importance of the E-Meter in auditing, Free Zone Scientologists are able to choose from a large number of E-Meter models. Ron's Org, for example, does not develop its own E-Meters, but makes use of models developed by Scientologists outside the CoS. Speculating that 'below 5% of people [in the Free Zone] use the Meters of the Church', Hanson stated that Ron's Org is open to using almost any E-Meter, due to the importance of the auditor's ability above the use of the E-Meter:

> If someone comes in with an E-Meter we test it a bit, but this is not a scientific test of it, just [to] see if it works. As I said to you before, the E-Meter is not that important as the Church makes you believe. The auditor, with two-way communication, is much, much more important than anything else.

The number of E-Meters available to purchase online is considerable, with several of these models, created by Free Zone Scientologists innovating the tech, containing different abilities and features, thus creating an online marketplace for independent auditors (see Free Zone Earth 2007). For example, Tracy has previously used CoS models of the E-Meter as a Free Zone auditor, but currently makes use of the Ability Meter. An Ability Meter is an E-Meter developed in the Free Zone which is advertised to 'accurately [reflect] what is actually happening within the mind of the subject with no inertial "swings" of the needle' (Free Zone Earth 2002: online) by placing an emphasis on high-quality needles. This distinguishes it from other E-Meters which attempt 'to artificially simulate the same response by electronic means [which] result in unnatural needle responses' (Free Zone Earth 2002), thus causing inaccurate responses to the emotions of the Preclear.

The Ability Meter also features what could be described as a more 'retro' aesthetic in comparison to the futuristic design of the Mark Ultra VIII (currently used by the CoS). This draws a distinction between the more 'independent' nature of Free Zone Scientologists developing their own devices on the one hand, and the lavish nature of the CoS on the other. The sleek design of Mark Ultra VIII highlights not only the technological nature of the CoS but also the way in which it promotes itself in the spiritual marketplace as offering a more desirable lifestyle to practitioners, which can include financial success. Alternatively, the 'retro' aesthetic of the Ability Meter points to the ways in which individual Free Zone Scientologists are able to personally innovate and develop their own E-Meters according to their personal 'homemade' designs, and subsequently make these devices available for purchase in a marketplace unhindered by institutional restrictions on E-Meter specifications.

Inside a Church of Scientology Org

Buildings

The CoS makes use of a number material objects in relation to both religious imagery and spiritual practice. For example, the buildings of Scientologist Orgs around the world feature modern and sleek designs and receive large amounts of investment from the CoS; they are in themselves aspects of the material culture of Scientology. For example, the 2013 launch of the Flag Building in Clearwater, Florida, attracted much media attention for its cost of $145 million (Walker 2013). Beyond their lavish designs, however, Scientologist Orgs appear to have an importance in Scientology as not only the locations of religious rituals and services but also because they enjoy the status of providing practitioners with what the CoS views as 'true' Standard Tech (Figures 6.6 and 6.7).

Scientologist Orgs specialize in the application of Hubbard's Dianetic technology and auditing sessions, and these are delivered in private auditing rooms between an auditor and the Preclear. While the auditing process remains the primary focus of Scientologist practice, presenting Orgs as only being used by Scientologists for auditing would be simplistic. Newcomers

Figure 6.6 The Flag Building in Clearwater, Florida (photo by the author, 23 August 2015).

to Scientology will be encouraged to take the 'Life Improvement Courses' at their nearest Org, which aim to be applicable to everyday life, and coincide with Hubbard's vision of a workable technology, ranging from the *Scientology Tools for Overcoming Financial Stress* and *Setting and Achieving Your Goals*, to *Creating a Successful Marriage* and *Successfully Raising Children* (The Church of Scientology Los Angeles n.d.). These courses are open to all Scientologists at various stages of personal development, but my experience at the CoS has suggested that they are used as suitable introductions for newcomers to Hubbard's work, intended to prepare the Preclears for their journey on the Bridge to Total Freedom.

Since the early twenty-first century the CoS has been working on their 'Ideal Organizations' (Ideal Orgs) initiative, a project that aims to raise all Scientology Orgs worldwide to the highest possible standard. This attempts to ensure that each Org delivers what the CoS views as the complete and perfect application of Scientology services, and relies upon the fundraising efforts of Scientology practitioners (Lewis 2016: 475; The Church of Scientology International n.d.-h). It has been suggested (Lewis 2016: 476) that the encouragement of donations from CoS practitioners, who could otherwise spend their money on progressing

Figure 6.7 The entrance to the Flag Building (photo by the author, 23 August 2015).

Hubbard's Bridge, has resulted in a decline in CoS membership numbers, which in turn has resulted in a greater number of Scientologists establishing independent Free Zone groups. Indeed, the lavish CoS Orgs funded by practitioner donations has drawn criticism from Free Zone communities (Hellesøy 2016: 459). Several of my Free Zone participants argued that such buildings are not necessary, with some auditors choosing to meet their clients at their homes, or even in hotels, to conduct auditing sessions. Furthermore, some participants spoke of the lack of Free Zone Orgs as a tactic to practise Scientology 'underground', away from what they viewed as the scrutiny of the CoS.

For the CoS, however, Orgs are an expression of devotion to Hubbard, and as Hellesøy argues, also act as part of the routinization of Hubbard's authority 'by making buildings manifestations of his legacy' (2016: 459; see also Weber [1948] 1991b: 297). Yet these Orgs go beyond material expressions of devotion – they are visual and physical methods of marketing by the CoS. Their expensive nature and lavish style are supposed to be indicative of the life improvements Scientology offers its practitioners – that auditing can lead to personal success in one's career through improving personal abilities, leading to financial gain and a more 'desirable' lifestyle.

Super Power and Cause Resurgence Rundown

Throughout my conversations with several Scientologists, both in the CoS and Free Zone, it has been clear that the E-Meter is a device of significant religious and scientific importance in Scientology. Despite its central role in the auditing process, however, there are aspects of Scientology, particularly within the CoS, that adopt other physical devices to assist in auditing. Indeed, as I discussed in Chapter 4, CoS Orgs contain Purification Centres to assist Scientologists with the Purification Rundown, and prepare the body for standard auditing procedures. The Centre's use of exercise equipment, such as treadmills and saunas, further demonstrates the importance of material culture and objects in the practice of auditing. In addition to the Purif and the use of the E-Meter, CoS members engaging with the OT levels are given the opportunity to make further use of technological devices at the Flag Building, specifically purposed to 'help unleash the superpowers of the thetan' (Lockwood 2016: 188).

When it was opened in 2013, the Flag Building (often referred to as the 'Super Power Building') was intended to facilitate more than the standard auditing procedures (auditing through questions and answers using the E-Meter) found in other Scientology Orgs. New and highly advanced auditing procedures are now conducted on the fifth and sixth floors of the Flag Building. Known as 'Super Power' and the 'Cause Resurgence Rundown'. These were described by *Freedom Magazine* (published by the CoS) as being 'auditing procedures Mr Hubbard intended for every Scientologist' (2013: 32).

Utilizing 'entirely unique 21st-century spiritual technology' (2013), Super Power aims to address disassociation with the spiritual self, based on Hubbard's research on the corrosion of society in the 1970s. According to *Freedom Magazine*, Super Power is particularly relevant in an age of television and social media, and aims to reawaken the 57 'perceptics' (perceptions) of an individual, ranging from basic senses including smell, hearing and touch, to rhythm, blood circulation and time. Engaging with Super Power is believed to allow a more effective participation in life (2013).

The Cause Resurgence Rundown is described far more vaguely in *Freedom Magazine* (2013) as a practice that enhances the individual's energy and allows them a greater control of their life without the barriers of mental and spiritual factors. As with many advanced Scientology procedures, the specific details of Super Power and the Cause Resurgence Rundown are disclosed only to Scientologists who have been deemed ready to engage with the practice. Similar to the leaking of Scientology's highly guarded Operating Thetan documents, online sources have revealed details of these practices through the CoS' alleged artistic renderings of the devices used, leaked photographs from practising Scientologists and the testimonies of both ex-Scientologists and Free Zone Scientologists on Hubbard's work on the proposed Super Power programme.

It is important to bear in mind that these accounts (whether they are from anti-Scientologist journalists, ex-Scientologists or Freezoners) all come from sources outside the CoS. As such, they cannot be regarded as guaranteed accurate or complete accounts of practices taking place within the CoS. Much of the public information on what Super Power entails comes from prominent Independent Scientologist Dan Koon, a former CoS staff member who, during the late 1970s, was a member of the team compiling Hubbard's work on Super Power, and who has since shared his recollection of what it entails online. Hubbard's work on Super Power relates to the issue of Rock Slams (R/S), which Koon describes as the 'wild and crazy manifestation of the E-Meter needle' (n.d.: 2). In Scientology, an R/S is believed to display evil intentions on behalf of the individual holding the E-Meter cans. This was an issue Hubbard believed was inhibiting the expansion of Scientology, due to the number of Sea Org officers experiencing R/Ses. The most problematic officers (known as 'List 1 R/Sers') were temporarily relieved of duty and sent by Hubbard to the CoS' disciplinary programme, the Rehabilitation Project Force (RPF) (Koon n.d.: 2; Urban 2011: 125) (Urban 2011; Koon n.d.). Deciding that there were too many people being falsely 'RPFed' (sent to the RPF), and that staff productivity was still too low, Hubbard set out to create the Super Power programme. Koon (n.d.: 9) claims that this programme was always intended for staff use only, consisting of twelve rundown practices to improve the efficacy of the CoS' staff. In a document written ahead of the opening of the Flag Building (and introduction of the new Super Power floor), Koon argues that the CoS' offering of Super Power would be drastically different to the practice he helped compile in the 1970s:

> Undoubtedly, people at Int [International Base, LA] have recompiled Super Power and what eventually is released by the Church may bear little resemblance to what [I] laid out. . . . [I]f one reviews the various parts of the rundown it is obvious that LRH pulled extensively from tech or tech theories that already existed and sequenced it in an order that would accomplish the desired product of a competent, efficient staff member. Super Power was and always will be primarily for STAFF. Only secondarily is Super Power for Dianetic Clears. That is not to say that [the] public will not benefit from it. Anyone would. Yet, Super Power does not supplant anything on the Grade Chart [the Bridge to Total Freedom]. (Koon n.d.: 9, emphasis in original)

In addition to Koon's account of Hubbard's creation of Super Power, the launch of Super Power at the Flag Building attracted much attention from anti-Scientologists, particularly the journalist and exposé writer Tony Ortega, one of the most prominent anti-Scientology writers on the internet. In 2012, Ortega drew attention to leaked images of artist and architectural renderings and plans of the Flag Building from CoS materials, including detailed information and images of both the Super Power and Cause Resurgence Rundown floors (Ortega 2012a). A year subsequent to the leaking of CoS materials on Super Power, Ortega's website distributed photographs of parts of the Super Power Building taken and shared on social media by a Scientologist who 'defied the rules' (Ortega 2013b: online). These leaked photos include the 'Motion Quadrant' chair – a chair held within a spherical metallic structure – which uses gyroscopic technology to spin the person sitting in it. Most notably, Ortega's blog post included a discussion on the chair with former CoS member Chuck Beatty, who claims to have helped build a giant chair while working on the original Super Power rundown in 1990 (Ortega 2012b). Ortega drew attention to details of physical objects and devices used to train the perceptics of Scientologists, including a balancing device and a magnetic sense device. Further to these devices, Ortega highlighted rooms in the Super Power Building which contain specific technology to train certain perceptics. For example, taste and smell are trained through a 'taste wall' and 'smell wall' that display containers of substances to stimulate these senses, while the sense of touch is trained in a room containing an 'oiliness table' used for the 'oiliness drills' (Ortega 2013b).

A number of artistic renderings of the sixth floor (the location of the Cause Resurgence Rundown) of the Flag Building were also leaked by Ortega, yet the details regarding Cause Resurgence Rundown are far sparser than those of Super Power. In addition to a dedicated Purification Rundown facility, the sixth floor is alleged to include a room designed for 'the Running Program', which is believed to be part of the Cause Resurgence Rundown. Ortega (2012a) claims that the Running Program involves individuals running around an illuminated column in the middle of a darkened, dome-shaped room. He speculates that this practice is an extension of the Purification Rundown, and is geared towards the detoxification of the human body, but very little seems to be known about the Cause Resurgence Rundown.

The response to the leaked information of the Super Power and Cause Resurgence Rundown has attracted mixed responses from Scientologists in the Free Zone. Dan Koon, as previously mentioned, worked on compiling Hubbard's works on the Super Power programme, and believes the original

Super Power procedure to be a beneficial practice for Scientologists. Speaking of the original pilot tests for Super Power, Koon states that 'the results [of Super Power] experienced by the pilot [subjects] were pretty spectacular on this step of the overall rundown as well as the entirety of Super Power itself' (Koon, cited in Ortega 2012a: online). However, Koon is highly critical of the practice of Super Power at the Flag Building, suggesting that the 'space-age' presentation of its devices is an intentional marketing tactic to attract members to the CoS. Furthermore, he argues that the Super Power process would only be used during an unusual problem (such as a particular E-Meter reading) during an individual's auditing, and that its original purpose was as a tool for staff efficacy. This assertion is echoed by my fieldwork participant Chris, who explained to me that

> Super Power was researched by LRH as early as 1978, if I recall correctly. But it was set up to be delivered to staff first by a roving 'Universe Corps' of auditors. These personnel would only deliver this service (and others, like OT levels inside the Org) to staffs after they had achieved a certain level of expansion for their Orgs. After some time, Super Power would be delivered to public. And my understanding is that Super Power would then be available at Saint Hill Orgs. Instead, Miscavige chose to reserve Super Power delivery to Flag public (not staff) alone. And he insisted on having an entirely new, lavishly furnished building to deliver the rundown in.

Chris' statement suggests that there was an intention to provide a public Super Power programme beyond that for the CoS staff, particularly in Saint Hill, East Grinstead. Yet he is highly critical of the way it is exclusively practised at Flag, and its use of expensive equipment. Similarly, Tracy is also concerned about the Super Power procedure at Flag, placing a specific emphasis on the technological devices used during the process:

> I know [David Miscavige] has a Super Power scary machine. . . . [He] thinks he is going to improve perception by spinning a body around in a chair while directing the thetan to look at things. Horror story, complete inversion of tech. Dramatization of past track that we are trying to remove, not do. I don't know what their Cause Resurgence Rundown is but probably took some of the tech LRH wrote and made a package to sell.

Focusing on the Motion Quadrant chair, Tracy is concerned that engaging with Super Power could cause an individual to relive the 'past track' (past events on the time track), rather than remove their presence from the reactive mind altogether, as is the intention of auditing. My discussions of Super Power with Free Zone

Scientologists highlight the prominent theme that additionally emerged during our discussions on the *Golden Age of Knowledge* and *Golden Age of Tech*: the strong criticism of David Miscavige's leadership of the CoS. Expanding on her concerns regarding the Motion Quadrant chair and Super Power, Tracy said:

> Miscavige isn't very well tech trained. The whole thing is a dramatization of an earlier time Scientology was presented. That time those who had the tech kept others from having it, then altered it and did Black Scientology and damaged people. This time around the cat is out of the bag, all upper materials are available outside of the CoS . . . and we have hopes of freeing people while the CoS continues to worsen and misapply Scientology.

Tracy accuses the contemporary CoS of practising 'Black Scientology' through its method of conducting Super Power. 'Black Scientology' relates to the issue of 'Black Dianetics', a phrase that originated from Hubbard for the use of Dianetic technology to harm others. Hubbard's *Dianetics and Scientology Technical Dictionary* contains a short definition of Black Dianetics:

1. Hypnotism.
2. Unscrupulous groups and individuals have been practicing a form a Black Dianetics on their fellow man for centuries. They have not called it that but the results have been and are the same. There are those who, to control, resort to narcotics, suggestion, gossip, slander – the thousands of overt and covert ways that can be classified as Black Dianetics (Hubbard 1975: 32).

Black Dianetics can therefore expand beyond the specific use of Dianetics for immoral reasons, and was considered by Hubbard to be a term for all kinds of covert mental abuse. In referring to the CoS' current interpretation of Super Power as 'Black Scientology', Tracy suggests that the technology and devices used are not only distant from Hubbard's original intention but potentially harmful to those who take part.

Concluding remarks

Through using the theoretical method of lived and vernacular religion, this chapter has demonstrated that the material culture of Scientology is deeply entwined with the auditing process, and offers an avenue through which contemporary forms of Scientologies can be understood through the materials and objects involved in its application. Despite its emphasis on transcending all aspects of the physical MEST universe, the auditing process is predominantly conducted through engagement with a physical device – the E-Meter – which is viewed as an essential device to auditing in several contemporary forms of Scientology. Its presentation by the CoS as both a religious and a scientific device is indicative of the hybrid nature of auditing as a practice drawing discursively from religious and secular-scientific methods. For several Scientologies, particularly the CoS, the E-Meter is seen as infallible, with Hubbard himself apparently attributing agency to the device. Accordingly, the E-Meter becomes as essential to the auditing process as the auditor in the CoS, yet Free Zone attitudes towards the device are varied. While most of the Free Zone Scientologists I interviewed make use of the E-Meter in their auditing sessions, others (particularly those who audit outside of any organizational Scientologist body) simply view it as an aid. Unsurprisingly, this nuanced attitude towards the device has resulted in an increasing number of Free Zone Scientologists choosing to create and develop their own E-Meter models, incorporating features that fit their perceived vision of auditing, drawing us back to the issues of authenticity and innovation (as explored in Chapter 5). While some Free Zone Scientologists expressed caution regarding certain E-Meter models, generally my fieldwork participants hold a liberal approach to which device they use, provided its efficacy meets their expectations.

The E-Meter may be the focal point of auditing, and the most immediate example of Scientologist material culture, yet the expression of devotion to Hubbard and his tech is seen in the buildings in which auditing sessions can be practised, particularly in the CoS (Hellesøy 2016: 459). It has been suggested that CoS membership numbers are in decline, while there are increasing numbers of individuals practising Scientology in the Free Zone (Lewis 2016: 480), yet the CoS still holds the financial ability to build expensive and lavish Orgs worldwide, particularly through its Ideal Org initiative. These buildings and their use of Scientologist imagery and symbols, when compared to the Free Zone, give the CoS a more visible presence in the public domain, allowing it to market itself to new members. The Ideal Orgs initiative extends beyond branding efforts, however, with the concept of an 'Ideal' Org tying in with the application of Standard Tech, aiming to ensure that all CoS Orgs provide consistent and high-standard auditing to practitioners. This is particularly notable with the opening of the Flag Building in 2013, which has shown a development in contemporary auditing through the establishment of the Super Power programme and Cause Resurgence Rundown. These programmes, aimed towards the most dedicated

OT level Scientologists, make use of technological devices and objects that are currently only available at the Flag Building, with CoS members worldwide being encouraged to make the journey to Flag and engage with new methods of auditing.

All of these factors culminate in Scientology's significant and rich material culture, demonstrating the ways in which the auditing practice straddles a hybrid social environment of religious and spiritual development on the one hand, and scientific procedure through technological devices, such as the E-Meter, on the other. These devices have become more than a distinctive visualization of Scientology and the auditing process – to use them is to 'do' Scientology.

7

Moving forward

Reflections on Free Zone Scientology and the wider study of religions

The primary purpose of this book is to advance studies of Scientology and new religions by using the auditing process as a vehicle to explore the dynamics of contemporary Free Zone communities. However, in the process of conducting this research, it became clear that the methods adopted and data gathered point to modern issues and frameworks that can be applied to other studies of contemporary religions. This chapter will reflect upon how the data analysed in the previous three chapters demonstrate that a double-focus on Free Zone and CoS understandings of auditing has presented a series of specificities with wider implications for the study of fluid and contemporary religions.

NRM studies and Religious Studies

Sociology, rather than anthropology, psychology or philosophy, has played the most prominent role in the study of NRMs. These sociological studies have been dominated by questions concerning typologies, including establishing the definitions and characteristics of different NRMs, and patterns of organization and leadership, as well as debates around conversion, brainwashing, secularization, globalization and media. While the approach adopted in this study engages with these issues, in positioning the auditing process as a hybrid practice that combines religious and secular-scientific elements, this research acts as a demonstration of how the study of practices as key elements can illuminate understandings of fluid forms of contemporary religion. In achieving this, the approach adopted in this book builds a bridge between established methods in sociological NRM studies and the wider study of religions (Religious Studies) as an interdisciplinary category of non-confessional academic methods focusing on the subject of religion (see Remus 1988; Sharpe 1988).[1]

In designing this research, I regarded the notion of Scientologies as forms of 'contemporary religion', equal to any form of 'traditional religion', as an attempt to avoid pandering to the 'World Religions Paradigm' (WRP), helpfully defined by Cotter and Robertson as 'a culturally constructed symbol, metaphor, or tool, that functions to simplify, for "good" or "ill", areas of human behaviour that have been deemed "religious"' (2016: 13).[2] Despite persistent critique in recent decades (Cotter and Robertson 2016; Fitzgerald 2000), the WRP continues to be a prominent force and topic of conversation surrounding the study of religions. In fact, the CoS's scientologyreligion.org website states that '[t]he world's foremost experts in the fields of comparative religion, history of religion, religious studies and sociology agree that Scientology is a *world religion*' (The Church of Scientology International n.d.-g: online, emphasis added). While the CoS' motivation to seek religious legitimacy from the academy and adopt the term is understandable, the WRP is potentially damaging to the status of NRMs in public discourse. The WRP typically covers 'the big five' – Christianity, Judaism, Hinduism, Islam and Buddhism (Cotter and Robertson 2016: 2), which in turn have been typically studied as sui generis models through Abrahamic and Western understandings of religion, often by privileged white male scholars (Fitzgerald 2000: 21–3; Knott 2005: 245).

This approach to the study of religions creates a distinction between a 'World Religion' and 'New Religious Movement', resulting in the NRM being treated as 'other', or even lesser. Moreover, the WRP creates little room to accommodate the study of emergent and fluid movements (as discussed in this book), giving further credence to the flawed understanding of religions as institutional and 'traditional' entities. In avoiding this, the study of NRMs must be considered an equal endeavour to the study of any majority group, in which scholars must attempt to set aside any cultural biases. Accordingly, the study documented in this book demonstrates how scholars can adopt qualitative methods and the perspective of 'lived religion' to challenge generalities that are often prompted by not only the WRP but understandings of NRMs as institutional embodiments of charisma (Cotter and Robertson 2016: 12). As this chapter will continue to demonstrate, framing Scientology's central practice of auditing through the lens of the self, authenticity and material culture highlights modern issues for scholars and sociologists of religion, particularly when considering notions of boundaries/fluidity, legitimacy and everyday practices.

Free Zone fluidity and the breakdown of routinized charisma

Perhaps the most notable typology in previous studies of Scientology (and new religions as a whole) is the notion of the charisma. L. Ron Hubbard's role as the 'Source' of Scientology, and the 'Model OT' (Westbrook 2019: 22), has positioned devotion and adherence to the founder at the centre of most understandings of Scientology. Indeed, in this regard Hubbard is an archetype of the 'charismatic leader', understood in the sociological study of NRMs as a figure who both attracts converts and rallies the support and admiration of their followers, who '*believe* that he or she possesses a very special (possibly divine) quality and that the followers are, as a consequence, willing to grant him or her a special kind of authority over them' (Barker 1992: 13, emphasis in original).

The lack of tradition, rules or authority to dictate charismatic leaders' behaviours results in an often unpredictable and unorthodox style of leadership. Devoted followers can be led to live in entirely new areas, leave behind family and/or possessions, and allow a number of aspects of their personal lives to be dictated (Barker 1992: 13; Chryssides 1999: 17). The influence of charismatic leaders can extend beyond NRMs to other aspects of society, such as political and economic structures, as exemplified in Weberian models. Weber views charismatic figures as self-appointed leaders that become a source of comfort and knowledge for their followers (Gerth and Mills 1948: 52). Weber added that such a leader does not establish their position through democratic elections; rather, 'it is the *duty* of those to whom he addresses his mission to recognize him as their charismatically qualified leader' (Weber [1948] 1991c: 246–7, emphasis in original).

This recognition of Hubbard as the 'charismatically qualified leader' has been at the centre of institutional Church of Scientology (CoS) practices, activities and frameworks. Hubbard's irrefutable status as the originator of the precise application of Scientology is shown through adherence to the *Keeping Scientology Working* (KSW) policy (Westbrook 2019: 124). Moreover, personal commitment and devotion to Hubbard's work and cause of Scientology (to spread the tech) is perhaps most significantly demonstrated by the signing of the 'billion-year contract' for Sea Org members, a 'symbolic commitment of the individual beyond their present earthly existence' (Melton 2018: 34). Scholarly inspections of these aspects of the Scientology have been approached through institutional frameworks, most specifically the Weberian model of routinized charisma, which focus analyses not on charismatic figures themselves, but on the institutional and materialistic ways their charisma manifests itself in social history (Gerth and Mills 1948: 54). Charismatic leaders have the power to implement new laws and practices in these movements, such as KSW, some of which may be viewed as radical or unusual to the social environment of the time. Yet Weber argues that, particularly following the death of the charismatic leader, the movement and its practices would succumb to routinization, in which '*rules* in some form always come to govern' (Weber [1948] 1991b: 297, emphasis in original). Indeed, this Weberian approach to routinized/institutional understandings of Scientology has become a common feature of NRM studies as a whole. Since the death of Hubbard, the CoS' emphasis on rules and institutional structure has become even more rigorous, with the increased emphasis on offshoot organizations (such as the Religious Technology Center and the Church of Scientology International) (Lewis 2016: 479–80; Westbrook 2019: 165). As I argued in Chapter 5, the establishment of the Religious Technology Center as an institutional embodiment of Hubbard's tech has assisted David Miscavige in strengthening his authority as the leader of the CoS, in which he is now viewed as a 'tireless advocate for [Hubbard] and the rightful heir to lead the religion' (Westbrook 2019: 172). As such, he is not an equally charismatic figure as the founder; rather, he derives authority from Hubbard's charisma as routinized through the CoS. Much of contemporary scholarship on Scientology (in addition to other new religions) has drawn from this routinized/institutional model, yet an analysis of Free Zone Scientology demonstrates how examining fluid forms of religion can illuminate nuanced approaches to charisma and the ways in which the teachings of the founder are both valued and applied in everyday life.

I do not intend to imply that the study of Scientology from an institutional perspective is a flawed approach. Indeed, studies of the institutional frameworks of the CoS have been invaluable in developing a scholarly understanding of Scientology's history, while also providing a rigorous bed of knowledge which has contributed to my contrast between the top-down hierarchy of the CoS and fluid-horizontal nature of the Free Zone throughout this book. I do believe, however, that the study of Free Zone Scientology, particularly its contrast with the CoS, has pointed to a breakdown in routinized charisma, and a period of time since the death of the charismatic leader in which he is now regarded with varying levels of devotion across the Free Zone.

There is very little 'routine', bureaucracy or even institutions in Free Zone spheres. Perhaps the most comparable to the CoS is Ron's Org, the Free Zone group founded by Captain Bill Robertson intending to deliver its perceived vision of Standard Tech outside the CoS. The significant majority of Freezoners interviewed for this book, however, performs an individualized version of

Scientology. While the Free Zone can often be viewed as 'attempting in effect to regain the charisma that they originally saw in L. Ron Hubbard' (Singler 2017: 65), my research points to the prevailing presence of innovation, creativity and distancing from the charismatic presence of Hubbard as the originator of the tech. This creativity and deviation from the founder's teaching are exemplars of modern issues for NRMs; they point not only to how spiritual teachings have been interpreted or adapted but also the ways in which schisms emerge and interact with one another, particularly through online mediums. A potential consequence for the charismatic leader is the 'loss of charisma', the possibility that a leader may lose their charismatic image amongst followers, and as a result may lose authority within the movement (Wessinger 2012: 88). In this case, however, Hubbard has not lost authority within the movement he established (the CoS); rather, his practices are adapted and used within communities unbound by routinized and institutional structures, often by individuals introduced to the practice subsequent to his death. Fieldwork conversations cited in the previous three chapters demonstrate that this breakdown in organizational structures is directly related to conducting practices and 'doing religion'. Accordingly, studies of fluidity in new religions adapting to modern issues are enhanced by focusing on religion as it is lived, and not dictated by top-down routinized authorities.

Lived religion, objects and 'doing Scientology'

Top-down hierarchy has been a defining feature in not only how the CoS is bureaucratically organized but also how the organization intends for the practice of Scientology to be applied across the world. Initiatives such as the *Golden Age of Knowledge* and *Golden Age of Tech Phase II*, in addition to the building of Ideal Orgs, are intended to ensure a precise and identical application of auditing across all CoS Orgs. In terms of conducting a study of an NRM from the perspective of 'lived religion', the institutional aspect of the CoS (in addition to other groups) can present challenges, as Gregg and Scholefield observe, 'it is highly likely that you as an individual or a class group will be welcomed at any CoS around the world. . . . However, it is equally likely that you will only encounter a very limited aspect of the lived lives of Scientologists' (2015: 61).

Indeed, the CoS has become increasingly encouraging of scholars conducting fieldwork and organizing field trips for undergraduate students (see Westbrook 2019: 9), yet these experiences are likely to be highly structured, and even rehearsed, in advance. While a potentially frustrating aspect of examining religions in the field can involve 'ordinary' practitioners, in response to researcher's questions, deferring to texts or religious leaders whom they deem to be more knowledgeable (Harvey 2011: 234), my experience with the CoS was the opposite of this. During my field visits to the CoS I was not given the opportunity to meet a single 'ordinary' or 'everyday' practitioner not employed by the CoS. Rather, all my participants were current or former staff members. This prohibited me from gaining an understanding of the lived lives of ordinary members of the CoS, including learning of their personal experiences of the auditing process. Furthermore, when I expressed an interest in attending Dianetic training evenings that were advertised in the CoS, I was told that I would be welcome to attend but that it would need to be for my own personal benefit, not for scholarly interpretation.[3] Such challenges of being presented with 'the choir' when working with any institutional group are to be expected. However, the data gathered in the three previous chapters demonstrate how honing-in on non-institutional forms of contemporary and emergent religions can offer not only a more thorough avenue to explore the everyday lives of religious agents but also illuminate the fluidity of these movements.

Fluidity is prompted by practices, rather than devotion to a singular leader or teaching. The emergence of new types of Scientologies in the Free Zone demonstrates how fluidity and schisms can be prompted by the creativity possible through the lack of restriction from top-down hierarchies, and that the studies of this creativity are the key to understanding the dynamics between such groups. For example, Harvey explains that the most fitting approach to the study of religions is to 'treat religions as the lived realities of those who associate themselves with those lifeways – or even with the names people use to identify religions' (2014: 60), emphasizing the need to focus on studying religions as they are identified and practised by the individuals or communities in question. Indeed, as the breakdown of routinization in the Free Zone demonstrates, scholars should not consider the 'acts or ideals of founders and elites as definitive' (2014: 60), rather focus their attention on the lived reality of people's lives.

My analysis of fluid groups adapting to modern issues is rooted in Primiano's notion of 'vernacular religion', which he described as 'religion as it is lived: as human beings encounter, understand, interpret, and practice it' (1995: 44). In a critique of scholars that create a distinction between the personal lives of religious practitioners and elite religious institutions, Primiano combines all aspects of religiosity under the category of vernacular religion, which allows scholars to view religions not as 'institutionalized truths but in individual creativity' (Bowman and Valk 2014: 17). While the research conducted for this book predominantly adopted qualitative methods, it has been informed by the approaches of lived and vernacular religion. My conversations with Free Zone Scientologists, particularly those who do not belong to an organized Free Zone group, concerned how the nuanced practice of Free Zone auditing is informed by individual interpretation of Hubbard's work. This creative expression of auditing is a demonstration of contemporary Scientology as lived religion and the ways in which the dynamics of Free Zone Scientology and its practices are shaped by its practitioners.

One of the more effective methods of engaging with the lived realities of everyday individuals is close inspection of the objects and material culture with which they engage. For Free Zone Scientology, the creativity connected to the creation of new E-Meters (and occasionally a rejection of its use) is directly tied to Free Zone understandings of 'what Scientology is'. This results in simultaneous boundaries (between groups insisting on a specific application of Scientology) and fluidity (involving collaboration between Freezoners innovating E-Meters to their own specifications).

This study points to another modern issue concerning lived religion for fluid groups – the internet and online communities. On a basic level, Free Zone use of the internet acts as an interesting case study of a minority schism rebelling against an institutional body, specifically its public dissemination of Hubbard's works, teachings and publications – often with disregard for copyrights and potential litigation from the CoS (see Schorey 2016; Singler 2017: 65). This use of online resources is primarily concerned with controlling Hubbard's work and laying claim to the true tech, but it also acts as an outlet for Freezoners to publicly air grievances with the CoS.

Beyond the use of the internet and a tool for self-promotion, this research has explored examples of how the internet is used to 'do' Scientology (such as online auditing sessions). For a considerable number of Freezoners, the internet is their primary method of conducting auditing sessions and interacting with other Scientologists. Whether they are auditing Scientologist practitioners or 'clients' who do not identify as Scientologists, they are applying Hubbard's theories and practices through methods he could not possibly have anticipated when writing his original Dianetic theories. By interacting with Preclears online and establishing their own auditing practices, Freezoners often use their independence as an opportunity to discard teachings they do not deem useful and 'pick and choose' beliefs and practices from Hubbard's work.

For scholars of religion this introduces an interesting angle. In the same vein as social media's ability to connect individuals sharing niche interests across the globe (Stout 2012: 81), the internet is now entwined with the notion of lived religion and 'doing' religion. Recent years have seen the emergence of a plethora of communities revolving around the creation of online mythology and 'invented' religion (see Asimos Forthcoming: 2021; Cusack 2010; Singler 2017). The example of Free Zone Scientology, however, as a movement that existed before the establishment of the internet, is a valuable case study for scholars of new and emergent religions to witness the transition of a movement beyond the death of its founder and into the twenty-first century, wherein online methods are involved in shaping and developing its practices in new and often unexpected ways.

Concluding remarks

This chapter has demonstrated how the data and frameworks established in this book can be transported to other studies of contemporary religion. Approaching this study involved a distancing from the typologies that have dominated conversations in the sociological study of NRMs and making use of the 'lived religion' approach from the wider study of religions. Accordingly, honing-in on fluid-horizontal movements, rather than top-down institutional projections, allows scholars to explore emergent and schismatic forms of religions that emerge based on practices, objects and beliefs which are undictated by hierarchies. In the case of Free Zone Scientology, this has prompted a breakdown in the Weberian model of routinized charisma, wherein Freezoners have adopted Hubbard's practices in an individualized fashion, rather than practising strict adherence to the founder's teachings. Simultaneously, however, boundaries have emerged within this fluid environment regarding the issues of authenticity, the self and materiality. This has presented the Free Zone not as a singular unified movement in opposition to the CoS (as it is often understood in public discourse), but a broad range of groups and individuals with fluid approaches to Scientology.

This fluidity is best approached through the method of lived and vernacular religion. For scholars attempting to penetrate the often complicated and contested nature of fluid movements, the dynamics between such groups can be understood through their engagement with material culture and objects. Furthermore, issues pertaining to the internet and online communication point to global communication in minority groups and creative innovation in religious practices. This creativity contributes further to the fluid and diverse nature of contemporary religion. Simply put, focusing on the core practices of Free Zone Scientology acts as an informative case study for scholars seeking to explore the breakdown of institutional charisma and boundaries in the twenty-first century.

8

Conclusion

Throughout this book I have explored the fluid and non-hierarchical nature of Free Zone Scientology, as demonstrated by the nuanced nature of auditing in contemporary Scientologies, including both the CoS and the Free Zone. While conducting this research, it became clear that the present discourse across Free Zone Scientologies regarding the nature of auditing highlights three prominent aspects of contemporary Scientology – namely the Scientologist understanding of the self, issues of authenticity and the material culture of Scientology. By examining auditing in relation to these areas, this study has demonstrated the dominant role auditing plays in the dynamics of not only the CoS' relationship with the Free Zone but the emergence of new types of Scientologies within the Free Zone.

Auditing is a practice that lies at the core of Scientology. By establishing the process in *Dianetics: The Modern Science of Mental Health* (*DMSMH*) in 1950 as a method of overcoming mental neuroses, L. Ron Hubbard set in motion a movement that would grow worldwide. Despite Hubbard's original intention to position the process as a precise scientific practice, his continuation of research into the human mind resulted in his discovery of the thetan, the true spiritual self (Hubbard [1952] 2007c: 61). With his research on the thetan in place, the auditing process became repositioned as a hybrid practice of religious and scientific discourses and led to the establishment of Scientology in the form of the CoS.

One of the challenges faced by scholars researching Scientology is the lack of academic work from which they can draw their research. Beginning with Roy Wallis' *The Road to Total Freedom* in 1976, scholarship on Scientology has been sparse, yet it has been observed that of late more scholars are beginning to turn their attention towards Scientology as a subject for academic study (Westbrook 2019: 10). I argued at the beginning of this book, however, that academic research on Scientology has been dominated by studies of the institutional CoS.

This can be attributed to the prevailing narrative of the CoS, which positions itself as being synonymous with the concept of Scientology (see also Gregg and Thomas 2019: 350).

The scholarly community has paid little attention to the Free Zone, with all existing monographs on Scientology concerning the institutional CoS. Following a brief period of inactivity after Wallis' work and Whitehead's *Renunciation and Reformulation* (1987), the beginning of the twenty-first century has seen a relative boom in monographs concerning Scientology. These studies, most notably those by Urban (2011), Melton (2000) and Westbrook (2019), provide comprehensive historical accounts of Scientology but are limited to the CoS. Similarly, edited volumes on Scientology (see Lewis 2009b) have also placed emphasis on vertical approaches to the study of Scientology. This book, however, has challenged this institutional understanding of Scientology by using the auditing process to demonstrate the horizontal and fluid forms of contemporary Scientology that exist in the Free Zone. Until now, the most detailed scholarly inspection of the auditing process was that of Whitehead (1987), which explored the process within the CoS during the 1980s. It is my hope that this book both compliments and builds upon Whitehead's work by exploring not only the changes in CoS auditing since its publication (particularly the *Golden Age of Tech Phase II*) but how the discourse surrounding the application of auditing has had a direct impact on the emergence of new and often-unregulated Scientologies outside the CoS.

While recent years have given rise to a small pool of scholarship on the Free Zone (Cusack 2016; Hellesøy 2016; Lewis 2013), the category remains largely unexplored. Accordingly, this research is intended to contribute to an academic conversation in its very early stages. It achieves this by considering the notion of 'Scientologies' – the existence of different types of Scientology in both CoS and Free Zone spaces. Through an examination of the nuanced nature of auditing across a range of Scientologies, this book sheds light on the diversity amongst different Scientologist communities pertaining to their understanding, interpretation and application of the practice. With the number of Scientologists practising in the Free Zone estimated to be rising (Lewis 2016: 480), the study of Free Zone communities is becoming increasingly important to the scholar considering the contemporary Scientologist landscape. Accordingly, answering the question of 'what Scientology is' requires more than an analysis of only the institutional CoS. Furthermore, this study of fluid and unregulated forms of Scientology points to wider issues in the contemporary study of New Religious Movements (NRMs), including the schisms and offshoots that can emerge following the death of the charismatic leader.

This book has drawn from established qualitative methods in the study of religions, with a particular emphasis on vernacular and lived religion, focusing on religion as something people 'do' (Primiano 1995; Bowman and Valk 2014). Using this approach, this research has examined the lived reality of auditing across different Scientologies by balancing institutionalized understandings of 'what auditing is', with a bottom-up approach of how auditing is practised by everyday Scientologists, both within the CoS and Free Zone. Throughout my research I conducted fieldwork with Scientologists, albeit through different approaches. During my work with the CoS I visited two Orgs – the Church of Scientology of London, and the Saint Hill Advanced Org at East Grinstead, UK. Visiting these locations gave me the opportunity to conduct participant observation, meet with CoS members and engage with Scientology's material culture. Due to the wide scattering of small Free Zone groups and individuals across the world, however, my fieldwork with the Free Zone was conducted entirely online. Through this method, I was able to conduct formal interviews through online programmes, such as Skype, and additionally maintain conversations with participants via email in the months following our interviews.

Auditing and notions of self

When conducting a study of Scientology, scholars are introduced to a wealth of specialized and often complex writing by Hubbard. Engaging with these materials becomes essential in a study of auditing, as they provide the theoretical foundations upon which Hubbard based the auditing process. Of particular importance to the contemporary practice of auditing across Scientologies is the Scientologist understanding of the self. In his theory of the 'Parts of Man', Hubbard ([1956] 2007: 65) taught that the individual consists of the body, the mind and the thetan. Despite consisting of these three parts, Scientology teaches that the thetan, the spiritual self, is the 'true' self in Scientology, with the body and the mind being mere aspects of the physical MEST universe. The liberation of the thetan from MEST, as achieved through auditing, is the ultimate goal of Scientology, granting the thetan complete control of the mind, body and all other aspects of the physical universe. Building upon his work on the spiritual nature of humanity, Hubbard ([1951] 2007d) developed a series of specialized theories on the nature of the self, such as the ARC Triangle and Tone Scale, which have become the foundations of how auditing is conducted. Understanding these methods has become a crucial aspect of the Scientologist's journey on the Bridge, particularly those who are training to be professional auditors. Accordingly, the Scientologist understanding of the self informs the application of auditing, with its meshing of spiritual and theoretical ideas demonstrating the process as a hybrid practice of religious and secular-scientific methods.

Previous scholarship on auditing (Harley and Kieffer 2009; Whitehead 1987) has concentrated on the process in its 'traditional' form in the CoS, namely the question and answer method laid out by Hubbard ([1950] 2007b) in *DMSMH*, with a focus on the treatment of the human mind. However, my fieldwork with the CoS demonstrated that the contemporary understanding of auditing extends beyond sessions between an auditor and a Preclear. My participants emphasized the importance of the Purification Rundown, the Scientologist detoxification programme, to the auditing process, stating that one's engagement with the auditing process would be less efficient without 'doing the Purif'. Most notably, one CoS staff member remarked that the Purif is a form of auditing in itself.

Through engaging with the Purification Rundown's specialized diet, exercise routines and spending time in a sauna, Scientologists prepare for spiritual development by removing remnants of drugs and toxins in the body. This focus on working on the body through the Purif is particularly noteworthy, presenting a contrast between Hubbard's work on overcoming the physical universe, and the ways this is achieved through physical methods. Accordingly, the notion of 'auditing' in the contemporary CoS is more nuanced than it may at first seem, with the Purif being positioned as an essential practice.

The importance of the Purif in the CoS is enhanced by the presence of Purification Centres at its Orgs, which give practitioners access to the equipment and facilities needed to engage with the programme. This is a contrast to many Scientologies in the Free Zone who, for the most part, do not operate in established Orgs. Most of my participants, particularly those who audit independently, view the Purif as simply a supplement to Scientologist practice, rather choosing to encourage healthy lifestyles to their clients instead. For example, Ron's Org makes use of public saunas in its Purif programme, yet does not view the practice as vital, choosing instead to emphasize the importance of progressing Hubbard's Bridge to Total Freedom through standard auditing methods.

The primary purpose of the auditing process is to traverse the Bridge to Total Freedom, developing the spiritual self through the stages of Preclear, Clear and Operating Thetan. Across the different Scientologies I encountered in my fieldwork, this was the most important aspect of Scientology to my participants. While some Free Zone Scientologists do not follow Hubbard's Bridge precisely, the emphasis on spiritual liberation and overcoming mental neuroses remains the primary purpose of their practice. Accordingly, the Scientologist notion of the self, both physically and spiritually, lies at the core of auditing and offers an avenue through which contemporary forms of Scientology can be explored.

Authenticity and innovation: Standard tech, squirrelling and the control of Hubbard's work

The practice of auditing across contemporary forms of Scientology, I have argued, is the primary factor in clarifying boundaries between different types of Scientologies. By publishing the *Keeping Scientology Working* policy in 1965, condemning those who alter the tech and practise Scientology outside the CoS, Hubbard established the foundations of the notion of 'squirrelling', a form of Scientological heresy (Hubbard 1965a: 6; Schorey 2016: 341). It has been previously observed that Free Zone communities have drawn their legitimacy from adherence to Standard Tech, accusing the contemporary CoS of squirrelling through altering Hubbard's original work (Hellesøy 2016; Lewis 2016). Throughout this book I have built upon this understanding, demonstrating that the notion of the 'Free Zone' is a diverse category of different views and interpretations of Standard Tech, with some Free Zone groups accusing one another of squirrelling, a term previously applied by the CoS to all Free Zone Scientologists.

While the research of Hellesøy (2016) and Lewis (2016) focuses on institutionalized Free Zone organizations, specifically Ron's Org and the Dror Center, I have positioned my research to pay close attention to individualized forms of Free Zone Scientology, particularly independent auditors who practise Scientology with no connections with a regulatory body. Through this approach, I discovered that the Free Zone is a fluid social environment, in which Scientologists and auditors unrestricted by administrative institutions use the opportunity to develop their own versions and applications of Hubbard's tech. This results in the contemporary practice of auditing being dominated by the issue of authenticity and innovation, creating boundaries between Scientologies that lay claim to a 'true' understanding of Hubbard on the one hand, and those choosing to innovate the tech on the other.

Laying claim to the 'true' Hubbard for several Scientologies involves the development of strategies for the interpretation of his work. This is particularly evident in relation to the recent *Golden Age of Knowledge* and *Golden Age of Tech*

Phase II initiatives launched by the CoS and its current leader, David Miscavige, through which Hubbard's work has been entirely republished to create Hubbard's true 'canon'. This has resulted in changes in how auditors are trained and how auditing is conducted. These amendments are positioned by the CoS as not only being a more efficient method of auditing but also being the entirely correct application of the tech according to the intention of Hubbard. Through Miscavige's leadership of the Religious Technology Center, an institution dedicated to preserving the tech according to Hubbard's alleged intentions, the CoS demonstrates Weber's ([1948] 1991b) routinization of charisma by becoming the institutional embodiment of Hubbard's work.

Free Zone reactions to the *Golden Age* initiatives have been less than favourable, with several of my fieldwork participants expressing caution regarding the republishing of Hubbard's work, as exemplified by Ron's Org's use of the 1969 edition of *DMSMH*. Yet the boundaries based on the application of the tech are particularly prevalent in Free Zone Scientology itself, as exemplified by one of my fieldwork participants' assertion that 'there are people who are with "with-LRH". And the people who are not'. While Free Zone boundaries can't be summarized with this level of simplicity, this observation displays the ways in which Hubbard's work can be used by Scientologists in establishing their superiority as 'true' Scientology. This is particularly highlighted by the division between the 'Free Zone' community associated with Captain Bill Robertson, typically Scientologists who left the CoS in the early 1980s, and the 'Independent Scientologists' (or 'Indies'), who left the CoS during the leadership of David Miscavige (Lewis 2016: 466).

The data analysed in this work demonstrate that the notion of 'Free Zone Scientology' cannot be simply defined as 'Scientology outside the CoS', with the category covering a large number of boundaries and understandings of 'what Scientology is', and different perceptions of where significant divisions lie. These boundaries all depend on how auditing is practised within these groups, creating divisions between 'purists' controlling Hubbard's work in asserting their status as Scientology according to Hubbard, and the those using the freedom of the Free Zone to innovate Scientology according to their own ideas.

Technology, devices and things

A distinctive aspect of Scientologist nomenclature is the use of the word 'tech' as an overarching term for both Hubbard's theories and practices, in addition to the technological devices used in Scientology. Similar to the treatment of the body through the Purif, the focus on spiritual development in auditing is assisted and executed through the use of material objects in the physical universe. The discourse of authenticity across Scientologies is reflected in the material culture of Scientology, with technological devices and objects being utilized in both the CoS and Free Zone communities, intended to assist in the auditing practice.

Auditing sessions conducted through the use of technological devices are primarily achieved through the use of the E-Meter, a device that is believed to detect the presence of engrams in the human mind across the whole track, the complete timeline of an individual's current and past lives. Hubbard presented the E-Meter as an entirely infallible device, even attributing agency to it in his recorded lectures (Hubbard [1961] 2013). Accordingly, professional auditors are rigorously trained to use the E-Meter correctly, with the device now becoming an essential tool in auditing in the CoS, in addition to other Scientologies in the Free Zone.

During my fieldwork I was given a stress test on the Mark Ultra VIII, the latest model used in the CoS. However, there are a significant number of different types of E-Meters being used in the Free Zone. Many of these models can be purchased online, resulting in a marketplace of various E-Meters with different features and customizations. Although the E-Meter has become widely recognized as an essential device in auditing practice, my fieldwork indicated a more relaxed attitude towards the use of the device in the Free Zone when compared with the CoS. My interviews ranged from Free Zone Scientologists who view the E-Meter as a beneficial, yet not essential, device, to those who view the device as completely unnecessary. Perhaps most notably, Owen stated that the E-Meter is simply an aid for inexperienced auditors and has ceased to use the device altogether, choosing to audit his clients via online video chat methods, a radical departure from the 'traditional' method of auditing in-person. The different interpretations of the importance of the E-Meter point towards different methods of auditing in contemporary Scientology, demonstrating that previous understandings of auditing do not necessarily reflect the realities of everyday practice amongst Scientologists.

Further to the use of the E-Meter, the CoS has recently introduced the Super Power programme and Cause Resurgence Rundown at the Flag Building in Clearwater. These programmes, intended to enhance the spiritual capabilities of the thetan, have been presented by the CoS as being new methods of auditing for advanced Scientologists who have reached the OT levels, and make use of technological devices, such as the Motion Quadrant chair (Lockwood 2016: 188; Ortega 2012a). These devices, when coupled with the E-Meter, point to the hybridity of auditing as a practice drawing from religious and secular-scientific methods, and as a process considered to be equally religious and scientific. Thus, the material culture of Scientology is more than a visual expression of Scientology; it is at the centre of the auditing process, and is an essential aspect of the contemporary Scientologist landscape.

Future studies of Scientology and contemporary religions

If Lewis (2016: 480) is correct in his assertion that CoS membership is indeed in decline, while numbers of Free Zone Scientologists continue to rise, then scholars wishing to understand the contemporary Scientologist landscape must consider the practice in both CoS and Free Zone spheres. The auditing process, as this book has argued, serves as a useful method for understanding the complexities of present-day Scientology, illustrating the nuanced nature of the practice across Scientologies, including the boundaries, objects, methodologies and theories involved in its application.

Beyond its value to the study of Scientology, this work makes a significant and original contribution to the wider study of religions. Through adopting the approach of lived religion, this research moves away from the typologies that have previously dominated the sociology of NRMs, that have stressed the power of institutionalized new religions over their followers (charisma and brainwashing) and (at the same time) the powerlessness of religions in the face of a globalizing modernity (the secularization thesis). In this book I have contrasted the vertical, top-down authority of the CoS against the flatter, more horizontal forms of auditing to be found in the Free Zone. Maintaining a double-focus on this vertical-horizontal axis has opened the study of Scientology to new questions and a new emphasis on lived Scientologies outside the CoS, complicating questions of power and authority and re-framing them in terms of authenticity, innovation and materiality. These new frames are portable and can be applied beyond the CoS and the Free Zone. They possess broader societal implications in relation to understanding how institutions try to control and protect knowledge and methods, and the ways in which people attempt to sidestep and subvert this.

Appendix A

A timeline of key Scientologist events and publications

1911: L. Ron Hubbard is born on 13 March.

1923: Hubbard meets Joseph 'Snake' Thompson, who introduces him to the psychology of the human mind.

1934: Hubbard's first pulp fiction novella, *The Green God*, is published in *Thrilling Adventures*.

1938: After establishing himself as a popular writer, Hubbard begins to publish for *Astounding Science Fiction* magazine.

1938: Hubbard writes his *Excalibur* manuscript, in which he documents his near-death experience that he believed revealed esoteric knowledge regarding the human goal of human survival.

1948: Hubbard documents his initial work on (and outline of) Dianetics and the human mind in *The Original Thesis*, which is circulated privately amongst friends and the science fiction community.

1950: The first public article on Dianetics and auditing, *Dianetics: A New Science of the Mind* is published in *Astounding Science Fiction* magazine.

1950: Soon after the popular response to the account in *Astounding Science Fiction*, Hubbard published *Dianetics: The Modern Science of Mental Health*, the first publicly available book on Dianetic theory and auditing. It arguably continues to be the most important book in Scientologist practice to the present day.

1951: Following the growth of the Dianetic movement, Hubbard develops the auditing process and establishes the practice of Scientology.

1952: Hubbard publishes *What to Audit* highlighting the increasing religiosity of the auditing process. In this book Hubbard introduces the concept of the thetan, Technique 88, the use of the E-Meter during auditing and the relationship between the thetan and MEST universe.

1954: Hubbard opens the first Church of Scientology in Los Angeles, California.

1958: *Have You Lived Before This Life?* is published, consisting of accounts of past life experiences from Scientologists during their auditing sessions.

1959: Hubbard purchases the Saint Hill Manor, which would go on to become a pilgrimage site for Scientologists and the location of the Saint Hill Advanced Org.

1975: The Church of Scientology's spiritual headquarters, the Flag Service Organization (Flag) is established in Clearwater, Florida.

1982: Captain Bill Robertson, a close friend and ally of Hubbard's, claims to have received extra-terrestrial knowledge that leads to the establishment of the 'Free Zone', the practice of Scientology outside the institutionalized Church of Scientology.

1984: Ron's Org, the first major Free Zone movement, is formed by Robertson, with an emphasis on preserving Hubbard's work and the 'Standard Tech'.

1986: On 24 January L. Ron Hubbard dies.

1987: David Miscavige is elected to the role of leader of the Church of Scientology, a position he holds to the present day.

1991: *Time Magazine* publishes its highly controversial account of the Church of Scientology – *Scientology: The Thriving Cult of Greed and Power*.

1993: The Internal Revenue Service (IRS) grants tax-exempt status to the Church of Scientology in the USA.

2005: David Miscavige announces the *Golden Age of Knowledge*, a restoration Hubbard's original texts and lectures

2008: A confidential Scientology promotional video featuring Tom Cruise is leaked online and becomes the subject of much publicity.

2013: David Miscavige announces the *Golden Age of Tech Phase II*, the distribution of Hubbard's tech according to the *Golden Age of Knowledge* as standard practice in all Scientology Orgs.

2013: The Flag Building opens in Clearwater, Florida, featuring dedicated facilities to be used in the Super Power programme and Cause Resurgence Rundown.

2015: The controversial anti-Scientologist film, *Going Clear: Scientology and the Prison of Belief*, is released.

Appendix B

Key terms

Analytical Mind: The conscious part of the human brain that rationally processes information.

Auditing: The practice upon which Scientology was founded. A form of psychotherapy that involves the removal of engrams from the patient's mind through a series of questions and answers regarding personal traumas.

Auditor: A trained individual that conducts the auditing sessions and leads the Preclear through a series of questions.

Clear: A state achieved through auditing; when the Preclear is no longer affected by their engrams.

Dianetics: L. Ron Hubbard's theory on the human mind, upon which auditing is based.

E-Meter: An electronic device used to measure and detect the presence of engrams during auditing session, thus improving its efficacy.

Engram: Hubbard's term for the traces of negative psychoses in the human mind, which can be removed through auditing.

Fair Game: A policy targeting enemies of the Church of Scientology.

Free Zone: An umbrella category for certain Scientologists (and Scientologist groups) practising Scientology outside the institutional Church of Scientology.

Lock: The past experiences of mental pain with which the engram is associated.

MEST: 'Matter; Energy; Space and Time'. The physical aspects of the universe which contain and damage the thetan.

Operating Thetan (OT): The advanced stages of spiritual development attained beyond the state of Clear through auditing.

Org: The Scientologist name for a missionary church.

Preclear: An individual that is affected by the negative consequences of their engrams.

Reactive Mind: Also known as the 'engrams bank'; a subconscious part of the human brain in which engrams are stored.

Religious Technology Center: An organization aims to ensure the precise application of Hubbard's tech across all Church of Scientology Orgs worldwide.

Scientology: The name given to Hubbard's New Religious Movement, meaning 'knowing about knowing' or 'science of knowledge'.

Sea Org: A community of the most prestigious members of the Church of Scientology, known for being a form of naval force with its own sea vessels.

Squirrelling: A Church of Scientology term for the act of practising Scientology outside the institutional Church.

Suppressive Person: An individual declared an enemy of the Church of Scientology.

Tech: All-encompassing term for Hubbard's theories and practices.

Technique 88: The method of identifying, locating and auditing the thetan.

Thetan: Considered by Scientology to be the 'true self', comparable to the concept of the soul.

Time Track: A complete timeline of an individual's memories.

Whole Track: The complete collection of an individual's time-tracks across the entirety of their past lives.

Xenu Documents: A collection of highly controversial documents containing esoteric knowledge allegedly distributed amongst Scientologists who have reached Operating Thetan III (OTIII) and beyond. They are said to describe the narrative of the arrival of thetans on Earth through the intervention of an intergalactic warlord named Xenu.

Notes

Chapter 1

1 INFORM is a charity-based organization, founded by Eileen Barker, specializing in the public dissemination of information on new and minority religions. Informed by academic research, INFORM responds to public enquiries, works directly with sensitive issues involving NRMs and informs government bodies.
2 There are large volumes of leaked Scientologist documents available on websites such as 'WikiLeaks', including organizational, legal and financial documents (WikiLeaks n.d.-b).
3 Following the completion of my PhD, one of my Church of Scientology contacts expressed a slight disappointment that I had acknowledged the existence of the OT III documents in my thesis. He did, however, seem to be pleased that I did not quote from the documents and also acknowledged the potential of the documents having been edited to discredit and undermine Scientologist beliefs.

Chapter 2

1 More detailed and comprehensive accounts of Hubbard's early life can be found in Christensen (2005), Westbrook (2019) and Melton (2009).
2 *Dianetics: The Original Thesis* was publicly published in 1951, a year following the release of *Dianetics: The Modern Science of Mental Health* (see Hubbard [1951] 2007b).
3 Such pejorative terms and attitudes were also adopted by Hubbard, who described gay Preclears as 'sexual pervert[s]' in *Dianetics: The Modern Science of Mental Health* ([1950] 2007b: 125). Hubbard's views and work concerning the LGBTQ+ community, and approaches to sexuality in Scientologies (both Free Zone and CoS) are explored further in Chapter 4.
4 During the early Dianetics period Hubbard was critical of organized religion, particularly institutional forms of Christianity, claiming in 1952 that they manipulated their practitioners through forced-guilt via the concept of sin (Urban 2011: 57).
5 The term 'Scientology' is derived from the words 'scio' (Latin for 'knowing') and 'logos' (Greek for 'study of') (Hubbard [1956] 2007: 5).

6   Most Sea Org members in the contemporary CoS operate on land, yet still hold naval titles and wear maritime uniforms (The Church of Scientology International 1998: 323). The Sea Org still makes use of ships, however, most notably the *Freewinds*.

Chapter 3

1   The Basic Books are *Dianetics: The Original Thesis* (1948 – publicly in [1951], 2007b); *Dianetics: The Evolution of a Science* ([1950], 2007a); *Dianetics: The Modern Science of Mental Health* ([1950], 2007b); *Science of Survival* ([1951], 2007d); *Self Analysis* ([1951], 1983); *Advanced Procedure and Axioms* ([1951], 2007a); *Handbook for Preclears* ([1951], 2007c); *Scientology: A History of Man*, originally published as *What to Audit* ([1952], 2007c); *Scientology 8-80* ([1952], 2007a); *Scientology 8-8008* ([1952], 2007b); *The Creation of Human Ability* ([1954], 2007a); *Dianetics 55!: The Complete Manual of Human Communications* ([1954], 2007b); and *Scientology: The Fundamentals of Thought* ([1956], 2007).

Chapter 5

1   Throughout my research, the only Scientologists I have witnessed referring to the founder as simply 'Hubbard' are in the Free Zone.
2   A Scientologist disciplinary programme intended to improve behaviour (Urban 2011: 125).

Chapter 6

1   Introduced by Hubbard during the 1950s, the eight-pointed Scientology Cross bears, according to Urban, a 'striking resemblance' (2011: 67) to the eight-pointed cross of the Hermetic Order of the Golden Dawn, a group based on occultism and magic which included Aleister Crowley, with whom Hubbard was acquainted. The CoS is keen to note, however, that the Scientology Cross is distinctive in its use of its eight points to demonstrate the 'Eight Dynamics' of human existence (The Church of Scientology International n.d.-j), which Scientologists aim to work through via auditing.
2   The TRs are the specific skills utilized by the auditor during the session and are all numbered for the specific skill they denote. These TRs include TR-2, which is a

practice of acknowledging the communication received from the Preclear, and TR-4, which allows the auditor to distinguish between the 'originations' and personal distractions of the Preclear (Whitehead 1987: 138–9).

Chapter 7

1. When discussing the interdisciplinary category of 'Religious Studies', I often make use of the term 'Study of Religions' in an attempt to avoid confusion between a 'religious' theological study, and a non-confessional study of religions. Other scholars (see Fitzgerald 2000, 2003) have expressed similar concerns regarding the term 'Religious Studies'.
2. The World Religions Paradigm has previously been useful as an introductory teaching tool for undergraduate students, particularly the work of Ninian Smart (1993), yet this can present generalities. Much like how 'many "Christianities" become "Christianity"' (Cotter and Robertson 2016: 12), focusing instead on lived religion allows for a study of Scientologies rather than only the institutional CoS.
3. My personal conversations with other scholars of NRMs have pointed towards similar experiences of a lack of opportunity to speak to 'everyday' Scientologists when conducting fieldwork at CoS Orgs.

References

An Introduction to Scientology (2006), Dir. Unknown, USA: Golden Era Productions.

Anonymous (2008), 'Message to Scientology'. Available at https://www.youtube.com/watch?v=JCbKv9yiLiQ (accessed 16 March 2020).

Asimos, V. (Forthcoming 2021), *Digital Mythology and the Internet's Monster*. Bloomsbury.

Atack, J. (n.d.), 'Possible Origins for Dianetics and Scientology'. Available at http://www.spaink.net/cos/essays/atack_origin.html (accessed 5 March 2020).

Bainbridge, W. S. (1987), 'Science and Religion: The Case of Scientology', in D. G. Bromley and P. E. Hammond (eds), *The Future of New Religious Movements*, 59–79. Macon, GA: Mercer University Press.

Bainbridge, W. S. (2009), 'The Cultural Context of Scientology', in J. R. Lewis (ed.), *Scientology*, 35–51. New York: Oxford University Press.

Bainbridge, W. S. and Stark, R. (1980), 'Scientology: To Be Perfectly Clear', *Sociological Analysis*, 41 (2): 128–36.

Barker, E. (1984), *The Making of a Moonie: Brainwashing or Choice?* Oxford: Blackwell.

Barker, E. (1992), *New Religious Movements: A Practical Introduction*. London: HMSO.

Barker, E. (2014), 'The Not-So-New Religious Movements: Changes in "the Cult Scene" Over the Past Forty Years', *Temenos: Nordic Journal of Comparative Religion*, 50 (2): 235–56.

Berger, A. I. (1989), 'Towards a Science of the Nuclear Mind: Science-Fiction Origins of Dianetics', *Science Fiction Studies*, 16 (2): 123–44.

Bowman, M. (1999), 'Healing in the Spiritual Marketplace: Consumers, Courses and Credentialism', *Social Compass*, 46 (2): 181–9.

Bowman, M. and Valk, U. (2014), 'Introduction: Vernacular Religion, Generic Expressions and the Dynamics of Belief', in M. Bowman and U. Valk (eds), *Vernacular Religion in Everyday Life: Expressions of Belief*, 1–19. Oxon: Routledge.

Bridge Publications (2012), *Philosopher & Founder: Rediscovery of the Human Soul*. California: Bridge Publications.

Bridge Publications (n.d.), 'The Materials of Dianetics and Scientology'. Available at http://www.bridgepub.com/introduction/materials-of-dianetics-and-scientology.html (accessed 5 March 2020).

Bromley, D. (1994), 'Expertise on Confidential Religious Writings'. Available at http://www.theta.com/copyright/bromley.htm (accessed 9 May 2020).

Bromley, D. (2009), 'Making Sense of Scientology: Prophetic, Contractual Religion', in J. R. Lewis (ed.), *Scientology*, 83–101. New York: Oxford University Press.

Butz, M. 'Gender Schmender'. *Scientologists Taking Action Against Discrimination* [Blog]. Available at https://www.standleague.org/blog/gender-schmender.html (accessed 19 March 2018).

Byron, K. D. (2015), 'Free Zone Scientology: The Social Structure of a Contemporary Reform Movement', *The Hilltop Review*, 7 (2): 122–31.

Carnegie Mellon University (n.d.), 'Inside the Mark Super VII'. Available at http://www.cs.cmu.edu/~dst/E-Meter/Mark-VII/ (accessed 14 March 2020).

Carnegie Mellon University (n.d.), 'OT III Course, Summary and Comments'. Available at https://www.cs.cmu.edu/~dst/OTIII/spaink-ot3.html (accessed 20 August 2018).

Christensen, D. R. (2005), 'Inventing L. Ron Hubbard: On the Construction and Maintenance of the Hagiographic Mythology of Scientology's Founder', in J. R. Lewis and J. A. Petersen (eds), *Controversial New Religions*, 227–58. Oxford: Oxford University Press.

Christensen, D. R. (2009), 'Scientology and Self-Narrativity: Theology and Soteriology as Resource and Strategy', in J. R. Lewis (ed.), *Scientology*, 103–16. New York: Oxford.

Christensen, D. R. (2016), 'Rethinking Scientology: An Analysis of L. Ron Hubbard's Formulation of Therapy and Religion in Dianetics and Scientology, 1950–1986', in J. R. Lewis and K. Hellesøy (eds), *Handbook of Scientology*, 47–103. Leiden: Brill.

Chryssides, G. D. (1999), *Exploring New Religions*. London: Continuum.

Chryssides, G. D. (2004), 'The Church of Scientology', in C. Partridge (ed.), *Encyclopedia of New Religions: New Religious Movements, Sects and Alternative Spiritualities*, 385–7. Oxford: Lion Publishing.

Chryssides, G. D. (2017), 'Changing Your Story: Assessing Ex-Member Narratives'. *The Religious Studies Project* [Podcast]. Available at http://www.religiousstudiesproject.com/podcast/changing-your-story-assessing-ex-member-narratives/ (accessed 8 May 2020).

Cort, J. E. (1996), 'Art, Religion, and Material Culture: Some Reflections on Method', *Journal of the American Academy of Religion*, 64 (3): 613–32.

Cotter, C. R. and Robertson, D. G. (2016), 'Introduction: The World Religions Paradigm in Contemporary Religious Studies', in C. R. Cotter and D. G. Robertson (eds), *After World Religions: Reconstructing Religious Studies*, 1–20. Oxon: Routledge.

Cowan, D. E. (2011), 'The Internet', in M. Strausberg and S. Engler (eds), *The Routledge Handbook of Research Methods in the Study of Religion*, 459–73. Oxon: Routledge.

Cusack, C. M. (2009), 'Celebrity, the Popular Media, and Scientology: Making Familiar the Unfamiliar', in J. R. Lewis (ed.), *Scientology*, 389–409. New York: Oxford University Press.

Cusack, C. M. (2010), *Invented Religions: Imagination, Fiction and Faith*. Farnham: Ashgate.

Cusack, C. M. (2012), 'Media Coverage of Scientology in the United States', in D. Winston (ed.), *The Oxford Handbook of Religion and the American News Media*, 303–15. New York: Oxford University Press.

Cusack, C. M. (2016), '"Squirrels" and Unauthorized Uses of Scientology: Werner Erhard and EST, Ken Dyers and Kenja, and Harvey Jackins and Re-Evaluation Counselling', in J. R. Lewis and K. Hellesøy (eds), *Handbook of Scientology*, 485–506. Leiden: Brill.

Dawson, L. L. (2006), *Comprehending Cults: The Sociology of New Religious Movements*. Oxford: Oxford University Press.

Donovan, P. (1999), 'Neutrality in Religious Studies', in R. T. McCutcheon (ed.), *The Insider/Outsider Problem in the Study of Religion: A Reader*, 235–47. London: Cassell.

Ex-Scientology Kids (n.d.), 'The Freezone/Independent Scientology'. Available at http://exscientologykids.com/freezone/ (accessed 17 March 2020).

Fitzgerald, T. (2000), *The Ideology of Religious Studies*. New York: Oxford University Press.

Fitzgerald, T. (2003), 'A Critique of "Religion" as a Cross-Cultural Category', *Method and Theory in the Study of Religion*, 9 (2): 91–110.

Flinn, F. K. (2009), 'Scientology as Technological Buddhism', in J. R. Lewis (ed.), *Scientology*, 209–23. New York: Oxford University Press.

Free Zone Earth (2002), 'Ability Meters International'. Available at http://freezoneearth.org/allmeters/scrapbook/abilitymeter.htm (accessed 27 April 2020).

Free Zone Earth (2007), 'All Meters: The Most Comprehensive Web about the Electro-Psychometer EVER!!'. Available at http://freezoneearth.org/allmeters/ (accessed 18 May 2020).

Free Zone Earth (n.d.), 'How to Fly the Rudiments (From Level Zero)'. Available at http://freezoneearth.org/Prometheus04/otOne/preot1/ruds_zero.htm (accessed 20 April 2020).

Free Zone Earth (n.d.), 'Solo-Auditing'. Available at http://freezoneearth.org/Prometheus04/otOne/preot1/ruds_zero.htm (accessed 23 April 2020).

Freedom Magazine (2013), *The Flag Issue: Celebrating Scientology's New Spiritual Center*. USA: Church of Scientology International.

Freezone Auditors (2008), 'Auditor List'. Available at http://www.freezoneauditors.org/auditor (accessed 15 August 2013).

Freund, P. E. S., McGuire, M. B. and Podhurst, L. S. (2003), *Health Illness, and the Social Body: A Critical Sociology (Fourth Edition)*. New Jersey: Prentice Hall.

Galactic Patrol (n.d.), 'The Free Zone Decree'. Available at http://www.galac-patra.org (accessed 17 March 2020).

Gerth, H. H. and Mills, C. W. (1948), 'Introduction: The Man and His Work', in H. H. Gerth and C. W. Mills (eds), *From Max Weber: Essays in Sociology*, 3–74. London: Routledge.

Graham, R. (2014), 'Are Academics Afraid to Study Scientology?'. Available at https://daily.jstor.org/scholars-on-scientology/ (accessed 10 May 2020).

Gregg, S. E. and Chryssides, G. D. (2017), '"The Silent Majority?" Understanding Apostate Testimony Beyond "Insider / Outsider" Binaries in the Study of New Religions', in E. V. Gallagher (ed.), *Visioning New and Minority Religions: Projecting the Future*, 20–32. Oxon: Routledge.

Gregg, S. E. and Scholefield, L. (2015), *Engaging with Living Religion: A Guide to Fieldwork in the Study of Religion*. Oxon: Routledge.

Gregg, S. E. and Thomas, A. J. L. (2019), 'Scientology Inside Out: Complex Religious Belonging in the Church of Scientology and the Free Zone', in G. D. Chryssides and S. E. Gregg (eds), *The Insider/Outsider Debate: New Perspectives in the Study of Religion*, 350–70. Sheffield: Equinox.

Grossman, W. M. (1995), 'alt.scientology.war'. Available at http://www.wired.com/wired/archive/3.12/alt.scientology.war_pr.html (accessed 17 March 2020).

Grünschloß, A. (2009), 'Scientology, a "New Age" Religion?', in J. R. Lewis (ed.), *Scientology*, 225–43. New York: Oxford University Press.

Harley, G. M. and Kieffer, J. (2009), 'The Development and Reality of Auditing', in J. R. Lewis (ed.), *Scientology*, 183–205. New York: Oxford University Press.

Harvey, G. (2011), 'Field Research: Participant Observation', in M. Strausberg and S. Engler (eds), *The Routledge Handbook of Research Methods in the Study of Religion*, 217–44. Oxon: Routledge.

Harvey, G. (2014), 'Elsewhere: Seeking Alternatives to European Understandings of "Religion"', *Diskus*, 16 (3): 57–68.

Hellesøy, K. (2013), 'Scientology Schisms and the Mission Holders' Conference of 1982', *Alternative Spirituality and Religion Review*, 4 (2): 216–27.

Hellesøy, K. (2016), 'Scientology Schismatics', in J. R. Lewis and K. Hellesøy (eds), *Handbook of Scientology*, 448–61. Leiden: Brill.

Hubbard, L. R. ([1950] 2007a), *Dianetics: The Evolution of a Science*. Copenhagen: New Era Publications.

Hubbard, L. R. ([1950] 2007b), *Dianetics: The Modern Science of Mental Health*. Copenhagen: New Era Publications.

Hubbard, L. R. ([1951] 1983), *Self Analysis*. Copenhagen: New Era Publications.

Hubbard, L. R. ([1951] 2007a), *Advanced Procedure and Axioms*. Copenhagen: New Era Publications.

Hubbard, L. R. ([1951] 2007b), *Dianetics: The Original Thesis*. Copenhagen: New Era Publications.

Hubbard, L. R. ([1951] 2007c), *Handbook for Preclears*. Copenhagen: New Era Publications.

Hubbard, L. R. ([1951] 2007d), *Science of Survival*. Copenhagen: New Era Publications.

Hubbard, L. R. ([1952] 2007a), *Scientology 8-80*. Copenhagen: New Era Publications.

Hubbard, L. R. ([1952] 2007b), *Scientology 8-8008*. Copenhagen: New Era Publications.

Hubbard, L. R. ([1952] 2007c), *Scientology: A History of Man*. Copenhagen: New Era Publications.

Hubbard, L. R. ([1954] 2007a), *The Creation of Human Ability*. Copenhagen: New Era Publications.

Hubbard, L. R. ([1954] 2007b), *Dianetics 55!: The Complete Manual of Human Communications*. Copenhagen: New Era Publications.

Hubbard, L. R. ([1956] 2007), *Scientology: The Fundamentals of Thought*. Copenhagen: New Era Publications.

Hubbard, L. R. ([1960] 1989), *Have You Lived Before This Life?* Copenhagen: New Era Publications.

Hubbard, L. R. ([1961] 2013), 'L. Ron Hubbard – The E-Meter (Scientology)'. Available at https://youtu.be/5D4PxUmAZNw (accessed 6 July 2017).

Hubbard, L. R. (1965a), 'Keeping Scientology Working'. Available at https://stss.nl/stss-materials/English/Courses%20Black%20und%20White%20Printing%20EN_BW_CR/EN_BW_CR_Keeping_Scientology_Working__KSW.pdf (accessed 17 March 2020).

Hubbard, L. R. (1965b), 'Safeguarding Technology'. Available at http://internationalfreezone.net/safeguarding-technology.shtml (accessed 17 March 2020).

Hubbard, L. R. ([1968] 2007), *Introduction to Scientology Ethics*. Copenhagen: New Era Publications.

Hubbard, L. R. (1975), 'Dianetics and Scientology Technical Dictionary'. Available at http://www.e-reading.club/bookreader.php/133981/Hubbard_-_Technical_Dictionary_of_Dianetics_and_Scientology.pdf (accessed 28 April 2020).

Hubbard, L. R. (1982), 'Understanding the E-Meter: A Book on the Basics of How the E-Meter Works'. Available at https://stss.nl/stss-materials/English/Books/EN_BO_Understanding_the_E_Meter_Monitor.pdf (accessed 11 November 2018).

Hubbard, L. R. (2001), *The Technology of Study*. Los Angeles: Bridge Publications Inc.

Hubbard, L. R. (2002), *Clear Body Clear Mind*. Copenhagen: New Era Publications.

Independent Scientology (n.d.), 'Beliefs of Independent Scientology'. Available at http://www.iscientology.org/about-us/beliefs (accessed 17 March 2020).

Independent Scientology (n.d.), 'Management of Independent Scientology'. Available at http://www.iscientology.org/about-us/management (accessed 17 March 2020).

International Freezone Association Inc. (n.d.), 'The Association of Professional Independent Scientologists'. Available at http://internationalfreezone.net/ (accessed 18 March 2020).

Jolly, D. (2016), 'Sexuality in Three Ex-Scientology Narratives', in J. R. Lewis and K. Hellesøy (eds), *Handbook of Scientology*, 411–20. Leiden: Brill.

Kent, S. A. (1996), 'Scientology's Relationship with Eastern Religious Traditions', *Journal of Contemporary Religion*, 11 (1): 21–36.

Knott, K. (2005), 'Insider/Outsider Perspectives', in J. R. Hinnells (ed.), *The Routledge Companion to the Study of Religion*, 243–58. Oxon: Routledge.

Koon, D. (n.d.), 'Super Power – Explanation by: Dan Koon'. Available at http://www.xenu.net/archive/SuperPower/Super%20Power-1.pdf (accessed 27 April 2020).

Lamont, S. (1986), *Religion Inc. The Church of Scientology*. London: HARRAP.

Leah Remini: Scientology and the Aftermath (2016), [TV programme] A&E.

Lewis, J. R. (2009a), 'Introduction', in J. R. Lewis (ed.), *Scientology*, 3–14. New York: Oxford.

Lewis, J. R., ed. (2009b), *Scientology*. New York: Oxford University Press.

Lewis, J. R. (2012), 'Scientology: Up Stat, Down Stat', in O. Hammer and M. Rothstein (eds), *The Cambridge Companion to New Religious Movements*, 133–49. Cambridge: Cambridge University Press.

Lewis, J. R. (2013), 'Free Zone Scientology and Other Movement Milieus: A Preliminary Characterization', *Temenos: Nordic Journal of Comparative Religion*, 49 (2): 255–76.

Lewis, J. R. (2016), 'The Dror Center Schism, The Cook Letter and Scientology's Legitimation Crisis', in J. R. Lewis and K. Hellesøy (eds), *Handbook of Scientology*, 462–84. Leiden: Brill.

Lewis, J. R. and Hellesøy, K. (2016a), 'Introduction', in J. R. Lewis and K. Hellesøy (eds), *Handbook of Scientology*, 1–15. Leiden: Brill.

Lewis, J. R. and Hellesøy, K., eds (2016b), *Handbook of Scientology*. Leiden: Brill.

Lewis, J. R. and Tøllefsen, I. B. (2014), 'New Religious Movements and Gender: The Case of Scientology', in J. R. Lewis (ed.), *Sects and Stats: Overturning the Conventional Wisdom about Cult Members*, 131–9. Sheffield: Equinox.

Lindsay, R. (1986), 'L. Ron Hubbard Dies of Stroke; Founder of Church of Scientology', *TimesMachine*, 29. The New York Times.

Lockwood, R. (2016), 'Scientology as "Corporate Religion"', in J. R. Lewis and K. Hellesøy (eds), *Handbook of Scientology*, 173–99. Leiden: Brill.

Mahmud, L. (2013), 'The Profane Ethnographer: Fieldwork with a Secretive Organisation', in C. Garsten and A. Nyqvist (eds), *Organisational Anthropology: Doing Ethnography in and among Complex Organisations*, 189–207. London: Pluto Press.

Manca, T. (2010), 'Alternative Therapy, Dianetics, and Scientology', *Marburg Journal of Religion*, 15 (1): 1–20.

Melton, J. G. (2000), *Studies in Contemporary Religion: The Church of Scientology*. Salt Lake City: Signature Books.

Melton, J. G. (2009), 'Birth of a Religion', in J. R. Lewis (ed.), *Scientology*, 17–33. New York: Oxford University Press.

Melton, J. G. (2018), 'A Contemporary Ordered Religious Community: The Sea Organization', *The Journal of CESNUR*, 2 (2): 21–59.

Miscavige, D. (2013), 'LRH Death Event 02/16'. Available at https://www.youtube.com/watch?v=dgDa22Fx_V4 (accessed 23 April 2020).

Morgan, D. (2011), 'Thing', *Material Religion*, 7 (1): 140–7.

Morgan, D. (2014), 'Art, Material Culture, and Lived Religion', in F. B. Brown (ed.), *The Oxford Handbook of Religion and the Arts*, 480–97. Oxford: Oxford University Press.

My Scientology Movie (2015), Dir. John Dower, UK: Altitude Film Distribution.

Ortega, T. (2012a), 'Scientology: Secrets of the Super Power Building'. Available at https://www.villagevoice.com/2012/01/09/scientology-secrets-of-the-super-power-building/ (accessed 25 April 2020).

Ortega, T. (2012b), 'Scientology's "Super Power Rundown": What is it Anyway?'. Available at https://www.villagevoice.com/2012/01/11/scientologys-super-power-rundown-what-is-it-anyway/ (accessed 25 April 2020).

Ortega, T. (2013a), 'Independent Scientology: The Ballad of Captain Bill', *The Underground Bunker* [Blog]. Available at http://tonyortega.org/2013/03/30/the-ballad-of-captain-bill/ (accessed 25 April 2020).

Ortega, T. (2013b), 'The Oiliness Table, For Real! A Look Inside Scientology's Super Power Building', *The Underground Bunker* [Blog]. Available at http://tonyortega.org/2013/11/19/the-oiliness-table-for-real-a-look-inside-scientologys-super-power-building/ (accessed 25 April 2020).

Palmer, S. J. (1994), *Moon Sisters, Krishna Mothers, Rajneesh Lovers: Women's Roles in New Religions*. New York: Syracuse University Press.

Patheos (n.d.), 'Gender and Sexuality'. Available at http://www.patheos.com/library/scientology/ethics-morality-community/gender-and-sexuality.html (accessed 20 April 2020).

Peckham, M. (1998), 'New Dimensions of Social Movement/Countermovement Interaction: The Case of Scientology and its Internet Critics', *The Canadian Journal of Sociology*, 23 (4): 317–47.

Pellikaan-Engel, M. (1998), 'Humankind at a Turning Point? Feminist Perspectives', *Hypatia*, 13 (1): 232–40.

Primiano, L. N. (1995), 'Vernacular Religion and the Search for Method in Religious Folklife', *Western Folklore*, 54 (1): 37–55.

Puttick, E. (1997), *Women in New Religions: In Search of Community, Sexuality and Spiritual Power*. London: Macmillan Press Ltd.

Rathbun, M. C. (2011), 'Truth Revealed about OT VIII', *Moving On Up a Little Higher* [Blog]. Available at https://markrathbun.blog/2011/03/16/truth-revealed-about-ot-viii/ (accessed 23 April 2020).

Reitman, J. (2011), *Inside Scientology: The Story of America's Most Secretive Religion*. New York: Houghton Mifflin Harcourt.

Religious Technology Center (n.d.), 'Mr. David Miscavige Chairman of the Board Religious Technology Center'. Available at http://www.rtc.org/david-miscavige.html (accessed 24 April 2020).

Remus, H. E. (1988), 'Religion as an Academic Discipline (Part 1: "Origins, Nature and Changing Understandings")', in C. H. Lippy and P. M. Williams (eds), *Encyclopedia of the American Religious Experience (Vol. III)*, 1653–65. New York: Charles Scribners Sons.

Rigal-Cellard, B. (2009), 'Scientology Missions International (SMI): An Immutable Model of Technological Missionary Activity', in J. R. Lewis (ed.), *Scientology*, 325–34. New York: Oxford University Press.

Robertson, B. ([1983] 2012), 'Captain Bill Robertson at Crown Hotel Meeting 1983 East Grinstead scientology.avi'. Available at https://www.youtube.com/watch?v=tvfioivtY6c&t=2s (accessed 5 March 2020).

Robertson, D. G. (2016), 'Hermeneutics of Suspicion: Scientology and Conspiracism', in J. R. Lewis and K. Hellesøy (eds), *Handbook of Scientology*, 300–18. Leiden: Brill.

Ron's Org Bern (n.d.), 'The Movement of Alternative Scientology'. Available at https://ronsorg.com/wp-content/uploads/2017/06/ronsorgengl.pdf (accessed 17 March 2020).
Ron's Org Committee (n.d.a), 'Bill Robertson'. Available at https://ronsorg.com/bill-robertson/ (accessed 17 March 2020).
Ron's Org Committee (n.d.b), 'Myths and Facts about Captain Bill Robertson'. Available at http://ronsorg.com/roc/english/mythaboutcbr.html (accessed 20 August 2018).
Rothstein, M. (2009), '"His Name was Xenu. He Used Renegades . . .", Aspects of Scientology's Founding Myth', in J. R. Lewis (ed.), *Scientology*, 365–87. New York: Oxford University Press.
Ruskell, N. S. and Lewis, J. R. (2016), 'News Media, the Internet and the Church of Scientology', in J. R. Lewis and K. Hellesøy (eds), *Handbook of Scientology*, 321–40. Leiden: Brill.
Scherstuhl, A. (2010), 'The Church of Scientology Does Not Want You to See L. Ron Hubbard's Woman-Hatin' Book Chapter'. Available at 23 April 2020. https://www.villagevoice.com/2010/06/21/the-church-of-scientology-does-not-want-you-to-see-l-ron-hubbards-woman-hatin-book-chapter/
Schilt, K. and Westbrook, L. (2009), 'Doing Gender, Doing Heteronormativity: "Gender Normals," Transgender People, and the Social Maintenance of Heterosexuality', *Gender and Society*, 23 (23): 440–64.
Schorey, S. T. (2016), '"LRH4ALL!": The Negotiation of Information in the Church of Scientology and the Open Source Scientology Movement', in J. R. Lewis and K. Hellesøy (eds), *Handbook of Scientology*, 341–59. Leiden: Brill.
Scientologists at War (2013), [TV programme] Channel 4, 17 June.
Scientology (2020), 'Scientology TV Super Bowl Commercial 2020 Ad: Rediscover the Human Soul'. Available at https://www.youtube.com/watch?v=YE_zTlo72tM (accessed 14 March 2020).
Sea Organization Executive Directive 2104 (1984), 'The Flow Up the Bridge: The US Mission Holders Conference'. Available at http://www.robertdam-cos.dk/SOED_2104_INT.pdf (accessed 22 May 2017).
Sharpe, E. J. (1988), *Understanding Religion*. London: Gerald Duckworth.
Shelton, C. (2015), *Scientology: A to Xenu: An Insider's Guide to What Scientology Is Really All About*. Denver: pubd online E-Pub Date.
Shupe, A. (2009), 'The Nature of the New Religious Movements-Anticult "Culture War" in Microcosm: The Church of Scientology versus the Cult Awareness Network', in J. R. Lewis (ed.), *Scientology*, 269–81. New York: Oxford University Press.
Singler, B. (2017), 'No Leader, No Followers: The Internet and the End of Charisma?', in E. V. Gallagher (ed.), *Visioning New and Minority Religions*, 61–73. Oxon: Routledge.
Smart, N. (1993), *The World's Religions*. Cambridge: Cambridge University Press.
South Park: Trapped in the Closet (2005), [TV programme] Comedy Central, 16 November.
Squeeze My Cans (2017), [Play] by Schekelberg, C., dir. Anderson, S., Assembly Rooms, Edinburgh, 8 August.

Stark, R. (2007), 'Why Religious Movements Succeed or Fail: A Revised General Model', in L. L. Dawson (ed.), *Cults and New Religious Movements: A Reader*, 259–70. Oxford: Blackwell.

Stout, D. A. (2012), *Media and Religion: Foundations of an Emerging Field*. Oxon: Routledge.

Swainson, M. (2016), 'The Price of Freedom: Scientology and Neoliberalism', in J. R. Lewis and K. Hellesøy (eds), *Handbook of Scientology*, 200–23. Leiden: Brill.

The Church of Scientology International (1998), *What Is Scientology?* California: Bridge Publications.

The Church of Scientology International (n.d.a), 'The Auditor's Code'. Available at https://www.scientology.org.uk/what-is-scientology/the-scientology-creeds-and-codes/the-auditors-code.html (accessed 23 April 2020).

The Church of Scientology International (n.d.b), 'Celebrating Scientology's New Spiritual Center: A Turning Point for the Religion'. Available at http://www.freedommag.org/issue/201407-flag/a-turning-point-for-the-religion.html (accessed 24 April 2020).

The Church of Scientology International (n.d.c), 'Chronology: Significant Events in the Life of L. Ron Hubbard'. Available at http://www.lronhubbard.org/ron-series/profile/chronology.html?link=body-learnmore#part35 (accessed 9 February 2017).

The Church of Scientology International (n.d.d), 'The Creed of the Church of Scientology'. Available at http://www.scientology.org.uk/what-is-scientology/the-scientology-creeds-and-codes/the-creed-of-the-church.html (accessed 20 April 2020).

The Church of Scientology International (n.d.e), 'David Miscavige: Scientology Scripture Recovered and Restored in 25-Year Program Completed in 2009'. Available at http://www.scientology.org.uk/david-miscavige/renaissance-for-scientology/completion-of-the-golden-age-of-knowledge.html (accessed 24 April 2020).

The Church of Scientology International (n.d.f), 'Dianetics Auditing'. Available at http://neweradianetics.org.uk/page07.htm (accessed 5 April 2020).

The Church of Scientology International (n.d.g), 'Experts Conclude Scientology is a True World Religion'. Available at http://www.scientologyreligion.org/religious-expertises/ (accessed 5 May 2020).

The Church of Scientology International (n.d.h), 'New Churches of Scientology'. Available at http://www.scientology.org.uk/churches/ideal-orgs/ (accessed 27 April 2020).

The Church of Scientology International (n.d.i), 'The Tone Scale'. Available at http://www.scientology.org.uk/what-is-scientology/basic-principles-of-scientology/the-tone-scale.html (accessed 20 April 2020).

The Church of Scientology International (n.d.j), 'What Is the Scientology Cross?'. Available at http://www.scientology.org.uk/faq/background-and-basic-principles/what-is-the-scientology-cross.html (accessed 18 May 2020).

The Church of Scientology International (n.d.k), 'What Is the Scientology Position Regarding Women Ministers?'. Available at http://www.scientology.org.uk/faq/scientology-ministers/scientology-position-on-women-ministers.html (accessed 23 April 2020).

The Church of Scientology Los Angeles (n.d.l), 'Scientology Tools: The Vital Knowledge of Life'. Available at http://www.scientology-losangeles.org/beginning-services/scientology-life-improvement-courses.html#lic-survival (accessed 27 April 2020).

The Golden Age of Knowledge (2008), 'The Golden Age of Knowledge'. Available at https://www.youtube.com/watch?v=fLWsOjEA8gw (accessed 24 April 2020).

Thomas, A. J. L. (2017a), '"Insider Knowledge": Seeing the Bigger Picture with New Religious Movements'. *The Religious Studies Project* [Blog]. Available at http://www.religiousstudiesproject.com/2017/11/23/insider-knowledge-seeing-the-bigger-picture-with-new-religious-movements/ (accessed 8 May 2020).

Thomas, A. J. L. (2017b), 'Taking a "STAND": Scientology's Latest Campaign for Religious Legitimacy'. *The Open University: Contemporary Religion in Historical Perspective* [Blog]. Available at http://www.open.ac.uk/blogs/religious-studies/?p=377 (accessed 23 April 2020).

Tøllefsen, I. B. and Lewis, J. R. (2016), 'The Cult of Geeks: Religion, Gender and Scientology', in J. R. Lewis and K. Hellesøy (eds), *Handbook of Scientology*, 390–410. Leiden: Brill.

Tremlett, P.-F. (2013), 'The Problem with the Jargon of Inauthenticity: Towards a Materialist Repositioning of the Analysis of Postmodern Religion', *Culture and Religion*, 14 (4): 463–76.

Urban, H. B. (2006), 'Fair Game: Secrecy, Security, and the Church of Scientology in Cold War America', *Journal of the American Academy of Religion*, 74 (2): 356–89.

Urban, H. B. (2011), *The Church of Scientology: A History of a New Religion*. Princeton: Princeton University Press.

Urban, H. B. (2012), 'The Occult Roots of Scientology? L. Ron Hubbard, Aleister Crowley, and the Origins of a Controversial New Religion', *Nova Religio: The Journal of Alternative and Emergent Religions*, 15 (3): 91–116.

Urban, H. B. (2016), '"Secrets, Secrets, SECRETS!" Concealment, Surveillance, and Information-Control in the Church of Scientology', in J. R. Lewis and K. Hellesøy (eds), *Handbook of Scientology*, 279–99. Leiden: Brill.

Urban, H. B. (2017), '"The Third Wall of Fire": Scientology and the Study of Religious Secrecy', *Nova Religio: The Journal of Alternative and Emergent Religions*, 20 (4): 13–36.

Wallis, R. (1976), *The Road to Total Freedom: A Sociological Analysis of Scientology*. London: Heinemann.

Wallis, R. (2007), 'Three Types of New Religious Movement', in L. L. Dawson (ed.), *Cults and New Religious Movements: A Reader*, 36–58. Oxford: Blackwell.

Walker, T. (2013), 'The Church of Scientology's New $145 Complex has Generated More in Fundraising than it Cost'. Available at http://www.independent.co.uk/news/

world/americas/the-church-of-scientologys-new-145m-complex-has-generated-more-in-fundraising-than-it-cost-8950282.html (accessed 27 April 2020).

Ward, J. and Schneider, B. (2009), 'The Reaches of Heteronormativity: An Introduction', *Gender and Society*, 23 (23): 433–9.

Weber, M. ([1948] 1991a), 'Class, Status, Party', in H. H. Gerth and C. W. Mills (eds), *From Max Weber: Essays in Sociology*, 180–95. London: Routledge.

Weber, M. ([1948] 1991b), 'The Social Psychology of the World Religions', in H. H. Gerth and C. W. Mills (eds), *From Max Weber: Essays in Sociology*, 267–301. London: Routledge.

Weber, M. ([1948] 1991c), 'The Sociology of Charismatic Authority', in H. H. Gerth and C. W. Mills (eds), *From Max Weber: Essays in Sociology*, 267–301. London: Routledge.

Weinryb, I. (2017), 'Votives: Material Culture and Religion', *Material Religion*, 13 (1): 98.

Wessinger, C. (2012), 'Charismatic Leaders in New Religions', in O. Hammer and M. Rothstein (eds), *The Cambridge Companion to New Religious Movements*, 80–96. Cambridge: Cambridge University Press.

Westbrook, D. A. (2015), *A People's History of the Church of Scientology*. Unpublished PhD thesis: Claremont Graduate University.

Westbrook, D. A. (2016a), 'Researching Scientology and Scientologists in the United States: Methods and Conclusions', in J. R. Lewis and K. Hellesøy (eds), *Handbook of Scientology*, 19–46. Leiden: Brill.

Westbrook, D. A. (2016b), 'Walking in Ron's Footsteps: "Pilgrimage" Sites of the Church of Scientology', *Numen*, 63 (1): 71–94.

Westbrook, D. A. (2019), *Among the Scientologists: History, Theology, and Praxis*. New York: Oxford University Press.

Whitehead, H. (1987), *Renunciation and Reformulation: A Study of Conversion in an American Sect*. Ithaca: Cornell University Press.

WikiLeaks (n.d.a), 'Church of Scientology Collected Operating Thetan Documents'. Available at https://wikileaks.org/wiki/Church_of_Scientology_collected_Operating_Thetan_documents (accessed 29 June 2017).

WikiLeaks (n.d.b), 'Scientology Leaks by Date'. Available at https://wikileaks.org/wiki/Scientology_leaks_by_date (accessed 9 May 2020).

Wilson, B. (1982), *Religion in Sociological Perspective*. Oxford: Oxford University Press.

WISE International (n.d.), 'About L. Ron Hubbard's Management Technology'. Available at http://www.wise.org/en_US/l-ron-hubbard/what-is/ (accessed 23 April 2020).

Young, J. H. (1972), 'The Persistence of Medical Quackery in America: Some Reflections on the Complex and Subtle Interrelationship Among Three Parties: the Citizen as Patient, the Orthodox Practitioner, the Quack Himself', *American Scientist*, 60 (3): 318–26.

Index

analytical mind   44, 54–5, 68–9, 79, 81, 132, 171
Anonymous   17, 35–6
anthropology   6, 152
anti-Scientology   35, 75, 85, 120, 146–7, 170
Apollo (former Sea Org flagship)   27
ARC break   71, 140
ARC Triangle   69–71, 162
Astounding Science Fiction magazine   23–5, 74–5, 169
auditing   2, 4–13, 15–18, 25–6, 28–9, 32, 37–8, 52, 60–4, 66, 68–9, 71, 73, 77–81, 95–7, 101–2, 104, 106–9, 113–18, 130–2, 144–5, 148–53, 156–8, 160–7, 169–72, 174
   Book One   44–6, 57, 132–3
   in the Church of Scientology   109–13
   in the Free Zone   115–19
   the mind and   54–8
   solo   9, 47, 79, 81, 83, 85, 89, 139
   theories   40–50
auditor   12–13, 26–7, 41–5, 47, 68–9, 77–80, 85–90, 108, 111, 114, 116–19, 123, 127, 131–7, 139–42, 144, 148, 150, 163–6, 171, 174–5
   Free Zone   32, 77, 141
   independent   62, 87–8, 118–19, 141, 164
   solo   85
   training   10, 42, 71, 78–9, 81, 113–14, 117–19, 124, 135, 140–1, 157, 163
authenticity   5, 17–18, 23, 95–6, 98, 104, 107–8, 113, 124, 128, 131, 150, 153, 159–60, 164, 166–7

Barker, Eileen   96–7, 126, 154, 173
Basic Books   43, 101, 109–12, 114
biophysics   56–7
boundaries   2, 5, 14, 18, 27, 93, 95–7, 113, 116, 119–21, 123–8, 131, 153, 158–9, 164–5, 167

brainwashing   5, 18, 37–8, 152, 167
the Bridge to Total Freedom   13–14, 17, 46–8, 51, 58, 62, 64, 73, 78–83, 86–8, 90–1, 98, 107, 109–21, 138, 143–4, 146, 162–3

Campbell, Jr., John   24
Cause Resurgence Rundown   113, 145, 147–8, 150, 166, 170
celebrity   33–4
charismatic leader   1, 5, 18, 22, 27, 82, 96–8, 105, 126, 153–6, 159, 161, 165, 167
Christianity   48, 74, 106, 116, 153, 173, 175
Church of Scientology
   establishment of   25–7
   scholarly studies of   2–4
   and STAND   73, 106
clear   10, 44–7, 52, 78–82, 85, 87–8, 112, 119, 132, 139, 146, 163, 171
Clearwater   8, 82–3, 112–13, 142–3, 166, 170
communities   2, 4, 11–13, 22, 24–6, 28–9, 31–6, 39, 47, 49, 63, 66, 74–8, 82, 106, 108, 114, 119–20, 124–5, 127, 144, 152, 156–9, 161, 164–6, 169, 172–3
controversies   3, 6, 14, 17, 22, 31–2, 36, 38, 47, 76, 78, 86, 106, 108, 170, 172
cosmology   78, 81, 120, 134
counselling   40, 48, 80, 88–90, 108, 114, 118, 141
Cruise, Tom   33, 170
Cult Awareness Network (CAN)   34
cycle-of-action   64–7

Dianetics   3, 7, 17, 21–6, 40–7, 49, 54, 56–8, 67, 69, 74–5, 80–1, 87–8, 90, 99, 107–9, 111, 116, 128, 130, 132–3, 142, 146, 149, 157–8, 169, 171, 173–4

Dianetics: The Modern Science of Mental Health 21–2, 24–6, 40–2, 44–6, 56, 67–8, 76, 80, 91, 99, 102, 108, 111, 132, 160, 163, 165
Dianology 120
digital 12, 134
disconnection 30–1, 34, 123
documentary 31, 34, 37
drugs 3, 58, 60–4, 91, 163

East Grinstead 1, 7, 59, 135, 148, 162
Eight Dynamics 66–8, 174
Elray, Elron 120
E-Meter 7, 10, 18, 38, 44–5, 47–9, 52, 58, 61, 71, 80, 85, 114, 116, 118, 124, 128, 130–2, 145–6, 148, 150–1, 158, 166, 169, 171
engram 41, 44–6, 54–6, 61, 68–9, 79–82, 132, 134–7, 139–40, 166, 171
esoteric 2, 6, 14–16, 24, 36, 46, 68, 79, 90, 134, 169, 172
extra-terrestrials 28, 120, 170

facsimilies 54
fair game 30–1, 36, 171
fieldwork 7–8, 11–13, 16–17, 43, 54, 67, 73, 79–84, 90–1, 95, 97–8, 106, 113, 115, 126, 134, 148, 150, 156, 162–3, 165–6, 175
Flag Building 8, 113, 142–8, 150–1, 166, 170
Flag Land Base 7–8, 82–3, 113, 142–8, 150–1, 166, 170
Freedom Magazine 145
Free Zone
 emergence of 27–32
 scholarly studies of 4, 6, 11
Freewinds (Sea Org flagship) 174

geeks 74–5
gender 50–1, 71–4, 76–8, 91–2
globalization 5, 152, 167
Golden Age of Knowledge 27, 76, 109–13, 127, 149, 156, 164, 170
Golden Age of Tech 16, 27, 109, 112–15, 118–19, 127, 149, 156, 161, 164, 170

hagiography 22–3, 86, 98
heteronormativity 71–2, 75–6, 78, 91

hierarchy 5–6, 11, 18, 36, 51, 78, 81–2, 116, 118, 155–7, 159
homosexuality 24, 76–8, 91
Hubbard, L. Ron 1, 3–4, 7, 10, 14–15, 17, 21–2, 38–58, 60, 63–72, 74–82, 85–8, 90–1, 95–115, 119–23, 125–7, 130, 132–7, 144–6, 149–50, 154–6, 160, 162–6
 charismatic authority 96–101, 126, 164–7
 death 28, 40, 97, 99
 early life of 21–3
 near-death experience 17, 23, 38, 169
hybridity 2, 17, 40, 45–6, 49, 150–2, 160, 163, 167

immortality 73, 87
Independent Scientology 113–17
 and the Free Zone 91, 96, 103–4, 121–3
Information Network Focus on Religious Movements (INFORM) 8, 173
innovation 5, 17–18, 95–8, 107–8, 115–16, 120–2, 124, 126–8, 131, 141–2, 150, 156, 158–9, 164–5, 167
internet 12, 14, 30–2, 34–6, 147, 158–9

Keeping Scientology Working 29, 154–5, 164

legitimacy 22, 27, 38, 48, 95–6, 102, 104–5, 108, 120–1, 153, 164
lived religion 7, 18, 129, 131, 153, 156–9, 162, 167, 175
lock 44, 54–5, 61, 69, 136–7, 140, 171

material culture 5–7, 10, 12, 18, 44, 128–30, 140, 142, 145, 149–51, 153–4, 158–60, 162, 166–7
Mathison, Volney 132, 134
Matter, Energy, Space and Time (MEST) 45, 47, 52–6, 60, 64, 67–70, 81, 84, 87, 90–2, 99–100, 112, 133, 150, 162
methodological approaches 2, 6, 13, 16
ministers 26, 73, 97, 116
Miscavige, David 4, 27, 31, 76–8, 91, 99, 104, 111, 114–15, 124–5, 127, 148–9, 155, 165, 170
Miscavology 106, 109

Index

New Religious Movements (NRMs), 3, 5–6, 16, 18, 73, 78, 82–3, 92, 96, 126, 129, 152–6, 159, 161, 167, 173, 175

online   1, 6, 11–15, 17, 28, 31–2, 34–7, 60, 75, 81, 83, 85, 118, 141, 146, 156, 158–9, 162, 166, 170
Operating Thetan   9–10, 14–16, 28, 34, 36, 47–8, 78–9, 81–91, 99–100, 111–12, 120, 132, 138, 140, 145, 148, 151, 154, 163, 166
Ortega, Tony   120, 147–8, 166
orthodoxy   29, 96–7, 124
Oxford Capacity Analysis test   10, 32

past lives   25, 46, 61, 87, 134, 166, 170, 172
pilgrimage   10, 170
Preclear   25, 41, 43–4, 46–7, 61–4, 68–9, 71, 77–81, 85–9, 91, 115, 117–19, 132, 134–8, 140–3, 158, 163, 171, 173–5
psychology   2, 17, 21, 41, 47, 49, 80, 116, 152, 169
psychotherapy   23, 25–6, 38, 48, 80, 134, 171
Purification Rundown   10, 17, 58–64, 80, 91, 145, 147, 163, 166

Rathbun, Mark 'Marty'   31, 37, 82, 106
reactive mind   44, 46–7, 54–6, 68–9, 79–82, 118, 132, 136–7, 141, 148, 171
reincarnation   87, 125
religion angle   125, 130, 133
Religious Technology Center   27, 29, 31, 104–7, 109, 124, 155, 165, 172
Remini, Leah   34
Rinder, Mike   34
rituals   116–17, 125, 129, 142
Robertson, Bill   1, 17, 27–8, 39, 63, 87, 96, 101–2, 108, 119–20, 123, 125, 155, 165, 170
Ron's Org   1, 4, 11–13, 28–9, 32, 63–4, 86–7, 91, 96, 101–2, 108, 114, 117, 119–20, 124, 127, 140–1, 155, 163–5, 170
routinization   18, 82, 97–8, 105, 144, 154–7, 159, 165

Saint Hill Advanced Org   7–10, 59, 80, 82, 134–5, 148, 162
salvation   22, 78, 130

schisms   4, 18, 86, 156–7, 161
Scientologese   17, 110–11
Scientology
    creed of   72
    development of   24–32
    the media and   32–8
    nomenclature   17, 40, 57, 89, 90, 165
    women in   72–3, 76–7
secrecy   13, 15–16, 81, 83
secularization   5, 18, 152, 167
sex   66–7, 71–3, 76–8, 92, 133, 173
Skype   12, 60, 118, 141, 162
sociology   6, 18, 152–3, 167
somatic mind   54–6, 79
squirrelling   17, 29–31, 39, 96, 105–6, 109, 113–14, 119, 121–2, 124, 127, 164, 172
Standard Tech   17, 106–9, 113–16, 120, 126–7, 140, 142, 150, 155, 164, 170
study of religions   6, 18, 129, 152–3, 157, 159, 162, 167, 175
Study Tech   42–3, 49, 51, 78, 83
Super Power   113, 145–50, 166, 170
Suppressive Persons   29–31, 103, 172
symbols   9, 129–30, 150

tax exemption   26–7, 105, 126, 170
technology   2, 27–31, 39–42, 45, 49, 57, 67, 69, 74, 90, 101, 104–8, 114, 122–6, 130, 134, 142–3, 145, 147, 149, 155, 165, 172
Teegeeack   14, 28, 84
thetan   14, 17, 25, 45–6, 51–6, 58, 60, 64, 68–9, 71, 73–4, 76–8, 81, 83–92, 100, 112, 133, 145, 148, 160, 162, 166, 169, 171–2
Tone Scale   68–71, 137, 162
Travolta, John   33

Wallis, Roy   3, 7, 49, 78, 160–1
Weber, Max   46, 82, 97, 105, 126, 144, 154–5, 159, 165
World Institute of Scientology Enterprises (WISE)   101
World Religions Paradigm   153, 175

Xenu mythology   14–15, 36–7, 83–4, 86, 116, 172

YouTube   34–5

www.ingramcontent.com/pod-product-compliance
Lightning Source LLC
Chambersburg PA
CBHW070639300426
44111CB00013B/2168